New York Rising

New York Rising

An Illustrated History from the Durst Collection

Kate Ascher and Thomas Mellins

Contributors
Hilary Ballon
Ann Buttenwieser
Andrew Dolkart
David King
Reinhold Martin
Richard Plunz
Lynne B. Sagalyn
Hilary Sample
Russell Shorto
Carol Willis

The Monacelli Press
In association with
The Graduate School of Architecture,
Planning, and Preservation and
Avery Architectural and Fine Arts Library
Columbia University

First published in the United States
by The Monacelli Press
All rights reserved

Library of Congress Control Number 201851389
ISBN 9781580934619

Avery Architectural & Fine Arts Library:
Christine Sala, Architecture Librarian

Design by Yve Ludwig
Printed in Singapore

The Monacelli Press
6 West 18th Street
New York, New York 10011
www.monacellipress.com

Foreword

In *New York Rising*, authors Kate Ascher and Thomas Mellins demonstrate how the development of New York's built environment reflects the evolution of its commerce, politics, culture, and people. Over the course of four centuries, the city's physical evolution has been an organic process by which it has effectively adapted in the face of historical events and spurred the growth of industry and communities—from entertainment in Times Square to finance on Wall Street and the development of residential neighborhoods throughout the five boroughs.

As a visual history, *New York Rising* relies upon the Durst Collection, an archive of nearly 35,000 books, maps, prints, postcards, and other materials. For forty years, our father, Seymour B. Durst, collected and curated this archive, which he dubbed the Old York Library. Over time, the collection expanded and eventually took over his residence on East 48th Street. Spread throughout the four floors of his 12-foot-wide brownstone, this archive became the largest private collection of New York City history ever assembled. When we began to fear for the building's integrity, and thus his safety, he agreed to move the library to a brownstone on East 61st Street. Seymour received special dispensation from the IRS to use the non-profit Library as a private residence so he could continue living among his collection. For the last three decades of his life, Seymour Durst and the Old York Library shared a home.

This home was filled with books, from kitchen cabinets to a lavish bathroom which housed the salacious material he collected from buildings and enterprises in and around Times Square. He stored the many awards

Seymour B. Durst

he received over the years in a sauna that had been installed by the previous owners. The Old York collection became an exceptional resource for writers, journalists, and others interested in viewing New York City's history through a unique lens. Amazingly, if you inquired about a particular topic, Seymour would immediately pull out a book from the seemingly chaotic stacks surrounding him and open it to a selection that he knew would answer your query. Of course, the Old York Library was not merely Seymour's home. The collection reflected his robust intellectual curiosity, his infamous dry wit, and above all, his lifelong fascination with and reverence for the City of New York.

Seymour never stopped collecting and preserving, always enchanted by the content of new material. His collection grew as he secured tens of thousands items—attending auctions, acquiring photographs from the now defunct *Herald Tribune* archive, and purchasing books at various specialty bookstores and antique stores throughout the world. Many of these shopkeepers knew Seymour by name, and they would call our father when they acquired a new treasure that they knew would rouse his curiosity. He filed away building plans and marketing materials from real

estate developers. Sometimes, he preserved relics from the buildings the Durst Organization demolished to make way for new developments.

The magnificent reproductions selected for this volume provide a new dimension to New York's real estate history. Cartographers' maps reveal New York as it was and as it could be imagined. Etchings and engravings provide helpful visual markers of a skyline, or a view down a popular thoroughfare, at a particular moment in time. Such images help the reader understand the context of the period and the larger forces that influenced it. One of the collection's prize pieces, an original 1811 Commissioners' Plan map outlining the rectilinear street grid that would forever determine New York's future evolution, is presented here. Broadway's anomalous angle became one of the grid's few admitted exceptions, and a view from 1840 is accompanied by the original artist's note: "Broadway is a noble street, and on its broad side-walks may be seen everything that walks the world in the shape of a foreigner, or a fashion—beauties by the score, and men of business by the thousand."

The contributing historians and scholars who have collaborated in *New York Rising* are as unique and

Old York Library

multifaceted as their subject matter. Their expertise is apparent in the enthralling sidebars to the reproductions they have individually selected. There has never been such a comprehensive annotating of our father's collection. These captions are sure to present some forgotten drama or irresistible facet of the city's history, which we hope will invite further exploration. Each preserved moment of New York City's past leads us to consider its future.

Our father understood how real estate synthesizes the diverse demands of the people who inhabit a city with the buildings and spaces in which they dwell. He viewed history both as a way to understand the present and, more importantly, as a blueprint for how we need to adapt to the future. So even as he and his brothers shaped the skyline, our father preserved ephemera from everyday life that offers a glimpse into the city's constantly evolving landscape. The current generations running The Durst Organization always strive to sustain the vision of their forebears by honoring this relationship to our city's rich past. Each project we build and manage responds to the needs of the city both for today and for the future. From the outset, our family has always held posterity firmly in

mind when undertaking our development projects. "Generations of builders, building for generations" is how we describe our role in the continued growth of New York City.

Seymour Durst recognized one of the primary mandates of the real estate developer: to leave a mark in a very distinct way, to build something that conveys a sense of permanence holding fast amidst the tides of change. Part of his legacy would rest as much on the artifacts of New York that he preserved, as in the buildings and neighborhoods the family developed. We have always viewed the Old York Library as Seymour's personal contribution to what makes New York great. This collection has always been about actively touching this past, by turning the pages, or viewing the material placed in front of us. His Old York Library, today known as the Durst Collection at Columbia's Avery Library, continues to offer its many visitors an experience of engagement with New York unlike any other. And in capturing what our father set out to do, that is what the authors of *New York Rising* offer their readers.

Wendy Durst Kreeger
Douglas Durst

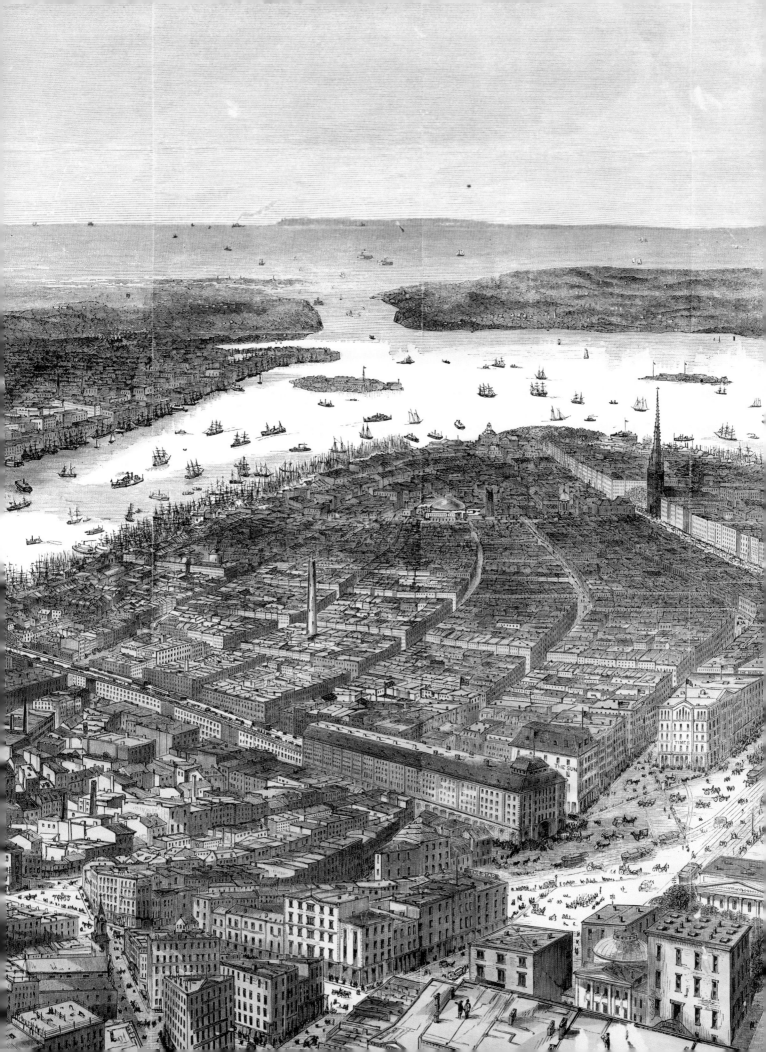

Introduction

Prior to 1898 and the unification of what we now know as the five boroughs of New York, Manhattan *was* New York City. Today, it remains both the epicenter of the region's economy and the heart of its real estate market. Manhattan's longstanding prominence is due to many factors, among them its density, reflecting the desire of so many people to live and work in such a geographically circumscribed place. That ongoing demand manifests itself in one of the world's most dynamic and efficient real estate markets.

New York Rising focuses on Manhattan's development in terms of both its built environment and the real estate transactions underlying its growth; additionally, the book examines aspects of the city's civic and cultural realms. Unlike in many cities, the forces that have shaped Manhattan's urbanism are not primarily natural ones: the fires, floods, and earthquakes that heavily influenced the appearance of cities such as Chicago and San Francisco have been largely absent from the history of New York. Instead, it has been people, politics, and money that have been responsible for the transformation of a small trading post at the mouth of a protected bay into one of the world's greatest and most vertical cities.

Perhaps no industry has shaped New York more than real estate, and no industry has been more dominated by a small number of families. Often denied opportunities in the traditionally lucrative areas of banking and finance, the immigrants who founded many of New York's real estate dynasties sought out and successfully exploited opportunities in land. Over time they made their presence felt in neighborhoods from one tip of Manhattan to the other, and in contrast to their peers in other world capitals, New York's real estate moguls went on to strongly influence their city in ways that went far beyond the physical, playing outsize roles in civic and cultural affairs for over a century.

The patriarch of one of New York City's most prominent real estate families, Seymour B. Durst, was a bibliophile and an avid collector of New York memorabilia for nearly three decades before his death in 1995. As a real estate entrepreneur, Durst well understood the city's architecture and urbanism. His archival holdings—once known as the Old York Library and now referred to as the Durst Collection—reflect his fascination with these subjects; the city's street grid, mass transit, port, parks and open spaces, as well as its monumental buildings and signature skyline, were of particular interest. The collection's oldest items, including maps, paintings, and drawings, vividly depict the rapidly changing appearance of the colonial city. As the real estate market developed in the nineteenth century, building prospectuses, advertisements, and other marketing materials became available, powerfully conveying the commercial forces that drove the city's development. In the twentieth century, land-based and aerial photographs served as visual tools for understanding the relationships between sites and burgeoning neighborhoods.

While of great value to scholars of architecture and urbanism, Durst's collection also reveals his appetite for the social and artistic dimensions of the city's history—its literature, theater, and cultural institutions—and its human side, in areas such as education, public health, and housing. It is the collection's documentation of the interplay between these forces that makes it an indispensable tool for understanding New York's rise as a world capital. Yet at its core, Durst's collection is more personal than academic or institutional. The breadth and variety of its materials tell us a great deal about the man who amassed them. Always fascinated by the people who lived in and visited New York, Durst collected more than 3,500 postcards that demonstrate not only the way New Yorkers once viewed their city, but also the way that out-of-towners experienced and memorialized it.

Other unexpected treasures in the collection include such unusual items as oversized aerial photographs of 1960s New York and memorabilia, including matchboxes, place cards, and napkins commemorating elaborate evenings at the great hotels and nightclubs of Gotham past. Collectively, these holdings conjure up a place and time—and one man's connection to his hometown in ways that many history books cannot.

In 2011 Seymour Durst's family donated his rich and varied collection, comprising over 35,000 items, to Columbia University's Avery Architectural and Fine Arts Library. We began thinking about this book, in cooperation with Avery Library and Columbia's Graduate School of Architecture, Planning, and Preservation, not long after the family gifted the collection. (Thanks to an accompanying financial contribution from the Durst family to Avery Library, many of the objects in the collection have been digitized, allowing them to both be accessed remotely.) Our initial goal was to celebrate and make more visible this magnificent collection to students of real estate, historic preservation, architecture, urban design, and planning—emerging professionals for whom the lessons of history will prove valuable in the future. But we also hope that the audience for this book, and for the collection it documents, will include aficionados of all that has conspired to make New York New York— the expansive views across its natural harbor, the legibility of its rectilinear streets, its welcome embrace of apartment living, its dizzying towers and remarkable density, to name but a few of its defining characteristics.

In this book, we trace the evolution of Manhattan, where the city began (and where the Durst family would ultimately make made its biggest mark), both chronologically and thematically. For each period, from the colonial era through the end of the twentieth century, we have selected themes that both highlight innovation and change in the city's architecture and urbanism, and showcase the breadth and depth of the Durst Collection. To make the archival materials come alive, we invited ten scholars—most on the faculty at Columbia or with a tie to the university—to draw on their knowledge of the respective periods to elucidate the principal themes of each chapter. Each contributor reviewed a "miniature exhibition" of material from the Durst Collection related to his or her area of expertise and selected those images which dovetailed with the story they wanted to tell, in some cases requesting additional images from other sources. They then drafted prose that contextualized each artifact for the viewer. Their perspectives are largely scholarly, but in some cases they are personal as well, echoing and reinforcing the subjective and eclectic nature of Durst's collection.

To provide a broader historical context for the chosen images and the captions that elucidate them, we prefaced each of the ten image portfolios with a summary of key events and milestones relating to the given theme. These texts are intended to provide a foundation for more fully understanding and appreciating both the images and the academic contributions that accompany them. The book's dual structure underscores the ways in which both students and scholars might use the collection in the future, with a perspective that is not singular but plural: different narrators, different subjects, and different styles of interpreting and remembering history.

Sit back and enjoy the visual journey you are about to embark upon, traveling to places and times that the Durst Collection documents so vividly. Indeed, we hope that reading this book and looking at its illustrations will not only evoke Durst's delight in collecting, but also simulate the pleasures of the flâneur, ceaselessly wandering the city's streets—both familiar and unknown—always savoring their beauty and pondering their complexities. It is perhaps fitting that we owe this experience to a lover of his city who developed real estate as a profession. For above all, the story of *New York Rising* is one of never-ending speculation and innovation—of the big ideas, big personalities, and big risks that collectively shaped a city like no other. As New Yorkers, we are grateful for the opportunity to tell that story.

1

Laying the Groundwork

1640–1800

My imagination is incapable of conceiving any thing of the kind more beautiful than the harbor of New York . . . I doubt if ever the pencil of Turner could do it justice, bright and glorious as it rose upon us. We seemed to enter the harbour of New York upon waves of liquid gold, as we darted past the green isles which rise from its bosom, like guardian centinels of the fair city, the setting sun stretched his horizontal beams farther and farther at each moment as if to point out to us some new glory in the landscape.

—Frances Trollope, 1832[1]

It is hard to imagine Manhattan as anything other than what it is today: a largely flat expanse of vertical towers, knit together in a decidedly deliberate and engineered fashion. There is almost nothing organic about it: even its parks and much of its shoreline are creations of man. Perhaps the most natural features remaining are the wide expanse of harbor that separates Manhattan from the Atlantic Ocean and the rivers along its shores, though they too rush about the island in ways that reflect the hand of man.

But before real estate development transformed the place in the nineteenth and twentieth centuries, Manhattan was pastoral landscape. Thick forests of oak, chestnut, and pine covered the island, with high hills pushing up at its center and to the north. Water features were abundant: streams ran from the center of the island to both the North (Hudson) and East

Rivers, large reedy ponds dotted the landscape, and fishing inlets and large tracts of salt marsh could be found along the eastern and southern edges.

To the Lenape and other Native Americans, who occupied Manhattan before the Dutch or the English arrived, nature provided amply. The rivers and bays were rich in aquatic life, and the largely temperate climate offered well-defined and reliable growing seasons. Hunting was productive, with abundant animal life providing food, shelter, and clothing. Skins and furs would prove particularly valuable in the Northern European market and hence become the primary medium of trade for well over a century.

To the European explorers, the Hudson River and its surrounds presented an attractive proposition. "The River is a mile broad…and there is very high Land on both sides…the land is the finest for cultivation that I have ever set foot upon," wrote Henry Hudson's first mate.[2] The mouth of that river, New York Harbor, was ideal as a protected location from which to support the fur-trading business to the north. The land itself, bounded by the Hudson and East Rivers and today of almost incalculable value, was of secondary importance to the waterways that allowed the fur trade to flourish.

The Dutch were the first Europeans to plant their flag in what we know today as the New York metropolitan region. The Dutch colony known as New Netherlands stretched from New Jersey north and east to upstate New York and Connecticut, with its boundaries first set in 1615. A monopoly on trade with this vast tract of land was given by the Dutch crown to a newly chartered "West India Company," mirroring the East India Company that had proven so successful in its ventures in Asia. The company's mission was to develop a productive and robust colony, extending the commercial power and wealth of the homeland.

The tip of Manhattan, from "Manahatta" (the Lenape word for hilly island), began as a way-station for vessels making their way north to Fort Orange (now Albany); it was a storehouse for convenience and refuge, and not much more. The original colonists lived not on Manhattan itself but on Nutten Island (Governor's Island), and used the fertile land across the lower East River solely for grazing. But as the number of settlers grew, the larger footprint of Manhattan and its adjacency to the trading activities to the north made it an obvious choice as a place for the settlement to expand.

The purchase of Manhattan in 1624, perhaps the most famous real estate transaction in American history, was only one of many land deals that the Dutch (as well as the English and French) made with the Native Americans along the Atlantic coast in the early seventeenth century. Although documentation of the original deal appears to have been destroyed, history books tell us that Peter Minuit, Director General of the Dutch West India Company for the area, exchanged 60 guilders of Dutch goods—likely tools, beads, and cloth primarily—for some 20,000 acres of tribal lands in Lower Manhattan. To the Native Americans who participated in the transaction, the exchange was less a sale than a lease-cum-defensive alliance: the Dutch would be allowed to live on and use the land, with an implicit commitment to support and protect the natives should other tribes threaten. The Lenape had no intention of ceding or leaving the land; they remained neighbors of the Dutch on Manhattan well into the second half of the seventeenth century.

New Amsterdam

The Dutch town that emerged from that transaction was named New Amsterdam. By most accounts, it was the fourth town founded in the New World, after St. Augustine, Jamestown, and Santa Fe. At its founding, the settlement was more a company village than a town—a few dozen wooden houses, windmills for sawing logs and grinding grain, the company headquarters (the only stone building), and an early attempt at a protective structure known as Fort Amsterdam. Residents were Dutch, Walloons from Belgium, and English. Freemen from these countries were given land upon which to live tax-free for ten years; subsequently they were taxed at one-tenth of the value each year, but did not receive title. They could farm, but they could not manufacture anything or engage in the fur trade. The company provided basic services—e.g., defense and schooling—and also provided a steady supply of Negro slave labor from Dutch colonies in the Americas and Africa for farming.

Colonists soon lost interest in farming land they did not own, and drifted to the more profitable businesses of smuggling furs, tobacco, or arms. Eventually, in 1639, the company relented on its land-ownership policies, and new settlers were granted land that they could own after a six-year rental period. The right to engage in commerce and manufacturing was given three years later to encourage growth and keep peace in the colony, but all foreign trade continued to be handled exclusively by the company through its maritime operations.

Various other incentives were put in place to grow and stabilize the colony. Entrepreneurial settlers moving outside of the boundaries of New Amsterdam were given four years to establish towns of at least fifty people. Known as "patroons," these settlers developed the land, took a fixed rent in stock or produce from their tenants, and could engage in any sort of commercial activity other than fur-trading, again with the restriction that the company's port facilities be used for all shipping.

On Manhattan itself, large farms or "bouweries" north of the southern tip of Manhattan were granted to settlers, known as "bouweriemasters" or "boss farmers," who paid rent to the company. By 1639 some thirty bouweries dotted land north of the island's tip, many of them along adjacent waterways and controlled by the wealthier or more prominent European citizens of the colony.

The growth of any form of governmental control or oversight did not really begin until after the arrival of Peter Stuyvesant as the fourth director general of the Dutch West India Company in 1647.[3] Taxes to pay for schools and services were levied, though defense was still provided by the company. Stuyvesant threatened the taking of unimproved land, instead levying a tax of one-fifteenth value on vacant land to incentivize development. New Amsterdam itself was incorporated in 1653; two years later, in 1655, the somewhat quirky

system of taxation was rationalized to one that taxed settlers based on their wealth.

At the same time, the town itself began to develop in a physical sense. Bowling Green, adjacent to the earliest fort, was the center and the starting point of two primary roads. De Heere Straat (Gentlemen's Street), now known as Broadway, traveled north. A second road, following along the alignment of Pearl Street, traveled east to the ferry connecting the colony to Breuklyn, located at roughly what is now Peck Slip.

Another notable feature was De Heere Gracht (Gentlemen's Canal), which ran along the lines of today's Broad Street from the East River to Beaver Street. Originally a swampy ditch that extended up to today's Exchange Place, it functioned as a canal after sheet piling stabilized its sides, and its shoreline became a desirable location to live. Other streets took descriptive names as well: Bridge Street led to the largest of the bridges over the canal, while Whitehall took its name from the governor's white mansion that abutted it. Pearl Street, paved with oyster shells, delineated the shore.

With the exception of official residences, most of the houses were small, two-story structures, often arranged as row houses. They featured two rooms—typically a shop or workspace on the ground floor with living space and a garret above. Attic storage within the familiar gable facade was facilitated by a hoist-type structure made from a beam extending from the timber members within the roof. The roofs themselves were typically made of thatch until it was banned in 1657.

Virtually all of these homes were well south of today's Wall Street, which at the time remained primarily pastoral and used for cattle grazing. In the early 1650s, a protective palisade, or wall, was erected along its length. The twelve-foot wall was sufficiently important to be paid for by a general levy, after it was determined that the town was vulnerable to attack from both Native Americans and the British and that its citizens could not be defended within the existing fort.

Development below the wall continued. In 1655 Captain Frederick de Koningh was authorized to make a survey of the town and requested that seventeen new streets be built and that several of the existing ones be straightened. The Staats Herbergh, the first tavern in the city, located at today's Coenties Slip and Pearl Street, was converted into City Hall (1653). Tiny Stone Street was the first to be developed with drainage and paved with cobblestone, via a tax levied on the wealthier residences that abutted it.

To the north, several areas were evolving. Bouwerie Lane ran along today's Bowery, connecting Lower Manhattan with Bouwerie Village (today's East Village and Stuyvesant Town). Further north, in roughly the middle of the island between 23rd and 90th Streets, was the area known as the "Common Lands." Low-value land that contained only a few farming leases, it was formally granted by the Dutch Assembly to the colony in 1658.

New York

Only eleven years after New Amsterdam was incorporated as a town, it disappeared as a Dutch entity. A commercial pawn in a much larger colonial trading game, the town was—with relatively little fanfare and no warfare—turned over to the English in 1664. The twenty-four "articles of capitulation" ensured that existing property, religious, and representational rights would continue, moving the town almost seamlessly into a new era as an English colony.

"New Amsterdam" gave way to the name "New York" in 1664, in deference to territory having been granted to the Duke of York (later King James II). But little else shifted on the political front for some time after the transfer. Dutch leaders remained largely in place for almost a year into English rule. Property rights were left intact, and the patroon system of property development, essentially unchanged, became known as the manor system. One important change was made: the limitations of the Dutch West India Company on commerce were lifted, allowing private enterprise to grow and become a new source of taxation for the British colony.

With the exception of a short period when the Dutch returned to govern the colony in 1673, the decades following the English takeover saw the colony of New York flourish, thanks to growth in maritime commerce; this would set New York's trajectory as a port city. A strategic piece of legislation known as the Bolting Act, passed in 1678, gave the town the exclusive right to the grinding and packaging of flour for export. Much to the consternation of those living outside New York's bounds, local millers and merchants rode to wealth on the back of this monopoly; their fleet of 18 boats in 1678 had grown to 125 fifteen years later.

With increasing wealth came a flurry of building: three hundred new buildings went up between 1665 and 1695, many related to the flour trade. Because the East River did not freeze, shipping activity was centered there rather than on the Hudson River; hence the town grew almost exclusively to the northeast. Two new wharves were developed on the East River and two basins or "wet docks" were established at the foot of Broad Street as the focal points for the growing cargo trade.

Expansion of the port and shipping activity was facilitated in 1676 by the Dongan Charter, which gave the town the rights to land under water and proved useful in expanding shipping facilities. A healthy market in "water lots" ensued: the town sold space in the water along the East River to adjacent landowners so that they might extend their landholdings, in return for an agreement to put in access roads and a public wharf at the seaward end of their property. Many of these new wharves were named after their owners, and traces of their legacy are still visible, for example at Peck's or Coenties Slip, in the area near the South Street Seaport.

The Dongan Charter also reaffirmed municipal control of the Common Lands. Although this tract was still of little value, being inland and remote from the center of commercial life, it would ultimately provide the city with a sizable supply of publicly owned land to both lease and sell as a source of revenue over the next two centuries.

By 1700 the population of New York had risen to five thousand. Still controlled by the English-appointed Governor, the town remained a cosmopolitan and liberal place, home to Dutch, French, Swedes, and Jews as well as English. Despite the extent of civil rights and religious freedoms maintained by the English, the residents included slaves, many of African or Native American descent, whose arrival in New York was a product of the increasing trade with the West Indies. The New York merchants who received these slaves as payment-in-kind often had little need for physical laborers and sold them on as farmhands or dock labor. In the eighteenth century, this trade in human beings centered around a slave market at the foot of Wall Street that operated between 1711 and 1747.

Through the first half of the eighteenth century, nearly all of what we might term "real estate development" remained the purview of the private sector. Land speculation grew, particularly in the rapidly expanding areas surrounding the docks. Maritime trade gave rise to counting houses, money-lending operations, and other businesses that would serve as the seeds of what would become a powerful financial district. What little civic rule existed largely served to facilitate property development: unimproved or vacant land that had been deeded to or taken by the city was sold to eager buyers.

Early Physical Development

When the English took over in 1664, only a handful of buildings existed outside of the colony's northern boundary defined by Wall Street. Along the western edge of town lay open land—gardens, orchards, and fields. Nearly all of the development radiated out in haphazard fashion from the busy docks along the East River. The winding streets that today can be found below Fulton and east of Broadway attest to the lack of planning: streets and alleys evolved around the perimeter of private houses placed wherever their owner desired. Though no houses from the seventeenth century remain, the streets that once surrounded them are essentially unchanged.

Much of Lower Manhattan was wet and boggy, and land grants were used to gift land to those who promised to fill and develop it. Broad Street was among

the most notable conversions from ditch to canal to road, but there were many other examples of swampy areas drained and surcharged to create primary access roads serving development along their edges. The one holdout over time would be the area around the Collect Pond, near today's Centre and Worth Streets, as it served as the sole source of freshwater for those unable to obtain a reliable supply of water from wells.

Initially indistinguishable from one another, the districts beyond the docks gradually took on independent characters as local industry grew. The first sugar refinery was opened by Nicolas Bayard in 1730 on Liberty Street. Shipbuilding had taken hold as well, with the bulk of ship construction activity located north of the area now occupied by the western footings of the Brooklyn Bridge. Wall Street's distinct and growing role in the commerce of the city soon made itself felt as well. No longer the settlement's northern boundary, it was paved in 1693 and became the location of the Stadt Huys.

During the early decades of the eighteenth century, a semblance of civic organization emerged. The colony, composed of roughly one thousand households, was divided into seven wards in 1731, six within the downtown core and the seventh encompassing both the Bowery and Harlem farmlands to the north. Of foremost importance was the Dock Ward, located at the foot of Broad Street not far from today's Hanover Square. Much of the wealth and shipping activity was concentrated here, or in the neighboring South and East Wards. The North and Montgomerie Wards to the north were less busy, and the West Ward—comprising the landholdings of Trinity Church—remained largely isolated from the life of the seaport town.

Trinity Church was not just any church; it was the representative institution of the Anglican Church in New York with the power to tax and enforce that tax via civil law. Chartered in the late seventeenth century, Trinity first built on lower Broadway in 1678. The "Queen's Farm" of 62 acres was added to its holdings in 1705, and additional land was subsequently given to enable the church to start a ferry, establish a school, and operate public markets.

The church's powerful hold on the West Ward did much to dampen and largely prevent development in this part of Lower Manhattan during the first half of the eighteenth century. Trinity would only lease land, a less-than-attractive commercial arrangement as land speculation began to fuel development around the port areas along the East River.

As a result, Trinity's holdings on the West Side became home to the workers and craftsmen engaged in building the young city—those who could not afford to purchase property. Carters with horses proliferated, as did stonemasons, bricklayers, and cabinetmakers. Many of these craftsmen would continue to live and work in one place long after the merchants had abandoned downtown living, their dwellings modest and primarily functional. Commenting on the physical appearance of the area, one commentator noted, "This proto-working class neighborhood was set off by more than distance from the wealthier East River wards. The discrepancy between the Georgian grandeur of upper-class brick residences and the rough-and-ready wooden housing of artisans was readily apparent—inside as well as out." Another observed that "the cobblestoned solidity of Hanover and Broad streets stood in marked contrast to the wet side's raw, unpaved roads, which frequently became quagmires of mud, garbage, and manure."[4]

Despite the increasing disparity between rich and poor, free and slave, New York remained a tightly knit and much-admired place. Jean de Crevecouer, a Frenchman, noted in the years just before the Revolution, "Here is found Dutch neatness, combined with English taste an architecture...the houses are finished, planned and painted with greatest care...Stone being scarce, nearly the whole town is built of brick."[5] Mid-eighteenth-century visitors admired the city's tidy cobblestone streets, stone pavements and the sidewalks of flat stone which had been laid on both sides of the streets.

To the north of the city lay largely undeveloped land, punctuated by roads and paths through farmland, swamp, and forest. On the west side of the island, Greenwich Street followed an older Native American path and led to Greenwich Village, a pastoral area of large estates that provided an escape from the hustle and bustle of the commercial heart of the town. Beyond that, the road continued to the small settlement of Harlem. To the east, Bowery Lane headed northeast to connect with the route to New England that would later become the Boston Post Road.

The American Revolution

The years of the Revolutionary War were a hiatus in the otherwise rapid physical development of New York. The number and duration of battles that took place in or around the town was limited. Indeed, for most of the war New York was a loyalist stronghold and remained a solidly British city. Nevertheless, the tensions between loyalists and patriots and the control of the harbor by the British slowed the pace of trade and investment significantly, interrupting the growth of the young colony.

Prior to the outbreak of the war, the population of New York was close to 25,000, but that number dropped dramatically as a result of the British occupation. As the middle class fled, the town became solidly Tory, giving rise to the nickname of "Torytown." Patriots who had supported groups like the Sons of Liberty and the New York–based Provincial Congress fell into the minority, and political protests were all but silenced.

By far the most momentous wartime event with respect to the city's early physical evolution took place in September 1776. A fire broke out in a wooden building known as the Fighting Cocks Tavern near Whitehall Slip. Spread quickly by the wind, the fire destroyed more than 500 buildings in the area west of lower Broadway and around today's Hanover Square, an estimated 25 to 40 percent of the buildings in the town at the time. Trinity Church was one of the more notable casualties.

For seven years following the fire, little physical development occurred in New York. Areas of downtown destroyed by the flames were not rebuilt by the British. This and a general uncertainty about the future undermined the vibrancy of the commercial core and greatly dampened the extent of trade over its piers. Operating more like a buttoned-down corporate headquarters than a dynamic port town, with the British wholly controlling its harbor and waterways, New York would not regain the commercial ambition that had characterized the pre-war years until well after the British surrender in 1783.

Physical Development after the Revolution

The physical impact of two fires and the Revolutionary War on the young city was significant. An Irishman who arrived in 1782 lamented, "What a pity it is to see such a fine City as this almost half Burned to ashes."[6] Yet the destruction would soon be remedied as the defeat and exile of the English buoyed the population and unleashed unprecedented levels of investment in the colony.

Duties on foreign trade were levied from 1789, providing funds, through the newly established Common Council, to begin to invest in infrastructure. Fort George was leveled, and improvements to both Wall and Greenwich Streets were undertaken. Broadway was paved, and a bridge over a tributary of the Collect Pond allowed the road to continue north. Both east and western edges of the town saw the construction of new waterfront boulevards to enhance mobility and rationalize the tangled web of ownership resulting from the sale of water lots; today they are known as South and West Streets respectively.

Perhaps most symbolically, the burnt-out district to the west of Broadway south of Barclay Street—largely filled with tents made of old ship canvases and shanties constructed of wood that housed the unlucky during the war—was finally rebuilt following the appointment by state representatives of the new American city's first mayor, James Duane, in 1783. On the east side of Broadway, old streets took new names signifying the break with the monarchy: King Street became Pine

Street and Queen Street, connecting the Battery to the docks, reverted to the name Pearl Street, evolving into the center of the dry goods trade. Buildings also took new names and purposes. The former Stadt Huys and City Hall was reincarnated as Federal Hall even before New York formally became the capital of the new republic in 1789. The first sitting of the Congress of the United States would take place there between 1785 and 1789, as would the swearing in of George Washington. Only a year later the nation's capital would be moved to Philadelphia in a deal to placate the southern states.

By 1790 an estimated 4,200 houses dotted the landscape of Lower Manhattan, homes to some 32,000 people, including 2,500 slaves. At least some of these were no longer wood-frame buildings; homes built south of Duane Street were required to be brick or stone to avoid a repetition of the fire that had savaged the city in 1776. But many wooden frames were simply clad in a facade of stone or brick, setting the stage for a second devastating downtown fire in 1835.

By 1800 the outer limits of the developed town had reached Houston Street, well beyond the area around the Collect Pond and Negro burial ground that had marked the northern edge of town. Immigrants and the indigent were drawn to the inhospitable area to the east of the Pond, where flooding and erosion was prevalent, homes suffered chronic sinkage, and houses were built cheaply and easily converted to multi-family dwellings. As early as 1797, cholera and yellow fever epidemics were frequent.

Yet the heart of the city was still very much around the docks and Wall Street; when the new City Hall was built on Broadway in the first decade of the nineteenth century, its south facade was elaborately clad in marble but its back, facing north, was plain brownstone. These lines of demarcation would not last long, however. By the time City Hall was completed in 1812, the Collect Pond had been filled, the Commissioners' Plan for the development of streets had been unveiled, and speculation around lands to the north was rapidly gaining pace.

American Bankers Association,
***Book of New York,* 1922**

The year was 1922: a gossamer time in New York City. Smoke-filled speakeasies were tucked into every street; the Babe was leading the Yankees. And that year, when the American Bankers Association held its convention in the city, the group produced a handsome historical guide to New York for its members from around the country, "as a reminder of what New York is, how it became what it is, and as a guide to some of the places of interest to visitors in this city." The New York bankers took pains in the catalog to link the city to America and to portray the burgeoning city as the humble servant of the nation: "the city has grown in size only as it has grown in usefulness, not usefulness alone to those of us who live here, but usefulness to every farm, village and city in this country and to you who come from every state."

The bankers couldn't resist exhibiting some then-and-now contrast in portraying the island of Manhattan for visitors. They chose for their catalog the so-called Hartgers View: the earliest depiction of Manhattan Island, from about 1628. They had an artist improve on the original by cleaning it up and correcting the view (the original showed the New Jersey shore on the east rather than the west side of Manhattan), but the features of the original view are the same: the fort, the windmill, the ships in the harbor, the peaceable natives in their canoes, and the little huddle of houses that constituted the Dutch city of New Amsterdam. Paired with the bucolic scene of New York's beginnings was an aerial photo of Lower Manhattan in its Jazz Age glory.

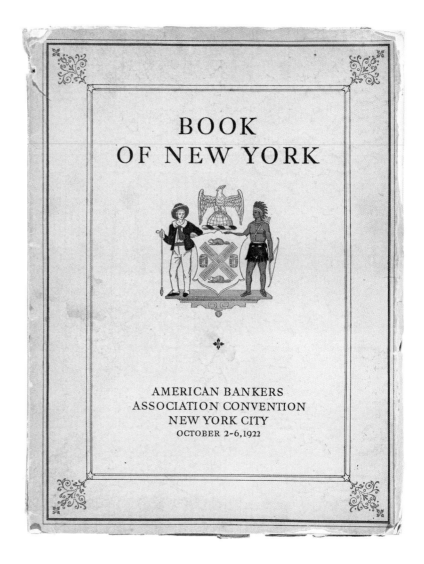

The "Hartgers View" of New York

The first view of New York ever shown to the world. Date depicted, 1626-8. It was drawn by Kryn Fredericks, engineer of Fort Amsterdam, and for years hung in Peter Stuyvesant's Council Room in the Stadt House. It was finally sent to Holland, and rescued from oblivion by Adriaen Van der Donck, who used it in the first book written on New Amsterdam, and published by Joost Hartgers, Amsterdam, in 1651. It is known as the "Hartgers View."

Courtesy New York Historical Society

© *Hamilton Maxwell*

New York, 1922

View of New York today showing the exact location depicted in the first or Hartgers view above. The Fort stood where the Custom House stands today. Skyscrapers replace the little houses clustered outside the Fort in the first picture.

Southern point of Manhattan, early 1600s

Of course, before there was a fort at the southern tip of Manhattan Island, there was wilderness. This nineteenth-century lithograph imagines the setting sometime between 1609, when Henry Hudson's *Halve Maen*, or Half Moon, first charted the Hudson River on behalf of the Dutch East India Company (and in the process claimed the territory for the Dutch Republic) and the construction of the fort in 1625 and 1626. The artist may have used the Hartgers View as a model. However, the terrain as depicted, both on Manhattan and in New Jersey in the background, is too hilly. The fort has not yet been built at the moment depicted, but the Dutch presence is indicated by the small ship (which, however, has features that would not be employed for another century), and the origins of New York as a trading hub are represented by Indians in canoes. Though there was apparently never a permanent native presence on the island prior to the Dutch arrival, a group of Delaware-speaking Indians known as the Wickquasgeck used it seasonally for hunting. They originated the trail that began at the southernmost tip (to the far left) and wound its way up the entire length of the island. The Dutch took over the trail and renamed it the Herenweg, or Gentleman's Way. Under the English, it became Broadway.

Broad Street, 1659

In the late 1800s and early 1900s, Americans were swept up in "Holland Mania," a passion for windmills, wooden shoes, and anything Dutch. Along with it came an interest in the Dutch founding of New York. In 1901 Julia M. Colton, who had previously published a book called *Annals of Switzerland*, followed it up with *Annals of Old Manhattan, 1609–1664*, focusing exclusively on the island's Dutch roots. The book, published by Brentano's, mixed history and folklore and featured fourteen illustrations, many of them recreations of precise locales in the Dutch period. Featured here is a central spot in New Amsterdam: the present-day intersection of Broad and Pearl Streets. When the Dutch arrived, they found a small inlet in the center of what would become their capital. They widened it into a *gracht*, or canal. In fact, it seems to have been more of a ditch; it probably never had the wooden reinforcements shown here. The neat, gabled brick houses, however, likely represent the look of the little port city. The bridge gave the name to present-day Bridge Street. Later, the canal was paved over, making the street the widest one in Lower Manhattan, hence its eventual name: Broad Street.

Governor Peter Stuyvesant House, 1658

For much of the life of the Dutch colony of New Netherland the directors lived inside the fort. When Peter Stuyvesant arrived in 1647, however, with a wife and a budding family, he had no interest in having his domesticity impinged by living in close quarters with dozens of soldiers. He built a fine brick house just steps from the fort, at the corner of Pearl Street. Legend has it that its high white walls gave the name to Whitehall Street. It is unlikely that Stuyvesant's property looked as quaint and tidy as this, nor was it walled off from the surrounding city. The heights of Breukelen (Brooklyn) rise on the opposite shore of the East River.

West India Company Building, Haarlemmer Straat, Amsterdam, 1623

New York began life as part of the Dutch colony of New Netherland, which extended across the territory of five future states: New York, New Jersey, Connecticut, Pennsylvania, and Delaware, and with its capital, New Amsterdam, at the southern tip of Manhattan. The colony was founded not by the Dutch government but by the West India Company, a seventeenth-century version of a multinational corporation. After the phenomenal success that the Dutch East India Company had in exploiting Asia trade, the West India Company was formed in 1621 to do something similar with the Americas. (In the nomenclature of the time, "West Indies" encompassed essentially North and South America as well as the Caribbean islands.) New Amsterdam was thus conceived of as one node of a vast Dutch presence in the New World. The directors of the West India Company planned and directed management of the colony from their headquarters on the Haarlemmerstraat in Amsterdam. The building still stands today.

View of City Hall, New York, 1670

As New Amsterdam grew, its residents chafed at the semi-feudal administration of the West India Company. The residents demanded, and in 1653 finally won, legal features of a Dutch province. Beginning in that year they were allowed to choose a city council. The city tavern—on the waterfront at present-day Pearl Street and Coenties Slip—became the council's meeting place, the first City Hall. This view of the building dates from early in the English period, but it shows typical Dutch features, including the gables on the houses.

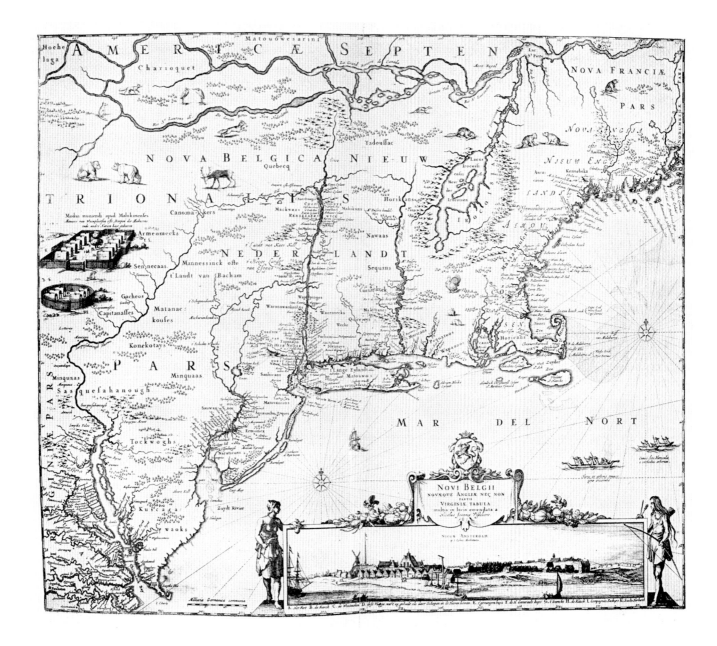

Jansson-Visscher Map of New Netherland, Virginia, New France, and New England, 1653

As part of the struggle between the inhabitants of New Netherland and their West India Company rulers, Adriaen van der Donck, the colony's only lawyer, traveled to the Dutch Republic in 1649 and made an elaborate appeal for the nation, then in the midst of its Golden Age, to take a serious interest in its North American property. Van der Donck commissioned a map from cartographer Johannes Jansson showing New Netherland and the neighboring colonies of Virginia, New France, and New England. The so-called Jansson-Visscher map (Claes Visscher would amend it) was reproduced in dozens of editions over the course of a century and became the standard image of colonial America. It gets plenty of things wrong (New Jersey was originally depicted as an island), but on the whole, it was a remarkably accurate and beautiful example of the cartographer's art. It shows many of the places that were named by the Dutch, from "Lange Eylandt" (Long Island) to Block Island to Cape May. It names native tribes and the areas they inhabited, shows the longhouse villages of the Iroquois and features flora and fauna typical of the region. The inset view at bottom gives a fine rendering of New Amsterdam as a peaceful New World community.

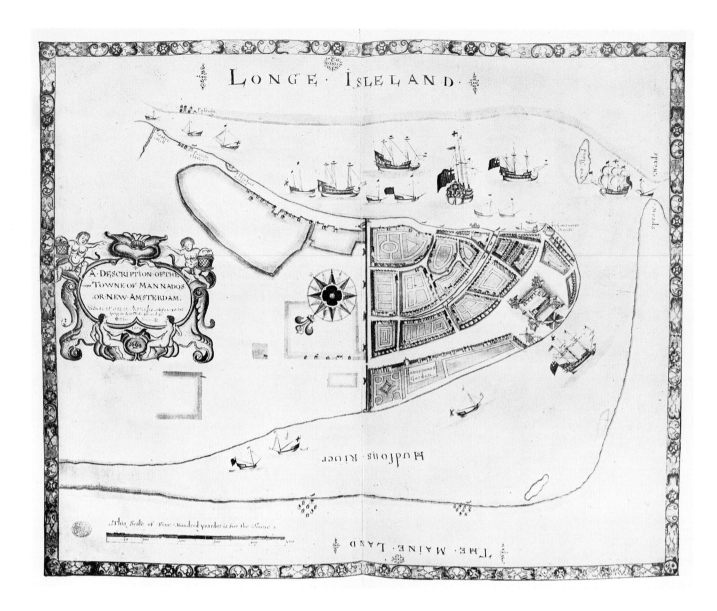

The Duke's Plan, 1664

In 1664 a small English invasion force appeared off Lower Manhattan and took the island, and the province of New Netherland, from the Dutch. The mastermind of the invasion was James, the Duke of York, brother of King Charles II. The king renamed the province and the town New York, after James. Shortly after the takeover, the English commissioned this map of their new city, which has become known as the Duke's Plan. It was drawn so soon after the takeover that it still refers to the city as New Amsterdam. The plan shows a neat-and-tidy town quadrant of civilization, with about fifteen streets, a canal, a fort, and gardens, all of it separated from the largely undeveloped land to the north by a palisaded wall. In fact, the original wall (at what would become Wall Street) was more of a log fence. At this point in New York's history, most of Manhattan island—exceptions being the community of "Nieuw Haarlem" and a settlement at present-day Greenwich Village—was still wilderness.

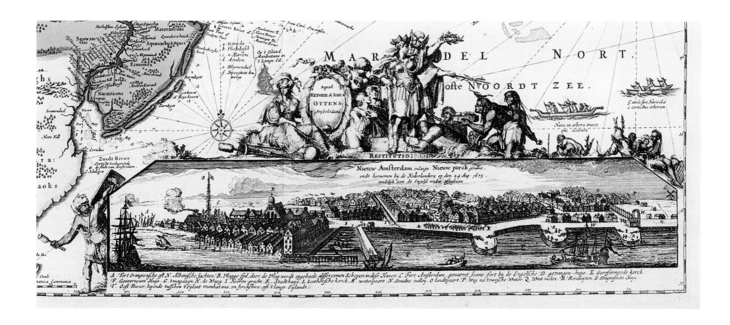

Detail of Totius Neobeigel Nova et Accuratissima Tabula, c. 1700

In 1673, nine years after the English took over the Dutch colony of New Netherland and its capital of New Amsterdam on Manhattan Island, they lost it again. As part of a new trade war between the two rival European empires—the third in that century—a Dutch fleet sailed into New York Harbor and wrested control of the colony. New York's name was changed again, this time to New Orange, after the House of Orange-Nassau. This inset view to a map of the East Coast, depicting the burgeoning city that was the subject of contention, shows the exact moment of the re-takeover. The "wall" that marks the northern boundary is at the far right. The canal at what would become Broad Street is near the center. The fort is at left, with a cannon firing. Soldiers are seen marching along Pearl Street. The title (in Dutch) tells the tale, including what happened next: "New Amsterdam, recently called New York, and retaken by the Dutch on the 24 of August 1673, finally returned to the English." After fourteen months in Dutch hands, in accordance with the treaty that ended the war, both sides agreed that the Dutch would return Manhattan to England. New York was New York once again.

**View of New York, looking west,
c. 1674**

This illustration, dating from the mid-nineteenth century, imagines a scene from ten years after the fall of New Netherland—that is, ten years into the life of New York City. The artist would appear to be on a ship on the East River facing west. The wooden fence on the right side of the image is the wall that the Dutch built in 1653; the street running along it was by this time already being called Wall Street. The bastion with cannon placed for defense (known at the time as a "half moon") did indeed exist by this period. Such bastions rimmed the city; those on the Hudson River were walled while those on the East River (as shown here) were exposed. The guardhouse was matched by another at the western end of Wall Street. The gate shown opened north-ward onto what was then known as Great Queen Street. Although New York was a bustling place, the illustration is probably correct in showing an essentially bucolic setting. The city itself was still largely confined to the area south of the wall. The land to the north was pasture and farmland.

Nº 1 The residence of Jacob Leisler on "the Strand" (now Whitehall Street, N.Y.)

THE FIRST BRICK DWELLING ERECTED IN THE CITY.

Jacob Leisler House, Whitehall Street, c. 1663

In 1660 a twenty-year-old German named Jacob Leisler emigrated to the Dutch colony of New Netherland and quickly went about establishing himself. He apparently didn't much mind the English takeover in 1664, when the place changed its name to New York, but, like many other New Yorkers, he bristled at the change that came in 1688. Two years earlier King Charles II began a radical reorganization of England's North American colonies, which united several of them under a single administration. The so-called Dominion of New England was then extended to include New York. The new government was loathed by the colonists. It restricted their long-held rights, deprived them of outright property ownership and limited their freedom to assemble. After the Glorious Revolution brought the Dutch stadtholder Willem III onto the English throne, Leisler led a rebellion in New York, under the belief that the new king would approve. Leisler's Rebellion, which lasted from 1689 to 1691, ended with its leader's execution. Leisler's red-brick house, shown here in the foreground, next to the one that had previously been the home of Peter Stuyvesant, stood just a stone's throw from the fort, which was the center of the Dominion power that he rebelled against.

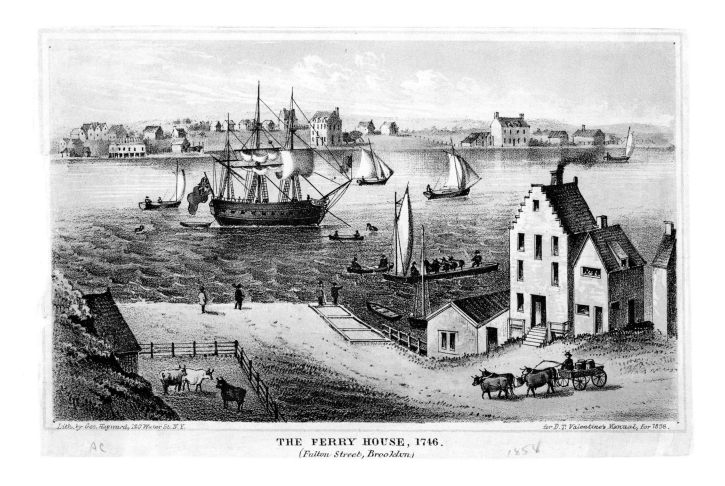

Lith. by Geo. Hayward, 120 Water St. N.Y.

for D.T. Valentine's Manual, for 1858.

THE FERRY HOUSE, 1746.
(Fulton Street, Brooklyn.)

George Hayward, *The Ferry House*, 1746

At about the same time that New Amsterdam became the capital of New Netherland, the village of Breuckelen, across the East River on Long Island, was established. Throughout the Dutch period it was mostly composed of farms. Its residents needed regular contact with New Amsterdam, and a ferry service began as early as 1642. Cornelis Dircksen, who owned an inn and tavern on the Manhattan side, began offering the service by having passengers rowed across the river. As the farms of Long Island grew in importance, the Ferry Road became the main thoroughfare of Brooklyn. This scene, dated 1746 but probably based on an image from decades earlier, shows the flat-bottomed ferry to the right, with the Manhattan shoreline opposite. The gabled ferry-house was burned in the 1740s, possibly by Brooklynites in protest over the fact that New York City retained ownership of the Brooklyn waterfront and the ferry itself.

VIEW of HARLAEM from MORISANIA in the PROVINCE of NEWYORK Septem.r 1765.

George Hayward, *View of Harlaem from Morisania in the Province of New York*, 1765

The principal Dutch settlement on Manhattan, New Amsterdam, lay at the far southern tip of the island. The leaders were always concerned about the island being invaded—by the Native Americans but most especially by the English—so besides fortifying the perimeter of the capital, they took steps to establish a village to the north, which could serve as a base from which to fend off attackers. A low-lying area along the East River appealed to several farmer/traders in the colony because it was relatively flat and had good soil. In 1658 the government issued a decree: "The Director-General and Council of New Netherland hereby give notice, that for the further promotion of agriculture, for the security of this Island and the cattle pasturing thereon, as well as for the further relief and expansion of this City Amsterdam, in New Netherland, they have resolved to form a new Village or Settlement at the end of the Island." They called the village Nieuw Haarlem, after the Dutch city of Haarlem. In time, of course, it became Harlem. This view, from 1765, shows it as still a rural settlement, more than a century after its founding. It was by this point a popular spot for wealthy residents from further south on the island to build country seats.

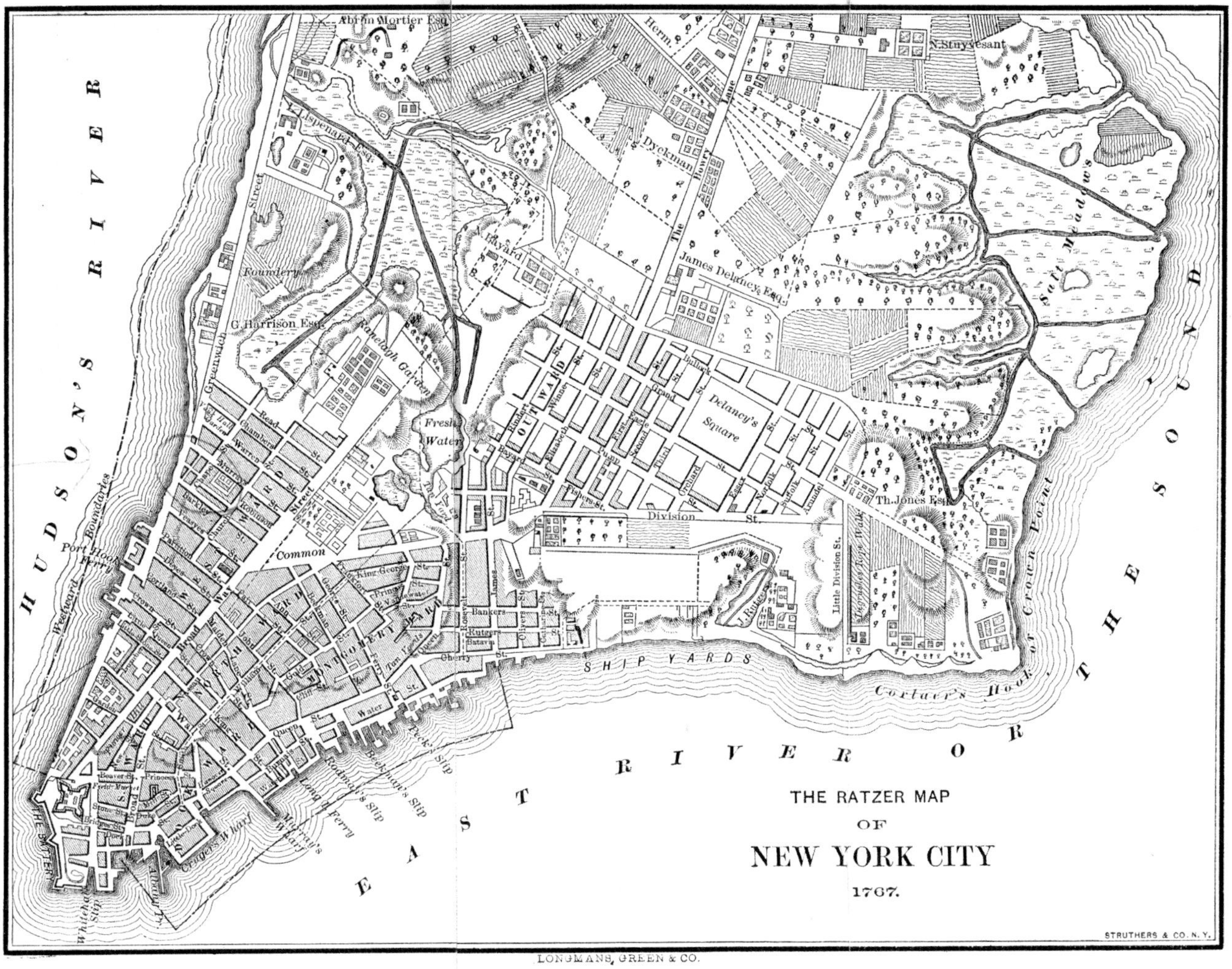

Bernard Ratzer, Maps of New York, 1767

By 1767 the city of New York had expanded to such an extent that it would have been unrecognizable to its first Dutch inhabitants. The area that comprised New Amsterdam is at the lower left, with Wall Street, its boundary, clearly indicated. This fragment is part of a larger map that was commissioned by the British army and shows barracks and other military sites. The main thoroughfare in New York, which the Dutch had called de Herenweg, or the Gentleman's Way, is now called Broad Way Street. The battery has been erected as a defensive work along the southern border, and the urban grid extends as far north as present-day Chambers Street, with most of the area north of that still farmland. Delancy's Square (as it is written), near the top of the grid, is something of a virtual place. The area around it was owned by the wealthy family of that name, which they had a plan to develop. But, less than ten years hence, they would side with the British in the Revolutionary War. Their lands were confiscated; Allen, Ludlow, and Orchard Streets were laid; and the square disappeared as the features of the Lower East Side came into being. Delancey Street remains as a testament to what was once a vast private estate.

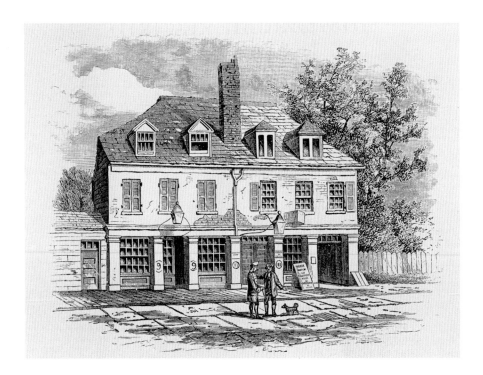

Burns's Coffee House, 1765

Coffee houses in colonial New York were much more than places for drinking. They were venues for meetings and public assemblies. When the popular innkeeper George Burns left the Kings Head Tavern in 1763 to take over the Province Arms, it instantly became known as Burns's Coffee House. It stood on Broadway near Trinity Church, in the heart of the city, and it was the preferred site for concerts and civic gatherings. In the summertime, people came to hear music in the garden behind the coffee house. (On at least one occasion a duel was fought in the garden—with swords— by two British officers.) In 1765, after the British Parliament implemented the Stamp Act, which imposed a tax on all printed matter, New York's outraged businessmen met at Burns's to decide on a response. They signed an agreement not to import British goods. Weeks earlier, patriotic protesters in Boston had begun calling themselves the Sons of Liberty. The day after the meeting at Burns's Coffee House a group of New Yorkers, who likewise took up the name the Sons of Liberty, marched down Broadway to Bowling Green where, in the face of waiting British troops, they tore down the park's wooden fence and staged a protest bonfire.

REPRÉSENTATION DU FEU TERRIBLE À NOUVELLE YORCK.

*Représentation du feu terrible à nouvelle Yorck, que les Américains ont allumé pendant la nuit du 19. septembre 1776. par lequel ont été brulés tous les Bâtimens du coté de Vest, à droite de Borse, dans la rue de Broock jusqu'au collège du Roi, et plus de 1000. maisons avec l'Église de la S.^e Trinité la Chapelle Lutherienne, et l'école des pauvres.
à Paris chez Basset Rue S.^e Jacques au coin de la rue des Mathurins.*

André Basset, *Représentation du Feu Terrible à Nouvelle Yorck*, 1776

One of the chief objectives of the British leadership in the early stages of the Revolutionary War was the capture of New York. On July 6, 1776, while his army was taking defensive positions in the city, George Washington learned of the signing of the Declaration of Independence in Philadelphia. Crowds of New Yorkers who also got the news toppled the statue of King George III that stood on Bowling Green. Washington's army of 19,000 was no match for the 32,000 British troops amassed on ships in the harbor. Faced with the imminence of British takeover, George Washington's troops abandoned the city in late summer of 1776, and the British entered on September 15. Six days later a fire broke out in Lower Manhattan and soon engulfed much of the most developed part of the city, including most of what had been New Amsterdam. By some estimates, 1,000 buildings—one quarter of all structures in the city—were destroyed. Before the British took over, American patriots had considered burning the city rather than let the British have it. That idea was rejected in official quarters, but immediately afterward rumors spread that the fire was deliberately started. One account says it began at a tavern on Whitehall Slip. The image above appeared in a French newspaper. The caption, in French and German, states frankly that the Americans themselves started the fire. Among the notable buildings of the old city that succumbed was Trinity Church.

Inauguration of George Washington as president at Federal Hall, Wall Street, April 30, 1789

In 1700 New York erected a City Hall building on Wall Street. For four years after the American Revolution, from 1785 to 1789, the building became the meeting place of Congress. In 1788 Pierre Charles L'Enfant, who would go on to lay out Washington, D.C., redesigned the building according to the new architectural fashion, which would become known as Federal style, and it was thereafter known as Federal Hall. The following year, George Washington was sworn in as the first president on the balcony of Federal Hall. After eight years of war and a hard-fought struggle to adopt a Constitution, Americans were ready for a celebration. People traveled for miles to attend; they lined the banks of Lower Manhattan to witness his barge, accompanied by several sailing ships, make the voyage from Elizabethtown, New Jersey. Beginning at dawn, they thronged Broad Street, which gives views onto the balcony of Federal Hall. For the ceremony Washington wore a brown suit with white silk stockings, and he had a sword at his side. Robert Livingston, the Chancellor of New York (the highest judicial officer in the state) administered the oath of office, and Washington repeated the words prescribed by the newly minted Constitution: "I do solemnly swear that I will faithfully execute the office of President of the United States, and will, to the best of my ability, preserve, protect, and defend the Constitution of the United States." Livingston let out an impromptu cry of, "Long Live George Washington, President of the United States!" Thirteen cannons fired a salute, and the crowd roared.

**Duel between Aaron Burr and
Alexander Hamilton, Weehawken,
New Jersey, July 11, 1804**

One of the most shocking events in the post-Revolutionary period was the duel between Alexander Hamilton and Aaron Burr on Kings Bluff in Weehawken, New Jersey, across the Hudson River from Manhattan. Burr was the sitting vice president; Hamilton, as the nation's first secretary of the treasury, had laid the foundations of its economic system. Both were brilliant; both had served in the continental army. And they hated one another. Hamilton believed that Burr would do anything to advance himself, even to the detriment of the country. He said of Burr, "I feel it is a religious duty to oppose his career." During Burr's campaign for governor of New York, Hamilton used every means to oppose him, and he spoke so vehemently in public against him that Burr eventually challenged him to a duel. Dueling was still fairly common as a means for gentlemen to settle disputes, but New York prosecuted the practice, so the city's elite often took their disputes across the river. On July 11, 1804, at 7:00 AM, the two met. One account says that Hamilton purposely fired his shot into the air. Another says he took aim at Burr and missed. Burr then shot Hamilton in the stomach; he died later of his wound. The event became one of the most talked-about and written-about affairs of the decade.

L.C. End of Battery   Whitehall Slip   T.Elizabethtown Ferry   Clinry   Delafields Stores   Exchange Back
    Tackanpt Slip

Old Slip (foot of W.Y.)   Counsellors Wharf   Crugers Wharf   Old Dutch Church   Jones Wharf   Trinity Church   Wall Street   Federal Hall   Tontine Coffee House   City Hotel   Burrows Wharf   Scotch Pres.t Church
    1.st Pew.d Ch.

A View of the City of NEW-YORK from Brooklyn Heights, foot of Pierrepont, S.t in 1798 by Monsieur C.B. Julien, de S.t Memin, with a P.

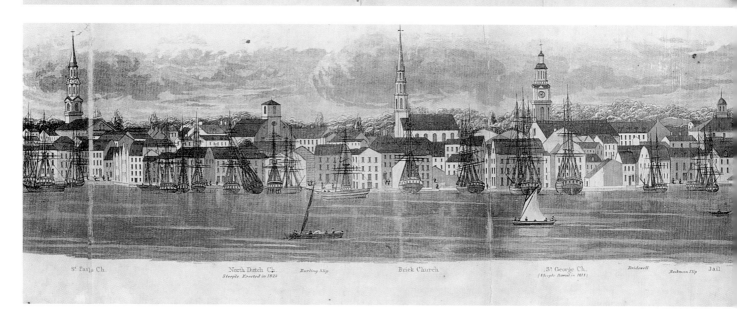

S.t Pauls Ch.   North Dutch Ch.   Burling Slip   Brick Church   S.t George Ch.   Bridewell   Jail
     Steeple Erected in 1828   (Steeple Burnt in 1814)   Beekman Slip

Charles Balthazar Julien Févret de Saint-Mémin, *A View of the City of New-York from Brooklyn Heights, foot of Pierrepont St. in 1798*

Charles Balthazar Julien Févret de Saint-Mémin, whose name suggests his aristocratic French background, fled the French Revolution and settled in the United States in 1793. He was destitute by the time he arrived, but he was a skilled artist and he had family connections. He thus was able to stay with John R. Livingston, whose brother had sworn in George Washington as president, in his Brooklyn home. The house had sweeping views of the harbor and the East River shore of Manhattan. "Charmed by the beauty of the landscape, M. de Saint-Mémin made a very exact drawing of it," Livingston said. Livingston informed the Frenchman that such an expansive view of the rapidly growing city was unique, and he suggested that if he were to make an engraving of it he would find that New Yorkers would be eager to buy copies. And so he did. The delicate image—broken here into three parts—manages to convey both the bustle of a busy port and a sense of tranquility. It shows how much the city had grown from its New Amsterdam beginnings. It is also remarkable that much of what Saint-Mémin depicts here was built since the fire of 1776.

2

The Formative Years

1800–1860

While many city plans are more beautiful in the abstract,
none has done more to facilitate the magnificent energy
of the flowing human city. The grid makes manageable the
messy humanity of millions.

—Ed Glaeser, 2011[1]

As the nineteenth century dawned, New York was an increasingly cosmopolitan place. With 60,000 residents, it was large in comparison to its Revolutionary War self, and 50 percent larger than its nearest rival, Philadelphia. And it was growing faster, with activity traced to the return of the patriot exiles and to a surge in economic and maritime commerce that followed the withdrawal of the British in 1783.

The steady growth in population after the war's close had pushed development as far north as Canal Street. The older, haphazardly placed streets at the southern end of the colonial town—many of which had once been Native-American trails or cow paths—were increasingly congested by the traffic associated with port businesses as well as domestic and retail life. Despite modest attempts to straighten and regularize these streets, it was clear that development on Manhattan Island could really only happen to the north—and doing so in a less erratic way would require some set of tools or framework.

Perhaps the earliest real attempt to bring some sort of planning to the growing metropolis of New York occurred in 1797, when Casimir Goerck, a veteran local surveyor, was hired to make a map of the city. Goerck died before he could complete the task, but his partner Joseph Mangin took the opportunity to represent in his map not "the plan of the City such as it is, but such as it is to be."[2] Mangin's improvements included new streets along the rivers' edges, widened and straightened streets at Manhattan's tip, and new streets laid out in five-acre grids that echoed private plans for dividing the existing farm holdings to the north. Included in it were three major 60-foot wide roads to the north: the "Bloomingdale Road" to the west, the "Eastern Post Road" to the east, and and the "Middle Road" between the two.

The Goerck-Mangin plan was ultimately rejected by its city sponsors, but it contributed to the idea of a grid-based plan for the city. Soon after, with the need for a planning tool increasingly clear, the State of New York set up an independent commission to plan the city's growth and more specifically to "unite regularity and order with the public convenience and benefit and in particular to promote the health of the city." Three commissioners—Gouverneur Morris, one of the respected "founding fathers" of the United States, former Senator and lawyer John Rutherford, and state surveyor Simeon DeWitt—were appointed to oversee the development of a plan for Manhattan from Houston Street to 155th Street, as far north as anyone could imagine people living.

The Commissioners' Plan

Over four years, every part of the island was surveyed by the Commissioners' appointed cartographer, John Randel Jr., with an eye to determining future street and block dimensions. The plan that was presented by the Commissioners in 1811 envisioned turning the rocky, hilly, and watery lands of Manhattan into a grid of north–south and east–west streets largely regular in their dimensions and precisely level, as if topography had no place in the future city.

The currency of the new grid would be its streets. Mistakenly thinking that most future traffic would move between shipping facilities on the rivers, the Commissioners drew up an extensive network of east–west streets, each 60 feet wide and 200 feet apart. A smaller number of 100-foot-wide avenues would stretch from north to south, with anywhere from 600 to 920 feet between them. The result was a series of rectangular blocks that could easily be subdivided into building lots.[3]

The unyielding efficiency of the grid was demonstrated in the absence of street names. New streets were numbered from 1 to 155 running to the north and and avenues from First to Twelfth running from east to west. The Cartesian system of X,Y coordinates made locating property, particularly for real estate transactions, easy and quick. It was a natural, albeit ambitious, extension of the numbering systems used in parts of Philadelphia and in Washington, D.C.

Beyond specifying street names and dimensions, the grid put forward by the Commissioners was not overly determinative. While the Commissioners noted that "straight-sided and right-angled houses are the most cheap to build and the most convenient to live in,"[4] they did not specify lot size; it was sufficient that the blocks were easily divided into 20- or 25-foot lots. It also did not speak to the massing or appearance of buildings, other than to specify that buildings on the wider avenues could rise to three stories high while those on the side streets would not extend beyond two stories.

Only a few exceptions to the proposed grid were incorporated in the initial plan. While recognizing the existing green spaces in Lower Manhattan, the Commissioners' Plan identified few future open spaces to the north. There was a sense that the island's unique location between two rivers at the mouth of an expansive harbor provided sufficient clean air and wind. As a result, the grid plan allocated only 470 of the available 14,600 acres for open space.

The most significant was a large Parade Ground, located between 23rd and 32nd Streets, running from Third to Seventh Avenues. In addition, the plan provided for an an armory and a large public market, the latter to be located on fifty-five acres of marshy (and presumably undevelopable) land between Third and

Seventh Streets at the East River. An observatory was slated for 42nd Street, perhaps as a holding place for a future reservoir.

The grid ignored existing property boundaries. The newly imagined streets cut right across farms, meadows, and estates. Roughly 40 percent of the buildings on Manhattan Island at that time were in the middle of one of the proposed streets. Given the island's topography, most buildings were either significantly higher or lower than the proposed street elevation: on the west side, buildings were an average of 118 feet above the new street level, while on the east side they were on average 46 feet higher. All would be leveled over time.

Equally brazen was the plan to pay for the "opening" of the new streets. Upon application by locals or on its own volition, the city would acquire the roadbed via condemnation, compensating the owners appropriately. It would then grade, pave, and open the street, recovering a portion of its outlays via assessments charged to property owners with frontage on the new street. Assessments would be levied up to three times: when the street was opened, again when it was paved, and once more when it was "improved" with sewers and other roadway infrastructure.

The proposed street grid touched every wealthy landowner in the city, in mostly unfavorable ways. Beloved homes in the middle of proposed streets would ultimately have to be moved or destroyed. No houses, except those in Greenwich Village and south of Houston Street, would be spared: in that sense, the grid was relentless and very democratic in its philosophy.

There were many challenges to implementation, mainly focused on the value of the building or street frontage and its relationship to the calculation of compensation or assessment. An extensive appeals process was established to adjudicate these disputes, and that remained in place over the next six decades as the grid plan was slowly brought to life.

For better or worse, the proposed leveling of earth made land an absolute commodity, something that could easily be traded, leveraged, and bought or sold. Without monumental squares or plazas or natural landmarks, any individual plot of land was very much like another: a potential buyer didn't really need to see it, or the physicality of the neighborhood around it, to understand its inherent value.

It is fair to say that the grid, in commoditizing land, became the engine that allowed real estate development to become New York's third industry after banking and maritime trade. It did not happen overnight, but rather over the course of the next century as immigration and industrial growth fueled demand for homes and workplaces. As historian Hilary Ballon noted, "The grid reconceptualized the island in one fell swoop, rationalized the real estate market, and enabled a change in the scale of development. In this sense, the 1811 grid gave birth to New York's modern real estate market."[5]

The implementation of the grid plan also propelled the evolution of the machinery of local government. It created revenue sources that the city could not have previously imagined, beginning with assessments associated with the opening of streets and extending to the growth of a significant property tax base. It also led to the initiation of municipal government oversight—to adjudicate claims, to regulate street openings, and ultimately to construct and manage these streets. This emerging regulatory and delivery function would be the forerunner of municipal governance as we know it in New York today.

Early Real Estate Development

As the city took on a larger role in its own expansion and development, the private sector began to perceive land as a new form of investment vehicle. Returns from real estate speculation could be as high as those of sending a cargo ship successfully abroad, with significant less risk. Amongst the earliest to recognize this opportunity was John Jacob Astor, a successful German fur trader whose small trading fortune would be dramatically magnified by his investment in land from the 1820s until his death in 1848.

Astor acquired and held vast tracts of land north of the city, including 250 acres in Greenwich Village, expansive farm holdings in what would become Midtown, and the legendary Vauxhall Gardens near today's Astor Place. He rented most of these properties to tenants, occasionally financing leasehold improvements that reverted to him at the end of the tenancy. Alternatively, he sold lots and provided financing to purchasers. By 1840 his 355 tenants were paying $128,000 annually, and his portfolio included farms, commercial property, houses, hotels, theaters, and grid and water lots. Among his most celebrated holdings was the Astor House Hotel, built in 1836 at Broadway and Vesey Street in Lower Manhattan. Six stories high, the hotel held eighteen shops and became a centerpiece of the social life of the town.

Astor was a towering figure in the earliest chapters of New York's real estate history, but he was not the only one. In contrast to Astor, whose primary mode of operation was to purchase and hold property until it became valuable, Samuel Ruggles used his civic status—as a statesman, a trustee of Columbia College, and a commissioner of the Erie Canal Corporation—to increase the value of his holdings. In 1830 he bought and then made ready for development a swath of property just north of 14th Street on the East Side, creating Gramercy Park at its center. Identifying 66 lots around this square, he began selling parcels with covenants that governed both height and building materials. In return, owners would collectively own the tax-exempt private park.

Ruggles knew the value of streets in opening up land values. He sacrificed six lots to introduce Irving Place to provide access to sites on the south side of Gramercy Park. He then convinced city and state officials to allow him to introduce a new north–south street between Third and Fourth Avenues, effectively extending Irving Place to the north. Lexington Avenue was the first named, rather than numbered, avenue in the gridded part of the city.

During this period, the city itself began to break with the grid plan, making the first move to retain Broadway's path through the island and extending it further north. Recognizing that the plan had not provided enough north–south capacity, the city then introduced Madison Avenue between Fourth and Fifth Avenues, opening up plots on either side to development. Both Lexington

and Madison Avenues were 75 feet wide, in contrast to the 100 feet that the grid had specified.

At the same time, the issue of open space began to be addressed. Between 1833 and 1836, Union Square, Tompkins Square, and Stuyvesant Square were all established. Madison Square, carved out of the Parade Ground identified on the plan, followed in 1847. Other parks included in the plan were not built, including Hamilton Square, on the East Side in the Sixties, Bloomingdale Square on the West Side in the Thirties, and Manhattan Square, along Central Park West at 77th Street, although the site is now the American Museum of Natural History. Harlem Square, intended to occupy land between Sixth and Seventh Avenues from West 117th Street to West 121st Street, was moved to an undevelopable rocky parcel at the top of Fifth Avenue, known today as Marcus Garvey Park.

The importance of land to the city's coffers was growing. In 1830 taxes on real estate produced $200,000 for the city. Seven years later, the city would receive more than five times that amount. As this revenue continued to grow, the city's ability to provide municipal services to address the challenges of rapid expansion and industrialization would grow as well, making real estate development a consistent priority across mayoral administrations.

Water for the City

The rapid growth of the city was marred by a devastating fire in Lower Manhattan in December 1835. Originating in a dry goods shop on Merchant Street (now Beaver), the fire was conveyed quickly by strong winter winds to other wooden structures in the area. Water taken by volunteer firemen from the rivers froze in the process of dousing the flames. Eventually gunpowder was used to blow up buildings in the fire's path, robbing it of fuel and bringing it under control some fifteen hours after it began. By then, most of the merchant district bordered by South, Wall, and Broad Streets was destroyed.[6]

The fire added momentum to the call for new water infrastructure for the city. With the filling-in of the

Collect Pond in 1811, firefighting relied primarily on some forty cisterns and a handful of neighborhood wells, supplemented by a modest-sized reservoir at 13th and Bowery. Whether for drinking or firefighting, it was rapidly becoming clear that Manhattan's continuing evolution would depend on its ability to tap into new and significantly larger volumes of water.

The Manhattan Company, pursuant to a 1799 franchise to develop new sources of water,[7] had implemented a limited delivery system, drawing water from a well near the Collect Pond and storing it in a 550,000-gallon reservoir near Chambers Street. Six miles of mains connected the reservoir to some 400 customers; the system would later be extended to 25 miles of mains reaching 2,000 customers.

Despite its monopoly on commercial water, the Manhattan Company's investments could not match the growing need for water across the city. A cholera epidemic in 1832 forced more than 100,000 people to temporarily abandon the city. Pollution and seepage from cesspools, privies, and street run-off was increasingly thought to be a contributing factor to the rising levels of disease.

The most promising solution was the proposal to dam the Croton River in northern Westchester and draw its water to the city through a gravity-fed aqueduct. The plan was ambitious in both concept and scale: a 400-acre lake created in Croton would use 40 miles of tunnels to bring water to a pair of receiving and distributing reservoirs in Manhattan, the former on a 35-acre plot between 79th and 86th Streets and Sixth and Seventh Avenues (now the Great Lawn of Central Park) and the latter on a smaller site at the southwest corner of Fifth Avenue and 42nd Street (today the site of the New York Public Library).

The engineering to bring clean Croton River water to Manhattan was herculean in scale. Sixteen tunnels had to be threaded through a variety of terrains, requiring condemnation of more than 500 acres of land. Reaching the Bronx, the water tunnels then had to cross the Harlem River, and the magnificent arched High Bridge was completed in 1848 to carry the water pipes to Manhattan.

Even before the completion of High Bridge, the Croton system was carrying clean water to the city; by 1844 more than 6,000 homes were connected. But the availability of water did not immediately overcome the threat of fire. In the summer of 1845, another fire broke out in Lower Manhattan, on New Street, one block south of Wall. Ignited in a whale oil and candle store, it spread to a nearby warehouse that exploded, blowing out windows as far as a mile away and setting adjacent buildings alight. By the time the fire was tamed eleven hours later, some 345 buildings had been lost, taking with them the last vestiges of Dutch architecture in the area.

Emerging Neighborhoods

By the 1830s, new divisions began to emerge in the city. Half a century earlier, there had been little separation of work and domestic life. Craftsmen and merchants typically lived where they worked, often providing housing for long-term apprentices or employees. By the early decades of the nineteenth century, however, with a growing and increasingly cyclical economy, few businesses wanted to be so committed to their employees. New forms of transportation facilitated this separation of work and domestic life, allowing downtown workers to commute from their homes in the north. Newly arrived immigrants took over the neighborhoods near the docks.

Whereas artisans, merchants, and financiers had all coexisted in the colonial towns of New Amsterdam and New York, by 1840 professions and crafts had scattered. Artisans relocated to areas along Canal Street. Broadway and Fifth Avenue became spines of retail and residential corridors respectively, lined with hotels, casinos, and upmarket stores. Brownstones appeared along Fifth Avenue north of Washington Square, adjacent to the new retail corridor along Broadway.

The wealth created by real estate would make itself felt in the architecture of both private and public buildings. The utilitarian character of federal period buildings was replaced by elaborate temples of commerce, such as the five-story Lord & Taylor building at

Broadway and Grand Street, which featured a marble facade with a two-story arched entrance. Private houses along Fifth Avenue alluded to European chateaux and villas, and civic buildings, like the Custom House, were modeled on Greek and Roman temples.

The contrast between the increasingly elaborate houses and commercial establishments to the north and the rapid deterioration of areas closer to the waterfront is seen best in the history of Five Points, a neighborhood that emerged on the site of the Collect Pond. For both topographic and geographic reasons, Five Points became the city's first slum.

The removal of the Collect Pond forced the relocation of tanneries, water-dependent factories, and other businesses. Though the land in that area was far from pristine—it flooded and shifted regularly—many of the commercial landowners held on to their property and allowed the construction of cheap residential structures to meet the growing demand for low-cost housing.

Immigrant workers, who could not afford to commute or buy land, needed to rent space in a central location close to their jobs, giving rise to the idea of a "tenant house" (and ultimately "tenement"). Leases were short, as neither owners nor workers felt secure enough in the new arrangement to extend beyond twelve to eighteen months at a time. As a result, the new neighborhoods had a transient feel, with families relocating every year or two.

The first "tenant house" was recorded in 1824 on Mott Street. The size of some of these tenements meant that they could be divided up into multiple dwellings, with homes ranging in size from a small apartment to a single room. Often a sub-landlord was hired to manage the turnover of transient tenants. Demand was rarely a problem; the swelling numbers of immigrants ensured a robust market. Returns to the owner were said to be in the range of 17 to 26 percent annually and to the sub-landlord up to 300 percent.

Conditions in Five Points deteriorated from the 1830s to the 1850s, as waves of immigration from Ireland and the German States accelerated and shabby tenements proliferated. Inner apartments often had no light and air, and all had poor sanitation. Tenants frequently took in random boarders to help pay the rent: it was not unusual to find a dozen or more people crowded into a low-ceilinged room with no natural light. Five Points owners had no incentive to invest in maintenance: demand was strong and improvements to buildings would only result in higher taxes.

Crowded tenements bred a variety of behaviors considered immoral by many. Streets were crowded with the detritus of residential and commercial life, the visible representation of neighborhood vice. As *Frank Leslie's Illustrated* newspaper noted in 1873, "FIVE POINTS! . . . The very letters of the two words, which mean so much, seem, as they are written, to redden with the bloodstains of unavenged crime. There is Murder in every syllable, and Want, Misery and Pestilence take startling form and crown upon the imagination as the pen traces the words. What a world of wretchedness has been concentrated in this narrow district!"[8]

So bawdy and notorious was Five Points that tourists were taken to witness its wonders: fighting, drinking, gambling, dancing, prostitution—a harbinger of what would be repeated in the Tenderloin and Times Square areas more than fifty years later. Ethnic flare-ups and riots were common, hardly surprising given the density of the area and the cultural differences among immigrants. But at least during the first half of the nineteenth century, there was no sense that slum life was a problem for government to solve; that would come later.

Central Park

The massive growth of population and the impact of industrialization in certain parts of the city confirmed what many observers of the evolving city-on-a-grid already knew: more space needed to be devoted to parks and recreation. William Cullen Bryant, the respected editor of the *New York Evening Post*, made open space his personal crusade. While most came to agree with his vision for a large, new park, where to put it was another question.

Jones Wood, a heavily vegetated area between Third Avenue and the East River and 66th to 75th Streets, was initially chosen, but commercial interests did not want to lose the riverfront to recreation. Real estate interests saw tremendous value in creating a larger, more centrally located park to push development farther north. The proposed site, extending from Fifth to Eighth Avenues and 59th to 106th Streets, was as derelict an area as could have been found in New York City at the time. Most of it was rocky and swampy terrain, punctuated by rock outcroppings and barren flats. Any original tree canopy was long gone, used as firewood by the assorted settlers in the area. African Americans could be found in Seneca Village on its west side and Native Americans and immigrants elsewhere, many living in impoverished conditions—lean-tos, shacks, and even caves. In addition to the estimated 5,000 residents of the 778-acre site, many of whom made their living scavenging, raising goats, or boiling bones, there were an estimated 100,000 animals roaming the area, among them horses, pigs, dogs, cats, chickens, and goats.

An estimated 1,000 workers were employed in cleaning out debris and taking apart the shantytowns and walls that had protected gardens from pigs. The Central Park police force was formed to oversee the job and deal with protests from the locals. Overseeing it all as Superintendent, from 1857, was Frederick Law Olmsted, who with Calvert Vaux would win an international design competition to bring life to the unattractive expanse of land. Their plan, known as the Greensward Plan, defied the functional street grid around it, the kind of streets that were "staked off," as Olmsted put it, "with a rule and pencil in a broker's office." As one observer noted, Olmsted's plan for Central Park was designed as an antidote to the city: "Here therapeutically romantic curves were to be the rule. Pedestrians and carriages would meander along paths affording ever-changing vistas, rather like a succession of Cole or Durand canvasses, intended to invoke decorous contemplation of nature, in a manner of Bryant's poems."[9]

Olmsted was not oblivious to real estate market forces. He noted that, while an expensive undertaking, the new park would "greatly accelerate the occupation of the adjoining land," pleasing wealthy Fifth Avenue landowners, and "increase tax revenues, a claim calculated to warm the hearts of city officials."[10] His claims were borne out, and quickly: land values and hence property taxes rose dramatically along the park's borders even before it was completed.

Olmsted and Vaux's Greensward Plan would set the standard for urban parks going forward. It featured a tri-functional system of pedestrian paths, horse trails, and carriage roads knit together in ingenious fashion by forty attractive stone bridges. Four sunken roadways tied the gridded streets east and west of the park together. The philosophy of the design was as democratic as the grid that embraced it: dozens of openings from surrounding streets were intended to bring different groups of New Yorkers together outdoors.

The city paid $5 million for the roughly 7,500 building lots in the park it condemned, and then a subsequent $1.2 million for land between 106th and 110th Streets, considered unbuildable because of the Harlem Meer. Some of the funding came from assessments on property owners whose land stood to benefit from the new park; the balance was raised via a "Central Park Fund" stock issue, secured by the land itself.

Central Park was just one, albeit the biggest, nineteenth-century departure from the Commissioners' Plan. Between its debut in 1811 and 1865, some thirty-eight state laws modifying the plan were passed, including three that secured the future of a special diagonal street intended to terminate at 23rd Street that we know today as Broadway.

By the end of the Civil War, the impact of the Commissioners' Plan was clear, not just in the physical fabric of the streets but also in the confidence it had given to real estate investors and speculators. Streets had been paved up to 59th Street, and the impending completion of Central Park ensured that speculation in properties to the north would continue. The city's role in securing land for the park implied its commitment to growth and a recognition of the wealth—for the city—that real estate development could bring.

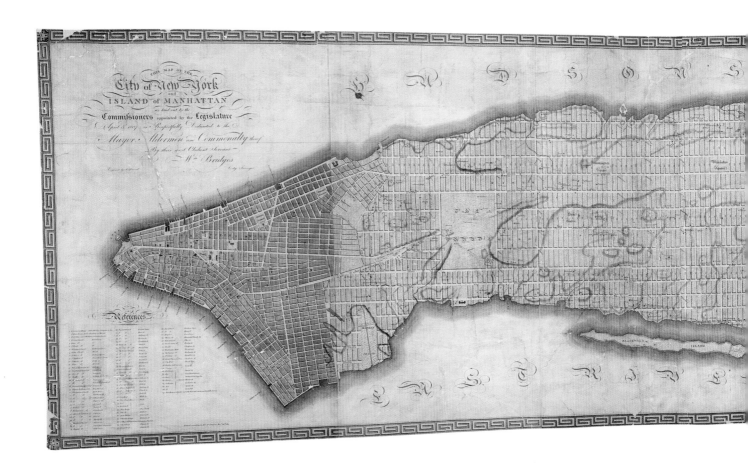

William Bridges, Map of Manhattan, 1811

William Bridges set a new format for maps of Manhattan with this stunning example of 1811. It records the plan for a grid up to 155th Street that a state-appointed commission, the city's first de facto planning board, had produced in March 1811. With the exception of the British Headquarters Map of 1782, earlier maps depicted only the southern tip of Manhattan. But inspired by the Commissioners' far-reaching plan, Bridges portrayed the full length of the island, in a landscape format stretching almost seven and one-half feet long (the map is made of six sheets). Like earlier mapmakers, he differentiated

the developed area, which is shaded, from the undeveloped area, which in 1811 was most of the island. Many nineteenth-century mapmakers adopted the horizontal format and shading convention to chart the filling in of the grid; derived from Bridges's work of 1811, this family of maps superbly visualizes the march of urbanization up the island.

Bridges was the first to produce a printed version of the Commissioners' Plan. The Commissioners issued their plan in three manuscript drawings that were probably executed by their chief surveyor John Randel Jr. The ink

drawings were uncolored, vertically oriented, and unadorned but for the signatures and wax seals that confirmed the legal status of the drawings as the official city plan. Bridges transformed their legal document into a magnificent picture of the city's ambition. Bridges, who was a city surveyor but played no role in Randel's extensive survey for the 1811 plan, scooped his rival by publishing this print and eliding his name, not Randel's, with the grid. Very few copies of the Bridges's map are known to survive. Daniel Haskell's 1931 inventory of Manhattan maps identified copies in four public collections, some colored, to

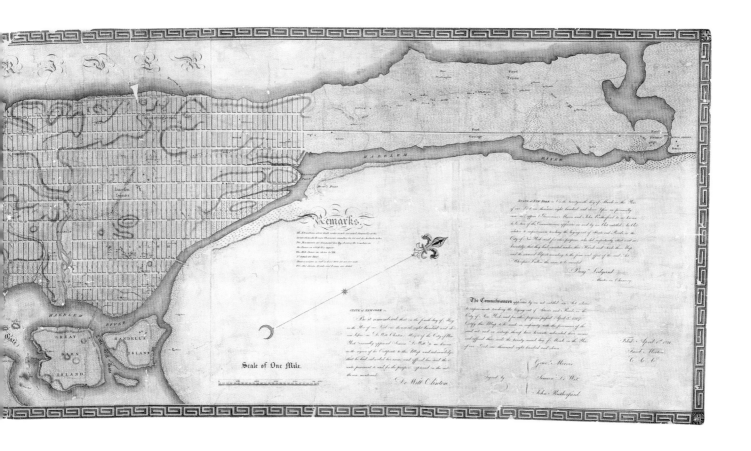

which can now be added this uncolored copy in the Durst Collection.

While faithfully recording the information on the Randel drawings, Bridges created a more powerful image that reads like a monumental scroll with layers of rich detail about topography, old streets, and structures as well as the future grid. But was Bridges or his fine engraver Peter Maverick responsible for the artistry? Bridges and Maverick, a prolific engraver in early nineteenth-century New York, had previously collaborated on a map in 1807, "Plan of the city of New-York: with the recent and intended improvements,"

also in the Durst Collection. The 1807 map, like virtually all earlier maps, concentrated on the populated southern tip of the island and included a proposal to grid the Lower East Side with several squares. Maverick's engraving shows a variety of linear effects that suggest contours in the land, marshes, rippling water, and roads condemned for removal. The shading of the rectangular city blocks on two sides give them relief, as if they were three-dimensional blocks, and the variety of lettering styles creates a subtle visual hierarchy.

Following Bridges's map, the landscape orientation of Manhattan became

one of the two primary formats in maps of the city, and by mid-century it would eclipse the partial view of Lower Manhattan as the city literally outgrew that format. Bridges included the islands in the East River and part of Long Island, and inscribed explanatory information where Queens lies. Thus, the map also anticipates the next evolution of the format to include the surrounding areas of Brooklyn, Queens, and New Jersey.

Samuel Marks, A New Map of the City of New York, 1827

As depicted in this map, drawn by Samuel Marks in 1827, the Manhattan grid is not oriented to true north; it is rotated about 29 degrees to the east. Marks's map exhibits the divergence by pointing north to the right and allowing the island to tilt diagonally downward. The grid is thus cut on a bias, running from West 31st Street to East 45th Street on the right edge of the map. Curiously a few blocks extend across the edge, evidently to include a "chemical factory" between 32nd and 33rd Streets on the waterfront.

Following a convention of earlier maps, the occupied city blocks are shaded and the undeveloped blocks are blank, which graphically emphasizes the edge of development. The city has filled in along Third Avenue, "the road to Haerlem," to 14th Street, and along Eighth Avenue to 20th Street. The map is one of the earliest to show Lafayette Street, which was opened in 1825, and Washington Square, also established in 1825.

At the bottom of the map are illustrations of two key city institutions: the Merchant's Exchange, where building

lots were sold, and City Hall. The map itself shows the footprint of relatively few buildings and traces of older streets, including Middle Road, Eastern Post Road, and Bloomingdale Road. The Durst Collection map has colored outlines of the fourteen wards; in other copies the ward boundaries are not colored. Samuel Marks was the publisher, but the map engraver is unnamed. He was a novice or poor copyist, judging by the artless design; note the overflowing margin, the inconsistently oriented labels, the floating, unimpressive map title, and abundant blank space.

The map accompanied James Hardie's guidebook, *The description of the city of New York* (New York, 1827). Crease marks indicate how the fold-out map was reduced to pocket size to tuck into the book. The map gives an overall picture of the city, which was useful for general orientation but not navigation, and reflects the status of the guidebook at this moment as a compendium of historical and current information about the city, but not as an in-situ guide to explicate sights for travelers.

Charles Magnus, New-York City & County Map with Vicinity Entire: Brooklyn, WIlliamsburgh, Jersey City, 1854

In this map of 1854, Charles Magnus depicts Manhattan as the spine of an expanding urban area. The map follows the landscape orientation of Bridges's 1811 map, but expands the scope to encompass the urbanizing environs, in particular the areas then known as Brooklyn, Williamsburgh, and Greenpoint as well as Jersey City and Hoboken, where Magnus lived. The expanded geographic area opens compositional space for other elements in the lower portion of the map: a view of City Hall on the left; a key to important buildings; an inset map of Long Island and Staten Island; and on the right, an inscription of the Declaration of Independence enclosed by medallions of the thirteen founding states. This patriotic inflection was not due to a milestone celebration; rather, the patriotic content may reflect personal or professional concerns.

Born in Prussia in 1826, Charles Magnus immigrated to New York City in 1848. After working for a German newspaper, he opened a lithography printing shop on 12 Frankfort Street in 1854, the year he became a naturalized U.S. citizen and published this map. Some versions of the map are dated 1854 or 1855. Other copies are undated, including this one, but the inscription ("in the 79th year") points to 1854. Until his death in 1900, Magnus was a prolific publisher of

ephemera: games, playing cards, letter sheets with views of American cities, song sheets, Civil War battle scenes, portraits, and views of New York City. His 1854 map might be seen as a calling card, a bravura demonstration of his expertise in lithographic publishing in the year he became an American.

The map uses the standard pictorial strategy of shaded blocks to show the northward growth of Manhattan, which has reached 50th Street except along Fourth Avenue, where the railroad drove development up to 93rd Street. The northern tip of Manhattan interrupts the decorative frame on the right; this interruption, which could have been easily avoided by a slight adjustment, serves to reinforce the idea of a dynamic, almost uncontainable city.

Published just before the creation of Central Park, the map depicts the infrastructure of the Croton system that would soon be incorporated in the new park: the original Receiving Reservoir between 79th and 86th Streets and the plan for a "New Receiving Reservoir," rectangular in shape, between 86th and 96th Streets, which was not yet built at this time. Two newly opened avenues are depicted: Madison Avenue runs from 23rd to 42nd Street and Lexington Avenue from 14th to 66th Street (at the south end it is called Irving Place).

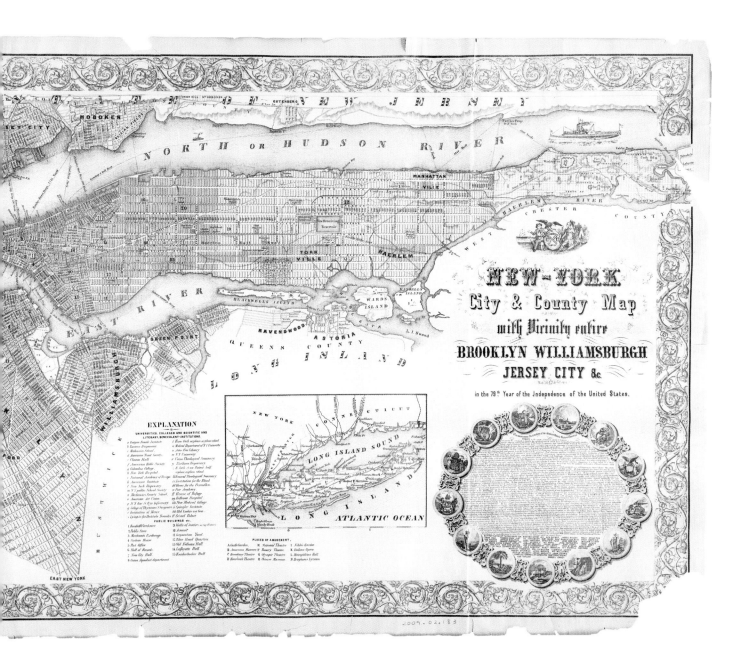

**David H. Burr, Map of the Country
Twenty-five Miles Round the City
of New York, 1831**

Drawn by David Burr, this circular map of 1831 locates Manhattan at the center of a metaphorical universe. The circle has ancient symbolic associations with the cosmos and was adopted by early-modern cartographers in representations of the eastern and western hemispheres, the north and south poles, and celestial charts. While circular maps of small areas were uncommon, Burr derived his map from a New York precedent: "Map of the Country Thirty Miles Round of the City of New York," drawn by cartographer Isaac H. Eddy, engraved by Peter Maverick, and published by Prior and Dunning in 1812.

Compared to Eddy's prototype, Burr intensified the focus on Manhattan. He reduced the radius from thirty to twenty-five miles, vividly colored the map, and outlined the grid so that the tip of Manhattan vividly reads as the center point of the region and water system where the bay meets the Hudson and East Rivers. This fortunate geography allowed New York to become the country's leading port city and accounted for its central role, as the map symbolizes. The compass frame degree markings locate the metropolitan region in relation to wider systems, with the longitude of the city compared to that of Washington, D.C., and Greenwich, England, the locus of mean time.

Burr's circular map was followed in 1846 by a more decorative version by J. H. Colton, who enlarged the radius to thirty-three miles. The density of lines and information as well as the distracting floral border diminish the visual impact of Manhattan on Colton's map. An 1849 circular map by J. C. Sidney regained clarity largely by tightening the focus and reducing the radius to twelve miles. Among this set of nineteenth-century circular maps, Burr's map of 1831 stands out for effectively conveying the idea of Manhattan as a metropolitan city.

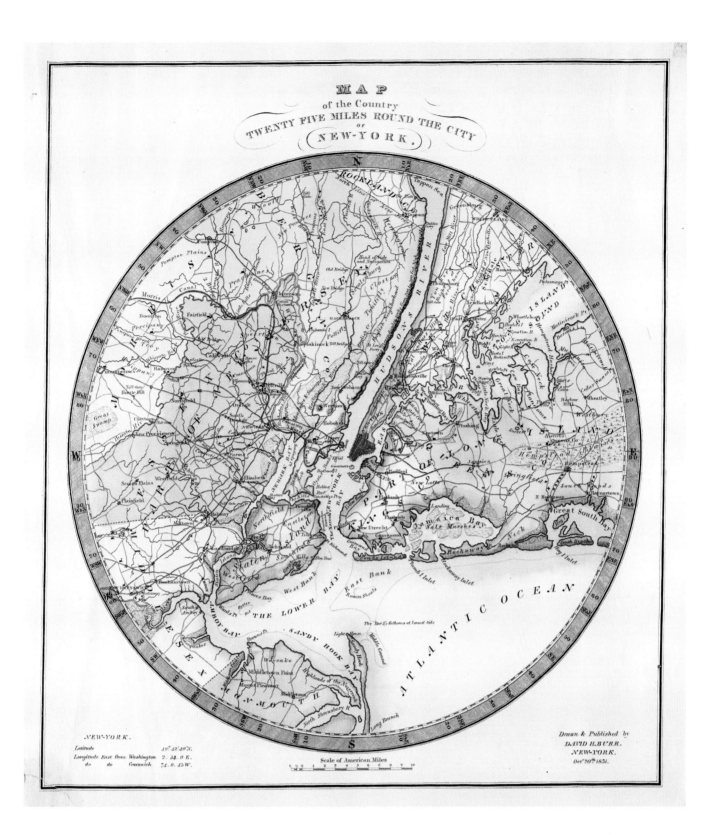

MAP
of the Country
TWENTY FIVE MILES ROUND THE CITY
OF
NEW-YORK.

NEW-YORK.

Latitude   40° 42' 40" N.
Longitude East from Washington   2. 54. 0 E.
do   do   Greenwich   74. 0. 45 W.

Scale of American Miles

Drawn & Published by
DAVID H. BURR.
NEW-YORK.
Oct. 20th 1834.

George Hayward, View of Fulton Street, 1828

In this image, the lithographer George Hayward positions the viewer at the East River waterfront looking west along Fulton Street. The slips and Brooklyn ferry pier are behind; Fulton Market is on the right, and the shops and warehouses of Schermerhorn Row, where horses line up loaded with barrels of merchandise, are on the left. This was one of the busiest commercial streets of the early nineteenth-century city, but the print shows a quieter scene of architecturally composed urban order. The vista is closed off by buildings along Water Street and beyond them rises the tower of St. Paul's Chapel, at the corner of Broadway and Fulton Street.

The Fulton Market, built in 1821 after a fire in the vicinity had cleared the site, was the city's finest market. The arcaded structure was managed by the Deputy Clerk, who resided in the pavilion over

the main entrance. Adjacent to the docks, the location facilitated the sale of cargo unloaded from boats, and visitors extolled the bounty of the foodstuffs sold at the market. But the early years of the market were marked by friction: butchers, the primary tenants, protested the city's high rents; they objected to the building design that required hoisting merchandise to a raised floor (see the tall steps on the right); and fishermen encroached on the market, along with their smelly mess.

The title dates the view to 1828, but the print was published in 1854 in the *Manual of the Corporation of the City New York*. An act of the state legislature called for publication of the *Manual*, which David Thomas Valentine, clerk of the Common Council, began in 1842 and continued with almost annual editions until his death in 1869 and after whom

these extraordinary records of the nineteenth-century city are known as *Valentine's Manual*. The first several editions had few illustrations, but in the early 1850s Valentine arrived at his preferred formula: a frontispiece map of the current city, hundreds of pages of information about the city, and scattered illustrations without explanatory text. Rarely depicting the modern city, the illustrations typically looked back to earlier decades. For many years, Valentine relied on George Hayward, who typically copied earlier prints. Hayward's source in this case appears to be an etching by William J. Bennett, published by Henry J. Megarey in 1834. The illustrations in *Valentine's Manual* have a nostalgic quality, recalling earlier scenes in a city fast erasing its history. The Durst Collection includes many prints from these volumes.

City Hall and the adjoining park, 1840s

This engraving depicts the civic hub of the city: City Hall and the park at its doorstep, framed by Broadway on the left and Park Row on the right. John McComb Jr. and Joseph François Mangin won the design competition for City Hall in 1802. After the design was modified to cut costs at the insistence of the Common Council, City Hall was built between 1810 and 1812. Its monumental form with columnar facade and cupola replaced a more modest structure on Wall Street, which was subsequently destroyed. City Hall was the iconic civic monument of nineteenth-century New York, often appearing on maps to represent the city's grandeur and order. When the Manhattan grid was established in 1811, measurements were recorded on the map from the new City Hall.

The park was an integral part of this civic space. Originally part of the commons and used for pasturage, the area was enclosed in 1792 and subsequently a portion of the land was transformed into a park. As seen here, the park is surrounded by an iron fence with four marble pillars dating from 1821. Paths cut across a lawn planted with occasional elm, plane, and willow trees. A file of poplars adorns the sidewalk. Shortly after this print was published, the simple water pump at the apex of the park was replaced by a sizable fountain supplied with Croton water beginning in 1842.

The print is enlivened by the street life: a militia marches down Broadway, horse-drawn carriages and trams and carts laden with merchandise fill the streets, pedestrians of distinctly different classes—working men, parasol-carrying ladies, and their gents—chat, stroll, and work. The buildings on Broadway are not visible, but the aerial perspective already suggests the urban impulse to build taller and to survey the urban spectacle.

The engraving by James Archer was after a drawing by William Henry Bartlett, a British artist. It comes from a series Bartlett made during a visit to the United States in 1835 and published in *American Scenery; or Land, Lake, and River. Illustrations of Transatlantic Nature* in 1840. (The Park and City Hall was first published in volume 1, p. 103, but this copy comes from a later edition; the inscription reads Vol. II, p. 393.) Willis's commentary includes a colorful description of Broadway: "Broadway is a noble street, and on its broad side-walks may be seen everything that walks the world in the shape of a foreigner, or a fashion—beauties by the score, and men of business by the thousand; but, besides every possible ingredient of peripatetics seen never on foreign *pavés* but in rare specimens—coloured dandies, and belligerent pigs." Not a single pig can be seen on the sanitized streets of Archer's delicate engraving.

N. W. cor of Fulton st + Broadway A.D. 1829

Northwest corner of Broadway and Fulton Street, 1829

This view of the northwest corner of Fulton Street and Broadway triangulates three key sites of the early nineteenth-century city. On the left, St. Paul's Chapel (1764–66) reveals its obelisk and Ionic portico, but the partial view downplays the monumentality of the Episcopal chapel. The artist instead draws attention to the billboarded wall announcing lotteries and sales and the pedestrian activity on the sidewalk.

The lively mix of Broadway is evoked by a horse-drawn cart before Bush's store, bonneted ladies on the arms of gentlemen, and street peddlers. In the distance rises City Hall, and on the right, is the American Museum at the corner of Ann Street and Broadway. Scudder's American Museum was established in 1810 and operated at a low level until it was purchased and reinvented by P. T. Barnum in 1841. Barnum also bought the

neighboring Peale's Museum in 1843 and enlivened the facade of his buildings with advertising and attention-grabbing decor. The undated print captures a moment before Barnum transformed the American Museum, and the two- and three-story buildings south of the museum were replaced by the five- and six-story buildings shown in prints of the 1840s. There is no other catalogued copy of this anonymous engraving.

Archibald L Dick, View of Broadway, 1831

This print of 1831 shows Broadway from Liberty Street looking south and revealing the buildings on the west side of the thoroughfare. In the distance, at left, and largely obscured except for its circular tower, is the original Grace Church, at the corner of Rector Street, built in 1808. Next to it is Trinity Church, its semi-circular portico, tower, and spire dramatizing the street facade.

In the center of the print is the City Hotel, built in 1794–96. According to Sarah Landau and Carl Condit, it is "the first newly built structure in America that qualifies as a hotel." Designed by John McComb Jr., architect of City Hall and St. Mark's-in-the-Bowery, the building had 137 rooms and was equipped with a range of entertaining spaces—a bar, coffee room, and concert and ballrooms. In 1828, just three years before this print was published, John Jacob Astor bought the hotel, his initial foray into the hospitality business. It led to a plan in 1833 to build a hotel on the site of his own house a block to the north, opposite City Hall Park, between Vesey and Barclay Streets. In 1834 Astor House opened, and Astor let the City Hotel run down.

At right, north of Cedar Street, are shops with wares displayed in the windows and legible street signs for Clinton's, J. L. Hewitt, Hewitt & Co., and R. & W. Nunns Piano Forte Warehouse.

This engraving by Archibald Dick was published in *Views in New-York and Its Environs from Accurate, Characteristic and Picturesque Drawings* by James H. Dakin and Theodore S. Fay. (The Durst Collection copy is removed from the volume.) It informed the print by George Hayward of the same scene published in *Valentine's Manual* of 1854.

Map of Croton aqueduct system, c. 1846

The construction of the Croton aqueduct system was the most extensive and ambitious public works project in New York during the first half of the nineteenth century. Largely executed between 1835 and 1842, the Croton system officially opened on July 4, 1842, with a grand celebration, although the High Bridge, which carried the aqueduct across the Harlem from the Bronx to Manhattan, was not completed until 1848. In *Providing the City with Water*, Theophilus T. Schramke, a draughtsman and member of the Croton corps of engineers, describes the engineering feat in plain language accompanied by line illustrations of each component of the system. Published by the author in 1846, with a second edition in 1855, the book appeared in English, French, and German. The Croton system was a critical investment in the city's infrastructure and a major advance in public health. Schramke's multilingual edition reflects pride in this achievement as well as interest in a European audience.

This hydrographic map, produced as a lithograph by Nathaniel Currier,

combines three elements. A regional map underscores the reach of Manhattan into the surrounding area and the reordering of the countryside to provision the fast-growing city. Traversing Putnam and Westchester Counties, the system channeled water from the Croton River, which was dammed to form Croton Lake, into Manhattan, covering a total distance of forty-five miles from the lake to the Battery. Outside the city the system was largely invisible because the aqueduct was underground, but in Manhattan it entailed a series of monumental infrastructures: the High Bridge, the Receiving and Distributing Reservoirs, two gatehouses and a fountain at Union Square, as well as an underground network of 134 miles of pipe. The sectional drawing at the top shows the elevation changes as the conduits crossed Manhattan; the system was gravity fed, the downward slope of the land propelling the flow of water. A corresponding plan shows the line of the aqueduct in Manhattan and calls out the reservoirs.

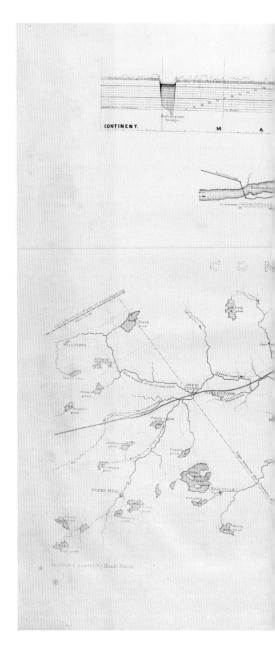

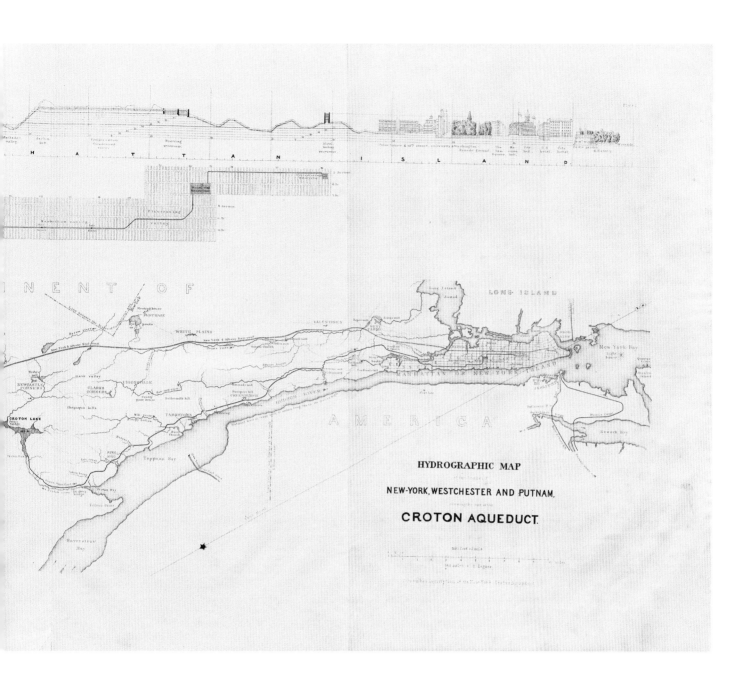

HYDROGRAPHIC MAP
of the boundary of
NEW-YORK, WESTCHESTER AND PUTNAM,
showing the course of the
CROTON AQUEDUCT.

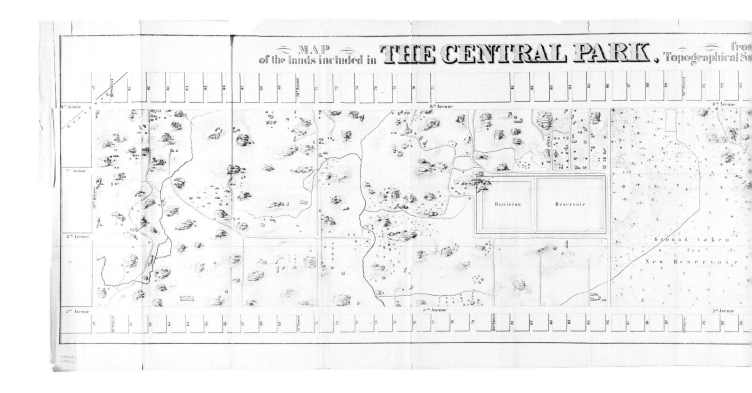

**Egbert L. Viele, Map of the Lands
Included in the Central Park, 1856**

In 1856 New York City Mayor Fernando Wood appointed Egbert Viele as chief engineer of Central Park. A West Point–trained engineer, Viele had served in the Mexican-American War and was working as the state engineer of New Jersey when he was recruited to work on the park. He oversaw a team of four surveyors and twelve axe- and chainmen who undertook the physically laborious work of measuring and mapping the 778-acre site, bounded by 59th and 106th Streets, Fifth and Eighth Avenues. The location was selected in 1854, in part because the city already owned substantial acreage and in part because the rugged ground reduced the acquisition costs of the remaining land. The city-owned land included the site of a new receiving reservoir, a rectangular area north of the original reservoir and lightly outlined on the plan.

Viele's plan published in 1856 depicts boulders, streams, pre-grid streets, and the footprint of extant structures, including the Arsenal, the Receiving Reservoir, Mount St. Vincent, and the smaller buildings of Seneca Village, the community of African Americans and Irish and German immigrants concentrated between 81st and 86th Streets on the west side of the reservoir. Viele's plan, however, gives little pictorial sense of the topographical conditions, the vegetation, the estimated 1,600 residents who lived on the park site, their habitations and workshops, nor the outlines of 7,520 lots that carved up the site and triggered the protracted eminent domain process by which the city acquired privately owned lots. By contrast, Viele's 1865 topographical and hydrographic map of the city, also in the Durst Collection but incom-

plete, is a magnificent, richly detailed record of both underground and ground conditions.

The survey work evidently kindled Viele's design ambitions, and he submitted a scheme for the park in the summer of 1856. It stood uncontested until the Central Park board decided in 1857 to run a design competition, which led to the selection in April 1858 of the Greensward plan by Frederick Law Olmsted and Calvert Vaux. The association of Viele, Olmsted, and Vaux continued at Prospect Park, where Viele also conducted the site survey, in 1860. Viele went on to an illustrious career of public service, serving as Brigadier General in the Union Army during the Civil War, New York City Commissioner of Parks, and representative for New York in Congress.

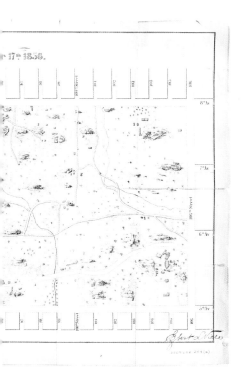

Matthew Dripps, Plan of Central Park, 1860s

This plan by Matthew Dripps illustrates the final design of Olmsted and Vaux, following the acquisition in 1863 of land that extended the park from 106th to 110th Street and increased its area from 778 to 843 acres. The plan also shows several other changes in the Greensward plan: the Green was reduced from 25 to 16 acres; a network of pedestrian pathways was developed apart from the wider carriage drives; a refectory near West 72nd Street and conservatory near East 74th Street were added, both delineated on the map in dashed lines to indicate they were not yet built.

After rejecting a plan to build monumental gates designed by Richard Morris Hunt in 1864, the Central Park board decided in 1866 to name the south gates. The Dripps plan documents a comprehensive naming scheme based on classes of people; Merchants, Artisans, Artists, and Scholars are the inviting names on the south side of the park, whereas the names on 110th Street—Strangers, Warriors, Farmers, and Pioneers—are fiercer.

Under the leadership of Andrew Haswell Green, the Central Park commissioners expanded their planning scope to areas north of the park. This plan hints at one of the commissioners' unrealized projects: the widening of Sixth and Seventh Avenues from 100 to 150 feet to convert them into European-style planted boulevards.

The uncluttered legibility of the Dripps plan, with selective information creating high visual impact, makes it a compelling record of Central Park, the city's great midcentury achievement, but it is unclear how widely circulated it was. The map is not in the other major New York City map collections.

SOUTH GATE HOUSE, NEW RESERVOIR, DURING CONSTRUCTION.
Viewed in the direction of the East Water Entrance.

Construction of the Croton aqueduct system's New Receiving Reservoir, 1862

Within a decade, the Croton system fell short of demand. In 1851, recognizing the need for additional storage capacity, the Common Council directed the Croton Aqueduct Department to build a new reservoir with a sixty-day holding capacity. The chosen site was between Fifth and Seventh Avenues between 86th and 96th Streets, directly north of the Yorkville Receiving Reservoir. As seen in Charles Magnus's 1854 map, the original idea was for a rectangular basin like the first reservoir. It took until 1856 for the city to acquire the land, by which time Central Park was underway, and the park designers reconceived a blocky reservoir as a lake with irregular, "natural" contours.

Constructed between 1859 and 1862, the New Receiving Reservoir could store 1 billion gallons of Croton water. The 1862 edition of *Valentine's Manual* marked the completion of the reservoir with three prints of the hydraulic engineering, including this lithograph by A. Brown & Co. of the South Gate, where the mains connect to the Old Receiving Reservoir. The view is from outside the reservoir, looking north, and shows six large mains, each 48 inches in diameter (the original Croton mains were 36 inches). In contrast to the typical picturesque, nostalgic images in *Valentine's Manual*, this print emphasizes the scale of the hydraulic infrastructure. Although the earthworks are vivid, the scene evokes a naval battleship, the mains like a battery of cannons overseen on the deck by their commanding engineers.

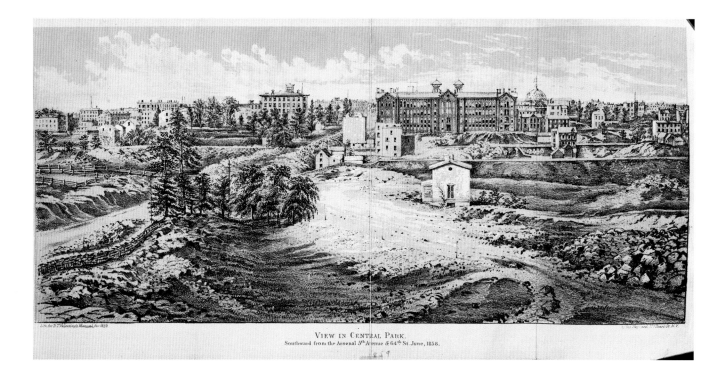

VIEW IN CENTRAL PARK.
Southward from the Arsenal 5th Avenue & 64th St. June, 1858.

George Hayward, *View in Central Park*, 1858

Dated June 1858, this print shows the city approaching the southeast corner of Central Park soon after the Park Commissioners selected Frederick Law Olmsted and Calvert Vaux's design in April 1858.

Olmsted and Vaux's design required extensive reshaping of the landscape. As Elizabeth Blackmar and Roy Rosenzweig explain in their book *The Park and the People*, in summer 1857, a workforce of twenty-six gangs, each with fifteen to twenty men, "stripped the land of its social and natural history, dismantling stone walls, clearing out old pig yards, digging up small boulders, and ditching clay mud." In November 1857, 1,000 workers were clearing the ground, with drainage work following in spring 1858. During the peak of construction, in 1859–60, approximately 4,000 workers per year were building the park, with as many as 3,600 workers on a peak day.

George Hayward, Valentine's preferred printmaker, is uninterested in the human labor making the park; his subject is the relationship between the city and park. The view is from the New York State Arsenal, one of the structures preserved in the park, at 64th Street and Fifth Avenue, and it looks south to the rising city. Fifth Avenue, cutting diagonally across the view, is not yet paved. In the distance, the grid is being imprinted on the land, with the outline of city blocks indicated by furrows in the land. The left side of the print shows stages of real estate development: a dense line of buildings rises in the distance, then come scattered, low-rise wood structures, and in the foreground a fence signals a bygone era of country farms and estates. Hayward includes shacks and other buildings to be destroyed for the park, although they outnumber what's shown on Viele's site survey.

Hayward compresses the distance to heighten the contrast between the encroaching city and the park, as if

to make a case for the necessity of Central Park. The monumental structure that appears to span most of the 920-foot block between Fifth and Sixth Avenues is St. Luke's Hospital, which opened on the block between 54th and 55th Streets in 1858. It marks the frontier of northern development. On the horizon behind the hospital is the dome of the Crystal Palace, on 42nd Street (it burned in October 1858). The large building with cupola east of Fifth Avenue is Columbia College, at 50th Street between Fourth and Fifth Avenues. It is unclear precisely where 59th Street lies, but the image suggests that development is nearly at the park's edge. To critics who complained about the northern location of Central Park, Hayward's print is a rebuttal: the city was closing in on the park and before long would surround it.

Entered, according to Act of Congress, in the year 1869, by D. APPLETON

**Asa Coolidge Warren, View of
Central Park lake, 1869**

This print of 1869 conveys the new recreational opportunities that Central Park offered. The vista depicts the lake and the Terrace (later called Bethesda Terrace), which the designers considered the most significant architectural feature of the park. The view from the elevated Terrace was an important consideration to Calvert Vaux, who claimed authorship of this element: it "would let the New Yorker feels that the richest man in N.Y. or elsewhere cannot spend as freely as is here spent just for his lounge— here he may lounge by the week if he pleases . . . his eye all purified." The print highlights not the prospect from the Terrace, but what it overlooks: boating on the lake, with incidental details illustrating other amusements, carriage rides, and promenading. Some rowboats are canopied, others plainer, but it is difficult to see any difference in the depiction of the families that crowd in them. Ducks, swans, and peacocks as well as the effulgent trees set the bucolic mood.

The artist Asa Coolidge Warren specialized in topographical prints, and the places he illustrated span the country. Warren's work remains to be catalogued, and, at this time, there are no other catalogued copies of this Central Park lithograph.

3

The Rise of
the Apartment

1860–1930

*Apartment life is popular and to a certain extent fashionable.
Even society countenances it, and a brownstone front is no longer
indispensable to at least moderate social standing.*

—Moses King, 1892[1]

At the end of the Civil War, New York was a study in extremes in terms
of where—and under what conditions—New Yorkers lived. Most affluent
Manhattanites lived in spacious private houses. Poor and working class
New Yorkers crowded into subdivided row houses sheltering many more
people than had ever been imagined. At the same time, tenements, generally five-story multi-unit dwellings put up as cheaply as possible, were
built throughout the rapidly expanding city, with the greatest density
in Lower Manhattan. The apartment building as we know it had yet to
appear in Manhattan, much less constitute the dominant housing type it
would become.[2]

Public concern about substandard housing in the city began as a public
health issue. A devastating outbreak of cholera in 1866 was widely linked
to the cramped, overcrowded, poorly ventilated housing in which many
New Yorkers lived. That year, the New York State legislature established
the Metropolitan Board Sanitary District, which included Manhattan; the
district was regulated by the Metropolitan Board of Health. The following
year, the legislature made its initial foray into what would later be identified as affordable housing, passing the Tenement House Law of 1867,

the first law of its kind in the nation. The law did not directly address the issue of cost, but, in an effort to address public health concerns regarding the spread of infectious diseases, it set legally mandated minimum building standards for housing intended for the poor.

Regulating Tenements

Despite its supporters' good intentions, the law proved difficult to enforce. Because it was conceived of and rendered as a health ordinance, not a building code per se, it was ultimately overseen by the Sanitary Board, which lacked internal bureaus of inspection or enforcement. Nonetheless, the law constituted a watershed; for the first time, the tenement building type was defined as a discrete housing type, distinct from a divided row house or a boarding house, and requirements were established for space, light, and ventilation. The law was soon amended to mandate the provision of fire escapes, and it was significantly revised again in 1879.

In the 1880s, following the Panic of 1873 and the ensuing depression of the real estate market, the construction of tenements exploded. Efforts to build so-called "model tenements," exceeding legal requirements, occasionally succeeded, but they were far outnumbered by standard fare. In 1890 the pioneering photojournalist Jacob A. Riis published *How the Other Half Lives*, a searing indictment of slum conditions on Manhattan's Lower East Side.[3] Suddenly, the dire slum conditions endured by many New Yorkers emerged as a central social and political issue confronting the city.

Governmental efforts to regulate tenement construction continued to evolve over the next decade. The Tenement House Act of 1901 marked another breakthrough. The legislation established the city's first real mechanism for enforcing housing regulations: a Tenement House Department, with its own Bureau of Records, Buildings Bureau, and Bureau of Inspection. For the first time, legally mandated enforcement became a widespread reality.

At the same time that tenements dominated housing for New Yorkers of modest means, another type of

multiple-unit dwelling, the residential hotel, played an important role in housing the middle class. In the 1860s and 1870s, the city's burgeoning population and the rapid spread of commerce had made it increasingly difficult for middle-income New Yorkers who eschewed tenements to own or lease private houses. The apartment hotel helped to fill that void, though some New Yorkers gravitated to boarding houses, others took in boarders, and still others moved to the expanding suburbs. Hundreds of apartment hotels were established in New York, though initially most were neither purpose-built nor intended for long-term family living.

Middle-Class Apartment Buildings

While tenements, boarding houses, and residential hotels offered an array of shared accommodations to a range of income levels, by the end of the nineteenth century, the middle- and upper-income apartment house, along with the private row house, would come to dominate Manhattan's residential architecture. In comparison to their European counterparts, affluent New Yorkers had been slow to favor the apartment building type, clinging instead to the British preference for private single-family residences. Parisians had pioneered multi-dwelling residential buildings for the affluent in the mid-nineteenth century, and the New York real estate community, eager to popularize the type in New York, often referred to them as "French flats."

A chief factor affecting the eventual acceptance of the New York apartment house was the incorporation of the elevator. In contrast to Parisian apartment houses, where wealthier families lived on the lower floors, with working-class families climbing common stairways to the upper levels, the inclusion of an elevator served to democratize real estate. While some early ventures in apartment house design and construction fell short of expectations, many developers remained convinced that the type constituted the future of the city.

Completed in 1870, the Stuyvesant Apartments complex on East 18th Street, developed by Rutherford

B. Stuyvesant and designed by Richard Morris Hunt, is widely acknowledged as the first middle-class apartment building in New York. Though at first dismissed by members of the city's elite as "Stuyvesant's Folly," the building was a commercial success, and it became an advertisement for the new residential building type. Reflecting New Yorkers' infatuation with all things French, the building synthesized the mansard roof seen on so many stylish Parisian townhouses with elements of the larger apartment buildings that lined Baron Georges Haussmann's grand boulevards in Paris.

In contrast to single-family houses, the era's apartment buildings, often housing more than ten families, collectively attracted intensified real estate activity and led to the development of new residential neighborhoods around town. Following Stuyvesant's lead, the Schermerhorn family played an important role in developing and promoting the Upper East Side east of Third Avenue as a middle-class apartment house enclave.

Throughout the 1870s, although the apartment building was increasing in popularity, it nonetheless remained a social experiment for which the results were not yet known. Would affluent New Yorkers ultimately adapt to apartment house living? In 1878 a lawsuit brought by an East Side homeowner sought to block the conversion of nearby houses into apartment buildings, arguing that local zoning restrictions prohibited tenements. (The court ruled against the plaintiff.) But despite reluctance and opposition, by the 1880s, New Yorkers across a broad economic spectrum were living in multiple-unit buildings.

One real estate innovation that contributed to the growing popularity of the middle-class apartment building was the Home Club. Based on the notion that an apartment building should form a type of community and not simply provide shelter, a Home Club was a cooperatively financed and managed venture in which like-minded individuals formed a joint stock company that developed an apartment building. Each stockholder would lease an apartment, the size of which related to the size of their investment. The apartment was intended for the shareholder's use, though units could be subleased. Other units in a

Home Club building were to be owned collectively and leased out to provide revenue with which to pay off the mortgage and operate the building. Often equipped with a wide variety of amenities, the buildings proved to be economically unsustainable.

Luxury Apartment Buildings

Though the demise of the Home Club movement hindered the construction of cooperative developments, conventionally financed high-end developments continued to be realized at ever-increasing size and luxuriousness, for ever-wealthier tenants. The Dakota, completed in 1884, hit a high-water mark for apartment design in the city and served, more than any other building before it, to persuade affluent New Yorkers that an apartment could be as opulent and private as a townhouse. The Dakota, which was fully rented upon its completion, reflected the developers' belief that the still sparsely built Upper West Side would become one of the city's premier residential neighborhoods, principally because of the extension of the Ninth Avenue elevated train line north from 53rd Street in 1879.

In 1885, a year after the Dakota's completion, the New York City Building Department, in a reflection of widespread concern regarding building height and density, imposed height limitations on residential buildings. Similar to regulations instituted by Napoleon II on apartment buildings in Paris, the legislation, known as the Daly Law, kept residential development to a maximum of 80 feet on avenues and 70 feet on cross streets. The law, which did not apply to commercial buildings, including apartment hotels, was repealed in 1901.

The adoption of the apartment house as a common and acceptable dwelling type for middle- and upper-middle class New Yorkers was as swift as it was, to many observers, surprising. By 1893, according to a census conducted by the Board of Health, more than 70 percent of New Yorkers lived in multi-family dwellings, though only 20 percent of those lived in non-tenement apartment buildings.

Once the twin effects of steel skeleton construction and the passenger elevator made tall buildings a ubiquitous feature of the cityscape, the popularity of the apartment-hotel type, which continued through the first decade of the twentieth century, was spurred by a particularity in the city's building laws. The height of houses and apartment houses was restricted, but the height of hotels, including those designed for long-term tenancy, was not. Examples of the type were especially plentiful on the west side of Midtown as well as on the Upper West Side. Many of the residents of apartment hotels were bachelors and single women, the latter of whom were, for the first time in the city's history, entering the workforce and living independently.

An interesting variant on the standard high-rise apartment building was introduced in 1901 by the builder William J. Taylor and the painter Henry W. Ranger: the studio apartment building. The type addressed the demand for live/work spaces among artists and often featured duplex units with double-height spaces and northern exposures admitting the muted light preferred by artists. Many of these buildings, built in the first two decades of the twentieth century, were cooperatively owned and managed, and located on primarily on the Upper West Side, adding to the area's vaguely bohemian air.

In the early decades of the twentieth century, the acceptance of the apartment house as the dwelling of choice for the wealthiest New Yorkers was nowhere more apparent than on Fifth and Park Avenues. The passage of the city's—and the nation's—first comprehensive zoning resolution in 1916 allowed buildings to rise to a height of 150 feet on Fifth Avenue, opposite Central Park. This regulation was highly controversial. In 1920 the Real Estate Board of New York, along with the Fifth Avenue Association and the City Club, lobbied to have a height restriction of seventy feet imposed. Such a regulation was passed the following year, but in 1923, following a campaign against the restriction waged by developers including Vincent Astor, the ruling was reversed. By 1931 Fifth Avenue was home to forty-three apartment buildings.

During the interwar period, Park Avenue, which had first been developed as an upscale residential district following the electrification of the New York Railroad's line in 1902 and the submergence of the railroad tracks, surpassed Fifth Avenue as the city's most prestigious apartment house address. Managed as cooperatives and often advertised as "mansions in the sky," many of the avenue's most elegant apartment buildings featured units outfitted to suit an individual buyer's tastes and requirements. The stock market crash in 1929, and the ensuing Depression, hit Park Avenue's most prestigious buildings hard and many went into bankruptcy.

In the late 1920s, the "race for height" that held the city in thrall as skyscraper office buildings transformed Manhattan's skyline was picked up by apartment building architects as well. Bypassing the restrictions imposed by the tenement house laws, architects and developers revived the residential hotel building type, resulting in soaring apartment buildings. The passage of the city's Multiple Dwelling Law in 1929 ushered in a proliferation of conventionally managed skyscraper apartment buildings, particularly along Central Park West, where soaring twin-towered apartment buildings became the avenue's architectural signature.

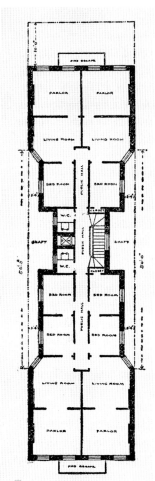

Model of hypothetical city block comprising "dumb-bell" tenements, 1900

Plan of typical "dumb-bell" tenement, 1900

TYPICAL DUMB-BELL TEN-EMENT, BUILT UNDER THE LAWS IN FORCE IN 1900.

According to the Tenement House Act of 1867, a tenement was any building housing more than three families, living and cooking independently; the definition was expanded in 1887 to also include buildings with three families. In common parlance, however, a tenement is a building erected as inexpensively as possible and with as few amenities as the law allowed. In the nineteenth century, tenements were almost always built on lots that were twenty-five feet wide, and they tended to be five or six stories, with two to four apartments per floor, mostly housing poor immigrants. These buildings were generally erected by small-scale, speculative developers, also largely immigrants, and they could be extremely profitable.

Construction was almost completely unregulated until the New York State Legislature passed the Tenement House Act of 1879 (commonly known as the "old law"), which required that every room have windows opening onto the street, a rear yard, or an interior air shaft. The most common result of these requirements was the "dumbbell," a building that was pinched in the center to create lightwells. Such shafts proved inadequate, providing little light and air to inner rooms, acting as flues in a fire, and becoming repositories for garbage. Yet, they remained the most common type in Manhattan until the "new law" was passed in 1901.

It was evident almost from the start that the 1879 law was a failure. Pressure to ban the construction of new dumb-bells increased at the turn of the century. The cardboard model illustrated shows a hypothetical block built up with dumb-bell tenements that could have housed four thousand people. It was displayed at a 1900 exhibition of the Tenement House Committee, a group of progressive housing reformers, which was instrumental in increasing support for the reforms instituted in the Tenement House Act of 1901.

THE GHETTO, NEW YORK CITY.

Orchard Street, c. 1900

Home and Tower Buildings, 1879

City and Suburban Homes, 1909

Kitchen in typical City and Suburban Homes apartment, 1909

This view of Orchard Street shows blocks lined with tenements of up to six stories, and a pushcart market in the street. By 1900 this area of the Lower East Side was so built up that, according to some housing advocates, it was thought to be the most densely populated place on earth.

Individuals and corporations concerned with housing conditions in the city erected model tenements to improve housing conditions for the working poor. These were experiments with how apartments in dense neighborhoods could be erected that were safe, clean, and sanitary, while assuring the investors made a profit, usually limited to 5 or 6 percent.

The earliest model tenements were the Home and Tower Buildings in South Brooklyn (now Cobble Hill), erected in 1876 and 1878 by Alfred Tredway White. These buildings had exterior fire stairs, cross-ventilated apartments with sinks and toilets, and large interior courtyards where laundry could dry and children could be safe. By the 1920s, John D. Rockefeller Jr. became deeply interested in housing reform and built several model tenement complexes, notably the Dunbar Apartments in Harlem, planned for African-American families and named for African-American poet Paul Laurence Dunbar. The six-story walk-ups, designed by Andrew J. Thomas, a proponent of reform housing, surround a landscaped courtyard.

Only a few individuals entirely funded model tenements. Others invested in stock companies that erected and maintained the buildings. The largest of these was the City and Suburban Homes Company, which built several buildings for African Americans, as well as two complexes on the Far East Side of Manhattan, each of which occupied an entire block. The Avenue A (York Avenue) Estate between 78th and 79th Streets, dating from 1901–13, was the largest such complex ever built and remains an island of affordable housing in Manhattan. Life in the small apartments centered around the kitchen, which was provided with up-to-date appliances and the amenities that few tenement dwellers enjoyed.

City Suburban Homes
78th. Street and Avenue A. New York.

Central Park with Majestic Hotel & Dakota Ap. N.Y. City

No. 314 National Art Views Co. N.Y. City.

**View from Central Park with the
Majestic Hotel on the left and
the Dakota on the right, c. 1900**

Designed in 1880, the Dakota was an investment by Edward S. Clark, whose fortune came from the Singer Sewing Machine Company. Henry Hardenbergh designed a picturesque building based on Northern European precedents, faced in bright yellow brick and sandstone from Nova Scotia of a similar hue. The Dakota was the first major building to rise above the treeline of Central Park and its upper floors, bristling with gables, chimneys, and tiny dormers, were clearly designed to be seen from the park.

The layout was influenced by Parisian apartment houses with their interior courtyards and multiple entries. The building has four separate entrances in the court, each originally with two apartments per floor. The units were lavishly appointed, with high ceilings, woodwork, mantels, and the most advanced technology. But the floor plans were somewhat awkward, with long narrow halls and a poor separation between public, private, and service spaces.

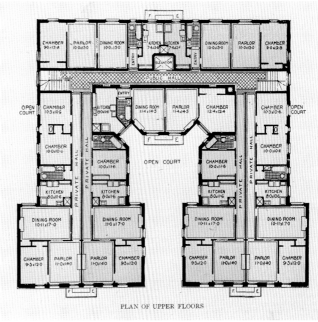

PLAN OF UPPER FLOORS

Kendal Court, 1903

The 1901 Tenement Act had a profound impact on the character of tenements and apartment buildings for working- and middle-class New Yorkers, mandating minimum room sizes, maximum lot coverage, and the size of light shafts and courts. Builders were certain that this law would make new construction uneconomical and that there would be no new and affordable housing in the city. However, with construction underway on the city's first subway line, opening in 1904, undeveloped neighborhoods such as Morningside Heights suddenly became accessible, and enormous numbers of modest apartment houses were soon under construction.

Kendal Court at 521 West 111th Street typifies the modest middle-class apartment houses erected soon after the

passage of the law. It was designed by Schwartz & Gross, a firm that designed hundreds of apartment buildings in the first decades of the century. The new-law buildings tended to occupy lots with street frontage of between fifty and one hundred feet and have I-, O-, or U-shaped footprints. Typically, middle-class buildings were six stories tall since the law required costly fireproof construction for buildings above that height. Some non-fireproof materials could be used on six-story buildings, but these had to have exterior fire escapes, as is evident on the Kendal Court.

In comparison to the contemporaneous, but more luxurious, Langham, the apartments are awkwardly arranged and the rooms small. The apartment layouts, seven per floor, were influenced

by lot size, legal requirements, and a desire to place the public rooms in the front, overlooking the street. Thus, the single elevator is toward the rear and the four front apartments are entered from the back. This explains the long, narrow, dark interior private halls that are ubiquitous in these buildings. Worse, from a social perspective, is the fact that in order to get from the door to the parlor in the front, a visitor would have to walk by the bedrooms, completely negating any separation between public and private spaces. Yet, these buildings had amenities to attract the middle class, including mantels, hardwood trim, and up-to-date plumbing, lighting, and telephone service.

CLINTON & RUSSELL, ARCHITECTS

The Langham, 1905

By the early years of the twentieth century, as builders erected well-planned apartments with large rooms and elaborate appointments, apartment living attracted more and more wealthy families. The Upper West Side became the center of luxury rental apartment development with the twelve-story Langham, at 135 Central Park West, among the most elaborate.

In 1904 Clinton & Russell received the commission from developers Abraham Boehm and Lewis Coon, and the firm designed an ornate limestone, brick, and terra-cotta building in the fashionable French Beaux-Arts style, complete with the sculptural ornament and tall mansard roof typical of this mode of design. Pedestrians entered from Central Park West, beneath an iron-and-glass canopy; an arch on 73rd Street marked the vehicular entrance to a drive with a Guastavino tile vault.

The building was divided into two wings, each with two apartments per floor and served by two passenger and two service elevators. The nine- and ten-room apartments were laid out with a smooth flow between the generously proportioned public rooms. The bedrooms were generally segregated along an interior hall, while service spaces were entirely separate, an arrangement that, the marketing proclaimed, "gives that privacy from servants that is essential in a home." The floor plan used in advertising the building shows reflected ceiling plans, indicating the variety of stylistic finishes in each apartment, including the beams of a "Colonial" dining room, the strapwork of an "Elizabethan" dining room, and the complex patterns of an "Adam" parlor, each illustrated by a small vignette.

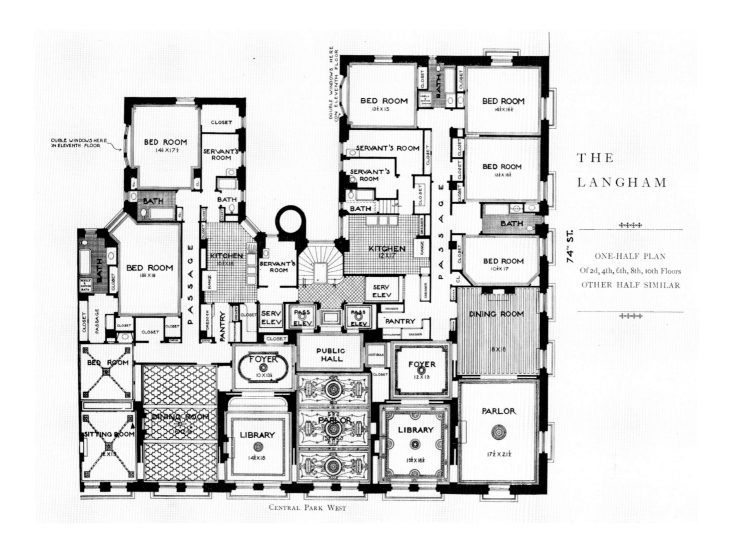

CLOSET

DOUBLE WINDOWS HERE IN ELEVENTH FLOOR

BED ROOM
14½ X 17½

SERVANT'S ROOM

BATH

BATH

BED ROOM
18½ X 18

BATH

PASSAGE

CLOSET

PASSAGE

CLOSET

KITCHEN
10 X 18

RANGE

SERVANT'S ROOM

PANTRY

CHINA

CLOSET

SERV ELEV

CLOSET

DRESSER

CHINA

SERV ELEV

PASS ELEV

PASS ELEV

CLOSET

BED ROOM

SITTING ROOM

EXIT

DINING ROOM
35 X DO 24

FOYER
10 X 13½

LIBRARY
14½ X 18

PUBLIC HALL

VESTIBULE

CLOSET

PARLOR
15 X 23

DOUBLE WINDOWS HERE ON ELEVENTH FLOOR

BED ROOM
13½ X 15

CLOSET

BATH

CLOSET

SERVANT'S ROOM

SERVANT'S ROOM

CLOSET

BATH

DRESSER

KITCHEN
12 X 17

RANGE

SERV ELEV

DRESSER

REFRIGERATOR

PANTRY

DRESSER

FOYER
12 X 18

LIBRARY
15½ X 16½

CLOSET

BED ROOM
14½ X 16½

CLOSET

CLOSET

BED ROOM
13½ X 16½

BATH

CLOSET

BED ROOM
10½ X 17

CL

DINING ROOM
18 X 18

PARLOR
17½ X 21½

THE

LANGHAM

⸎⸎⸎

ONE-HALF PLAN
Of 2d, 4th, 6th, 8th, 10th Floors
OTHER HALF SIMILAR

⸎⸎⸎

74ᵀᴴ ST.

CENTRAL PARK WEST

View of street lined with three-family tenements (left) and two-family tenements (right), 1909

Floor plan of typical two-family tenement, 1909

Floor plan of typical three-family tenement, 1909

As speculative developers sought ways to water down the 1901 Tenement House Act, lobbying for changes with state legislators, the Tenement House Department strenuously defended the reforms. One major issue was the regulation of three-family houses, which were considered tenements under the law and had to conform to its standards for light, air,

and fireproofing. Builders advocated for their removal from regulation so that they could be treated in the same manner as two-family dwellings.

The *Fifth Report of the Tenement House Department* from 1909 included a strenuous defence of regulating three-family dwellings, accompanied by a series of comparative photographs and plans. A survey had found that there were 19,822 three-family tenements in New York City, primarily located in outlying regions where land values were low. These buildings housed approximately 268,000 people. The report compared conditions in two- and three-family buildings, finding that because of their regulation under the tenement house law, three-family

units had windows in every room, while there were bedrooms with no windows in two-family houses. Three-family buildings also had well-lit stairways and adequate fire protection. "Light, air, sanitary conditions and protection of life and limb are all assured to the occupants of the tenement by the requirements of the law. Why then," asked the Tenement House Department, "should the dwellers in three-family houses be deprived of these beneficent conditions? . . . The interests of the speculative builders of three-family houses, a small number of persons, should therefore not be permitted to prevail against the interests in proper housing conditions of such a large proportion of our population."

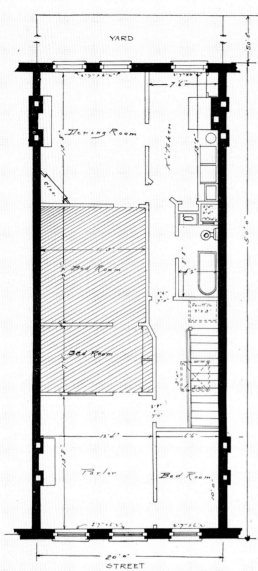

YARD

Dining Room

Kitchen

Bed Room

Bed Room

Parlor

Bed Room

STREET

TYPICAL FLOOR PLAN OF A TWO-FAMILY
DWELLING ACROSS THE STREET FROM THE
TENEMENT SHOWN ON PAGE 35.

NOTE:- TWO INTERIOR ROOMS ON
EACH FLOOR WITHOUT DIRECT LIGHT OR VENTILATION.

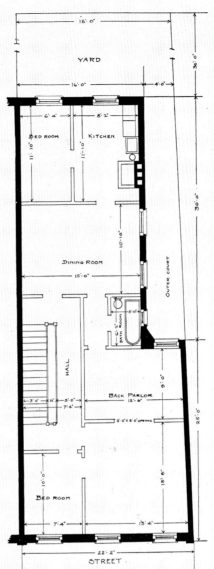

YARD

BED ROOM

KITCHEN

DINING ROOM

OUTER COURT

HALL

BATH ROOM

BACK PARLOR

BED ROOM

STREET

TYPICAL FLOOR PLAN OF
A THREE STORY THREE FAMILY
TENEMENT SHOWN BY PHOTOGRAPH
ON PAGE 35.

NOTE:- EVERY ROOM HAS
A WINDOW TO OUTER AIR.

998 Fifth Avenue, 1912

Completed in 1912 for developers James T. Lee and Charles R. Fleischmann, 998 Fifth Avenue, on the corner of 81st Street, was the first luxury apartment building on Fifth Avenue, and it was a harbinger of the changing character of upper-class life in New York as more and more wealthy households gave up their townhouses and mansions. McKim, Mead & White, the city's most prestigious architecture firm, designed the building with all of the amenities of a private house coupled with the conveniences of an apartment building. The grandeur of the exterior is evident from Central Park: an Italian Renaissance palazzo expanded to twelve stories, with a four-story, rusticated base, piano nobile on the fifth story,

and a deep copper cornice. The two street facades are clad in limestone, with yellow marble trim on the eighth and twelfth floors; entry is beneath a magnificently crafted iron-and-glass marquee.

The interiors rivaled those of the grandest townhouses, with expansive suites of public rooms, some up to thirty-five feet wide and seventy feet long, in the simplex and duplex apartments. The apartments were, to quote the advertising prospectus, "suited in size, equipment, design and finish to the most exacting requirements of those who demand the comforts and conveniences of the modern private residence, yet desire to simplify as far as possible the problems and vexations of housekeeping."

998 Fifth Avenue became a model for the lavish apartment houses that rose on the Upper East Side over the next few years. It changed the "deep-seated repugnance" that families of high social position had for apartment living. The seventeen apartments at 988 Fifth Avenue ranged from thirteen rooms and five baths to twenty-four rooms with eight baths. Unlike the apartment houses of the upwardly mobile on the Upper West Side, East Side buildings did not generally have names. 998 "is so famous," wrote the *New York Times*, "that even the name of the Avenue is not added. It is always spoken of, among the elect, as '998' and nothing more."

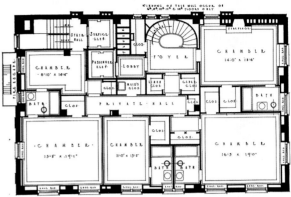

UPPER FLOOR OF TYPICAL DUPLEX APARTMENT.

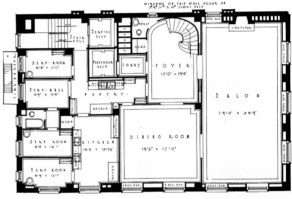

LOWER FLOOR OF TYPICAL DUPLEX APARTMENT.
APARTMENT HOUSE AT 898 PARK AVENUE, NEW YORK CITY.

898 Park Avenue, 1924

The construction of apartment houses with spacious rooms and luxurious appointments continued into the 1920s on Fifth Avenue, Park Avenue, and other streets that attracted the city's wealthiest households. Most of these were cooperatives and not rentals, meaning that residents owned shares in a corporation and could carefully vet all prospective residents, assuring that their buildings would be as exclusive as they wished. Indeed, such exclusivity was accented in the marketing of the apartments.

898 Park Avenue was erected by developers Henry Mandel and Seward W. Ehrich on a small plot at the corner of 79th Street in 1923–24, replacing two earlier rowhouses. John Sloan and Adolph E. Nast designed the Lombardy Romanesque building with irregularly colored, shaped, and textured buff bricks that from the time of the building's completion lent a sense that the facades had been weathering for hundreds of years. As with many other luxury buildings of the era, 898 Park has an interesting plan. There are only seven apartments, a second-floor simplex and six duplexes with public rooms and service spaces on the lower level and five bedrooms, or chambers, on the upper level, reached by a private curving stair. The focus of each duplex was a grand "salon," more than thirty-six feet long, stretching across the entire 79th Street frontage.

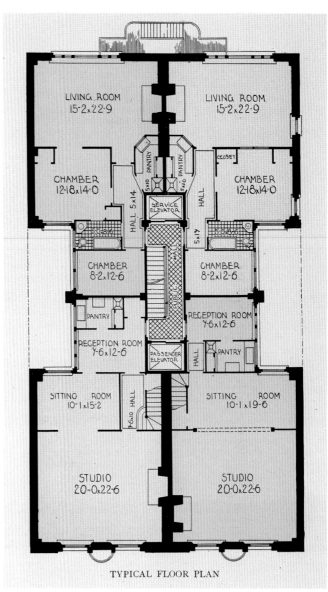

TYPICAL FLOOR PLAN

Gainsborough Studios, 1908

In the early twentieth century, artists, even the most successful artists, faced a real-estate quandary: they had to pay for their apartments, rent a studio in which to work, and find a place to display and sell their art. In 1901 landscape painter Henry Ranger initiated the idea of a cooperative apartment house that would combine living and working spaces and would be welcoming to potential clients and buyers. The first studio buildings on 67th Street between Central Park West and Columbus Avenue were so successful that similar studios appeared on other streets, including the Gainsborough Studios at 222 Central Park South.

Typical of the studio buildings, the Gainsborough contained well-decorated, double-height spaces, facing north, with large fireplace mantels, where artists worked and welcomed clients. The tall windows of the facade define the individual studios. At the rear of the building were small, single-floor, rental apartments that provided the cooperative corporation with revenue and allowed it to keep maintenance fees to a minimum. The Gainsborough was unusual in that it was actually an apartment hotel, so units did not have kitchens. Residents could eat in the ground-floor restaurant, or meals could be sent directly to an apartment via a dumbwaiter.

The Griffon, 77 Park Avenue, 1923

Following World War I there was a serious housing shortage in New York. The city's population had grown, but there was little new construction, as the labor and materials markets were both volatile. With prices rising and labor strikes frequent, banks hesitated to give mortgages. The shortage in upper-middle-class apartments began to ease in about 1923, as many new buildings rose on the Upper West Side, in Murray Hill, and elsewhere in Manhattan. Except at the highest end of the market, the new apartments generally offered smaller apartments with fewer amenities than in those erected before the war.

The Griffon typifies these buildings. While pre–World War I apartment buildings tended to have twelve stories, those built in the 1920s were the same height but, with lower ceilings, they squeezed in fourteen stories. The facade is modest with a limestone base and Georgian brickwork. While prewar apartment houses for wealthy households often had one or two apartments per floor, 77 Park Avenue has eight, ranging from two to six rooms. The living rooms were a comfortable size, but other rooms were small. Kitchens shrunk and dining rooms especially suffered. These relatively small apartments were largely rented to single men and women and childless couples.

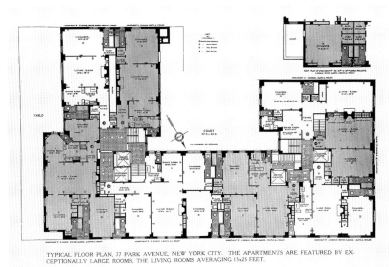

TYPICAL FLOOR PLAN, 77 PARK AVENUE, NEW YORK CITY. THE APARTMENTS ARE FEATURED BY EXCEPTIONALLY LARGE ROOMS, THE LIVING ROOMS AVERAGING 15x25 FEET.

The Oliver Cromwell Apartment Hotel,
32 Stories of Service—24 Hours a Day

Twelve West Seventy-Second Street, New York City.

THE SHERRY-NETHERLAND, *Fifth Avenue, at 59th Street, as seen from Central Park*

"THE PANHELLENIC", NEW YORK CITY
SHOWING NEW APARTMENTS UNDER CONSTRUCTION

The Oliver Cromwell, 1926

The Sherry-Netherland, 1926

The Panhellenic, 1927

The Oliver Cromwell, The Sherry-Netherland, and The Panhellenic were all apartment hotels that catered to long-term and permanent guests as opposed to more typical transient hotels. In design and planning, each apartment hotel catered to a specific audience. The Oliver Cromwell at 12 West 72nd Street on the Upper West Side, designed in 1926 by Emery Roth in his favorite Italian Renaissance style, sought a middle-class clientele, with its two- and three-room suites. Schultze & Weaver,

specialists in high-end apartment hotels, designed the 1926 Sherry-Netherland for a luxury audience, as befit its location at Fifth Avenue and 59th Street. The dynamic Art Deco Panhellenic at 3 Mitchell Place, designed in 1927 by John Mead Howells, was planned for the young, college-educated women who were flocking to New York for jobs. The name reflects the policy of renting rooms to women who had been members of Greek-letter sororities.

The construction of apartment hotels was extremely popular with developers during the 1920s because it was a way for them to evade the restrictions of housing laws. Hotels were considered commercial buildings and conformed to the zoning code rather than to laws governing multiple dwellings. At a time when apartment-house heights were capped, hotels could rise, with setbacks, to a far greater elevation. They could also occupy a larger percentage of their lot area. Since they did not have to be of fireproof construction, apartment hotels could not have legal kitchens. Instead, units had a serving pantry where food could be delivered from the hotel dining room. However, these pantries were easily converted into illegal kitchens. The city was well aware of this ruse, but it was not until 1929 that the apartment-house height limit was removed and most developers lost interest in constructing apartment hotels.

THE CLOISTER and THE MANOR - TUDOR CITY - NEW YORK, N. Y.

PROSPECT TOWER - TUDOR CITY - NEW YORK, N. Y.

Tudor City, 1925–28

Tudor City, the enormous apartment complex overlooking the East River, originally consisted of six middle-class apartment houses and four apartment hotels, all designed, constructed, financed, and managed by the Fred F. French Companies. Fred French began assembling the property on a bluff between 41st and 43rd Streets in 1925. The apartment houses line the side streets, while three of the apartment hotels face onto private Prospect Place (now Tudor City Place). The hotels faced west toward Midtown and away from the riverfront which, at the time, was lined with slaughterhouses.

The buildings are ornamented with sophisticated English Tudor detail, including stained glass and ornament copied directly from Tudor country houses. The focus of the community is a pair of small private parks. The landscaping, the choice of the Tudor style, and building names redolent of old England (Windsor Tower, Prospect Tower, Essex House, The Cloister, The Manor, Hadden Hall, etc.) provide the suburban ambiance that many middle-class people were seeking. But the density of the ten- and eleven-story apartment houses and especially the skyscraper apartment hotels create an intensely urban community. The message on the back of the postcard of Tudor City residents enjoying their park reads "Manhattan's largest apartment colony combining the charm of suburban atmosphere with Midtown convenience."

French instituted an extensive advertising campaign to attract middle-class New Yorkers to Tudor City. Ads were, of course, placed in local newspapers, but also in a new weekly magazine, *The New Yorker*, and in *Playbill*. Matchbooks and postcards were given away in an effort to increase awareness of the rental opportunities, which ranged from one-room studios in the hotels, with Murphy beds that folded into a closet and no legal kitchens, to traditional apartments of up to six rooms. All of the advertising focused on the convenience of the location; "NEW YORK's most remarkable Residential Community . . . just four minutes from Grand Central Station," reads the marketing text on the back of the three postcards illustrated here. Much of the promotion was especially adamant that Tudor City residents could walk to work in the new Midtown office center, thus saving hours of commuting each day.

A Glimpse of
the Private Parks in
Tudor City

4

Moving the People

1880–1950

It is a miracle that New York works at all. The whole thing is implausible . . . By rights New York should have destroyed itself long ago, from panic or fire or rioting or failure of some vital supply line in its circulatory system or from some deep labyrinthine short circuit. Long ago the city should have experienced an insoluble traffic snarl at some impossible bottleneck.

—E. B. White, 1949[1]

The Commissioners' Plan made clear the direction in which the city would grow. Demand for travel between new neighborhoods uptown and the downtown business district gave rise to the first forms of mass transit on the streets of New York in the 1820s. Omnibuses, an urban version of the horse-drawn stagecoaches that carried travelers between New York and Boston, brought riders to Harlem and Manhattanville or closer destinations within the denser parts of Manhattan.

Omnibuses were sizable, seating twelve to fifteen people. To signal a stop, passengers pulled a cord wrapped around the driver's ankle. These colorful vehicles ran on regular, fixed routes with published fares, schedules, and stops. So many ran up and down the avenues by the late 1830s that one commentator dubbed New York the "city of omnibuses."[2] While the omnibuses ran along fixed routes, they did not run on a fixed track. The first transit vehicles to do so were also horse-drawn, and were typically referred to as "horsecars" or "horse railways." These carriages were larger, holding up to forty people, and ran along metal tracks or grooves in the streets. They were also significantly faster—a speedy eight miles-per-hour compared to the omnibuses' six—and cheaper (five cents rather than ten).

The earliest horse railways appeared a decade or so after their omnibus competitors. Introduced by the New York and Harlem Railroad in 1832, the first horse railway traveled along the Bowery from Prince to 14th Street. Passengers signaled a stop by asking the conductor to ring a bell for the driver. Because it ran along a predetermined roadway, the ride was smoother and more comfortable than on the omnibuses.

Both modes of travel were extremely popular, and as residential development moved further away from the center of business and commerce, Manhattan's streets were increasingly jammed with horse-drawn vehicles. In 1860 some fourteen separate horse railways carried 38 million passengers and another twenty-nine omnibus lines ran more than 600 buses. There was no segregation by type of vehicle or direction on the street, nor were there anything approaching "lanes"; horses and their drivers could go anywhere they wanted. Often traffic backed up to a standstill. Manhattan was still hilly in places, and horses pulling great weight were often slow.

By the second half of the nineteenth century, neither omnibus nor horse railway travel was a particularly pleasant experience. In addition to congestion and horse manure on the streets, the cars themselves were crowded and people stood in the aisles. According to the *New York Herald,* "People are packed into them like sardines in a box, with perspiration for oil. The seats being more than filled, the passengers are placed in rows down the middle, where they hang on by the straps, like hams in a corner grocery."[3]

The combination of crowding both on communal vehicles and in the streets themselves spurred interest in more efficient forms of rapid transit governed by dedicated rights-of-way. Across the Atlantic, London had invested in a new form of mass transit known as "the underground"; the Metropolitan Line began rumbling under north central London in 1863. But various attempts to secure licenses to develop "undergrounds" in New York were stymied by the state legislature, largely because of the resistance of the influential horsecar companies.

Steam and electricity brought new forms of transit to the city. Cable cars began plying the Brooklyn Bridge soon after its opening in 1883, running down the center of the bridge on either side of the pedestrian walkway. A steam-driven engine moved wire cables beneath the roadway; above it, the cable car gripped and released them to move and stop. The power of steam was suited well to steep grades that were challenging for horses, and the cable-based system would—by 1890—be used by tens of millions of New Yorkers making the crossing.

But timing worked against the expansion of a cable-car system in New York. Electricity, piloted a stone's throw from the Brooklyn Bridge in the 1880s, would spur a street trolley revolution that would put cable cars out of business by 1910. But it did not happen immediately: the early trolleys, or "street railways," that relied on overhead or underground electric wires were cheaper than steam-powered cable cars, but moved at 6 mph. They generally ran on tracks down the middle of the street, which became more and more problematic as use of automobiles in the city grew. Ultimately, their routes were turned over to buses.

The "El"

The most significant form of new transit in the late nineteenth century was the "el," or elevated train, with steam-powered locomotives pulling rail cars on trestles above the avenues. The New York Elevated Railway began operation in 1871, running along Ninth Avenue. It was a classy alternative to the horse-drawn streetcar, with passengers seated rather than standing in the aisles. The ride was smooth and quick; the trains traveled at up to fifteen mph, twice as fast as the trolleys or cable cars. Getting a franchise to build and operate an elevated train was, however, a monumental task. The horsecar lobby was still strong, and many city politicians were reluctant to introduce a competitor. Furthermore, adjacent property owners objected to the elevated trestles, which contaminated the street-scape in front of their houses and businesses and left a residue of soot on everything below the rails. Even after the Rapid Transit Act of 1875 clarified property rights associated with elevated railways and established a mechanism to formally review applications for these trains, securing an el franchise was not easy.

In spite of constant legal challenges, additional elevated franchises were awarded in the 1870s, establishing the Metropolitan Railway along Second and Third Avenues and the New York Elevated Railway along Sixth Avenue. With this expansion, which reached into nearly every major Manhattan neighborhood, elevated train travel exploded. By 1880 these trains were handling some 150,000 riders each day. In 1881 the two elevated companies consolidated to become the Manhattan Railway Company (MRC) bringing further growth. The MRC lowered the fare from ten cents to five in 1883 to better compete with the street railways.[4] With greater speed and investment in clean, new cars and locomotives, the els began to dominate city transit. As *King's Handbook of New York* noted in 1892, "By its aid the New Yorkers fly through the air from end to end of their teeming island at railway speed and in comfortable and well-appointed cars . . . A ride on the London Metropolitan Railway is a depressing necessity; but a flight along the New York elevated rails is a refreshment."[5]

The tactical move to halve the transit fare worked as intended to expand the ridership of elevated transport. By 1890 New York's was the largest and most respected mass transit system in the world, with 94 miles of routes serving millions of people each day, with roughly 600,000 on the els and many more on the street-level railways. But the fare reduction would ultimately cause the downfall of the system as a whole. Despite tremendous inflation over the years, the five-cent ride would become a principle that New Yorkers would fight for, and succeed in retaining, for more than fifty years, much to the detriment of the financial stability of the transit system as a whole.

Though the els were highly efficient, they were undisputedly noisy and dirty. Some improvement came as electricity replaced steam as the fuel of choice, although the trains remained noisy and the tracks continued to block light. Other streets and the new bridges were equally compromised by congestion from all different modes of transport—horsecars, cable cars and soon electric streetcars. By the turn of the twentieth century, the Brooklyn Bridge featured cable cars, steam-powered trains, electric streetcars, and horse-drawn carriages.

Each mode of transport fought to defend its market from inroads by others. Nowhere was this behavior more pronounced than in opposition to the idea of underground transit. Despite London's early and successful experiments with its Underground, innovators and entrepreneurs who proposed bills allowing experimental subways were repeatedly rebuffed by the state legislature. The state Rapid Transit Commission refused to consider any proposals for underground transit, ostensibly due to concerns about the status of underground property rights. Street car and elevated operators lobbied heavily against them. So too did real estate owners, who feared the undermining of their buildings along proposed transit routes and, as an industry, did not want one company having a "monopoly" on any form of transit. Few wanted to see a subsidized underground franchise given to Tammany cronies of public sector officials, most notably Jay Gould, who already controlled nearly all of the city's elevated railroads and, according to the *New York Times*, had "an insatiable appetite for grabbing everything in sight."[6]

The Subway Arrives

By the 1890s, a variety of factors began to shift the debate over underground transit. The Great Blizzard of '88 had shown how vulnerable the above-ground system of streetcars and elevated trains was; steam engines found it impossible to cope with the snow and the city was paralyzed for days. The storm also highlighted the wisdom of burying cables underground. If electric and telecom cables could be operated underground, why not power the trains with electricity and bury them as well? Increasing congestion in the city forced many reformers and municipal officials to acknowledge the need to develop new housing markets outside of the boundaries of Manhattan. In theory, a subway could provide the means to absorb population growth by channeling it out to less settled areas within the city. In practice, the system could not be built fast enough. As the historian Benson Bobrick has noted, "The theory of urban redemption by means of the railroads was based on an idea of asymmetrical growth, of a population growing more slowly than the means of diffusing it, while the relation between the two was actually developing in reverse."[7]

The Rapid Transit Acts of 1891 and 1894 set the foundation for the first subway contracts, clarifying the issue of underground property rights and spelling out the parameters of the public-private partnership that would pave the political way for the subway. The city would cover a large share (40 percent) of the capital cost, and the private franchisees would support the rest. Ownership of the tracks would remain with the city, while the train operators would construct the system, buy the trains, lease the right-of-way, and operate the trains for a nickel a ride. Payments to the city out of their profits would retire the city's debt on the project. This public-private collaboration devised to build and operate the subway was structured as a "design-build-operate-maintain" relationship, with the city taking primary credit risk, but passing significant construction and other risks off on the private operator.[8]

Two companies were formed to carry out what was eventually known as Subway Contract 1: the Rapid Transit Subway Construction Company and the Interborough Rapid Transit Company. Bonds were issued to finance the city's capital contribution, and the Rapid Transit Subway Construction Company, later to become a part of the IRT, was contracted to build the line. The IRT, as private partner, would repay the principal and interest on those bonds, as well as a variety of other local and state taxes, after recovering its operating costs. The lease to operate on the public right-of way was initially for fifty years, with a twenty-five-year option.

The Interborough Rapid Transit (IRT) line that opened in 1904 was a wonder on many levels. Stations and trains were larger than those along the elevated train lines, and the trains were far less noisy. Cars were heated, and stations featured bathrooms and escalators. It was also fast: the new IRT route featured a four-track main line with both express and local tracks, greatly speeding up travel times. Built under what became known as Contracts 1 and 2, the line ran from City Hall to Grand Central on 42nd Street and then across to Times Square. From Times Square it proceeded north along Broadway to 96th Street, where one branch continued north and the other veered east through Harlem and into the Bronx. The response to the new lines was immediate and wholehearted. The new network reached its design capacity of 600,000 people/day within its first year, and by 1908 it was used by about 800,000 people each day.

Connecting the Boroughs

The impact of the new subway line on the evolution of the city was momentous. Opening up new areas to development outside of Manhattan, particularly large tracts of land in the Bronx, provided a significantly broader taxation geography. Tax revenues from areas newly connected by the IRT line would ultimately help fund the expansion of municipal services necessary to support the growing metropolis—police, water, fire, sanitation, roads, and various early social services. Almost immediately, planning for an extension of the system began under the same public/private construct as the initial work. Subway Contracts 3 and 4, signed in 1913 and known as the "Dual Contracts" or the "Dual System," outlined an expansion of the system into new areas of the Bronx and into Queens and Brooklyn. Again, the public sector would in effect subsidize a portion of the private sector's risk for building out the system. Track miles under the new contracts would be doubled, and the East River would be traversed by a new tunnel.

By 1920, when this second round of contracts had been completed, the system had become the largest and busiest in the world. For a nickel a ride, regardless of distance, workers could ride to their place of employment more comfortably and safely than ever before. Trains operated around-the-clock, at speeds up to three times the speed of the fastest elevated trains. New York was, almost overnight, on the move in a way it had never imagined.

The introduction of the subways facilitated real estate development beyond Manhattan's boundaries—from the North Bronx, across Queens, and into Brooklyn. The shift in population from Manhattan to these new areas was marked. Vast numbers of poor and immigrant families moved out of Manhattan slums and tenements and into new neighborhoods in places like Parkchester, Canarsie, Bay Ridge, and Elmhurst. Between 1910 and 1949, the number of residents in Manhattan fell by 19 percent while the city's population as a whole grew by 56 percent. Borough growth was staggering: the Bronx grew by 309 percent and Queens by 218 percent. By 1930 Brooklyn had more residents than Manhattan.

Notwithstanding the fall in population, areas in Manhattan were transformed by the new subway lines. Longacre Square, a rather seedy area of Midtown, saw new life as Times Square when the New York Times Company opened its building at the intersection of Broadway and 42nd Street in 1904. The round-the-clock operation of the subway served to support the area's evolution as a late-night destination; upmarket hotels arrived too, notably the Hotel Astor at 44th Street and Broadway. The Upper West Side was equally transformed. While the earliest elevated line along Ninth Avenue had spurred development along or adjacent to Columbus Avenue, the avenues further to the west, including West End, Broadway, and Riverside, remained largely undeveloped. With the opening of the new IRT line, speculators there were rewarded with a tripling of land values.

From Private to Public

While the system grew in popularity, the financial success of the companies operating the subways waxed and waned. The first casualty was the BRT, which

went bankrupt after an accident in 1918 and went into receivership a few years later; it would re-emerge five years later as the BMT. The IRT had more of a financial cushion, but the system nevertheless found itself in a worsening economic position, unable to raise prices in the wake of rampant inflation between 1917 and 1920. The situation deteriorated further after World War I. Operating losses meant that the lines could not meet their annual payments to the city. Requests to increase the nickel fare went unheeded, most notably by John Hylan, who ran for mayor in 1921 on a platform based squarely on keeping the nickel fare. His election cemented the five-cent ride for the next twenty-seven years.

The commitment to the nickel fare was fatal to the private subway franchises. Against a background of inflation and rising costs, they had little to invest, leading to a deterioration in performance. Falling levels of service were characterized as "inefficiency" as early as 1922 by politicians eager to promote a public takeover of the system. At the same time, the Public Transit Commission was calling for system expansion. Competition from cars and surface transportation—whose fares were not regulated—was growing. The companies asked the city to take over their franchises and simply contract out to them for operations, but the city refused. The Depression also had a significant impact, with demand dropping dramatically due to growing unemployment after years of rising passenger numbers. By 1932 the IRT had gone into receivership.

It is not entirely a coincidence that the "independent" subway (IND) operated by the city opened that year. The new line was an attempt to clean up the streets, and likely make room for the growing number of automobiles, by providing an alternative to the Sixth Avenue and Ninth Avenue elevated lines. The first IND line, which ran along Eighth Avenue (today the A, C, and E lines), began construction in 1925 and opened in 1932; within eight years, its sister trains (the B and D lines) were running along Sixth Avenue. Like the BMT, the IND trains were wider than the original IRT lines and could not be deployed at IRT stations, complicating subsequent integration of the system.

In 1940 Mayor Fiorello LaGuardia decided that the IRT's financial position was too precarious and that the system would function more efficiently as an integrated whole by merging public and private operations. The city took over the assets of the BMT and IRT, creating the framework for the integrated subway system we know today. While the subway remained a popular means of transport, the takeover did not reverse the decline in the financial position of the network. Operating expenses continued to rise, but the five-cent fare remained in place until 1948, when it was raised to ten cents. The increase was too little, too late. From 1946, the high-point of subway ridership, the number of riders declined as the automobile took hold, wages rose, and the migration to the suburbs gained pace.

In 1953 the New York City Transit Authority was established in response to calls for the creation of a dedicated authority to manage the system. As a quasi-governmental authority, its mission was to operate the subway on behalf of the city. With that remit, the Transit Authority set about unifying the system, offering free transfers and, slowly but steadily, constructing interchanges to simplify movement between the existing lines. Some platforms were extended to accommodate longer trains, but even today the rolling stock is not interchangeable.

Following unification, it was recognized that despite modest and regular fare hikes, the unified fare structure adopted would never cover the system's costs. In part because of the need for subsidy, the system was turned over to the state in 1968 and integrated into a larger umbrella entity: the Metropolitan Transportation Authority (MTA). This allowed subway operations to be cross-subsidized by more profitable bridge and tunnel operations carried out by the Triborough Bridge and Tunnel Authority division of the MTA.

The journey from a nascent industry with tremendous entrepreneurial spirit to one overseen and operated by a state bureaucracy took a century. It was not a straight path: the developers who once supported the new transit technologies as a means to increase the value of outlying lands would abandon advocacy for subway expansion when the automobile and highways came to the fore.

Yet there has been no force as important in the physical development of New York as transit. Streetcars, trolleys, elevated trains, and subways opened the boroughs to development, underpinning real estate values that encouraged developers to build housing that allowed New York to grow by accommodating waves of immigrants. Transit also shaped Midtown, with land values in the Grand Central area high enough to allow construction of skyscrapers in the early part of the twentieth century, defining its position as the city's foremost commercial district and cementing New York's place as a global capital.

Irving Underhill, Manhattan Bridge under construction, 1909

Between 1880 and 1950, the city saw the creation and destruction of elevated rail, electric streetcars, and cable cars. Streets morphed from places filled with people and commerce to thoroughfares designed to move cars and trucks as efficiently as possible. Yet although many technologies were short-lived, others endured, including the subway system, tunnels and bridges across the East and Hudson Rivers, buses and, of course, automobiles. Indeed, the era saw the development of the modern transportation infrastructure that continues to shape the growth and development of the metropolitan New York region today.

Charles Thompson Harvey's elevated rapid transit system on Greenwich Street, 1867

The development of transportation networks in the city was a process of experimentation. This image from 1867 shows the first known attempt at an elevated rapid transit system. This "car truck" system, separated from buildings and powered by a cable, was built by Charles Thompson Harvey, who made his name as the builder of the Soo Canal in the Great Lakes. Harvey was denied the patent rights to expand his system, however, and spent the next few decades embroiled in legal fights while elevated systems took over the city.

Building above the street was a logical response to the need to maintain commercial and existing transport activities at street level. Thus the trains above were built to supplement existing mobility, rather than as a replacement for it. A related question was where to build above the street. Should elevated trains be a second story directly above the street, or should they be attached to buildings above the sidewalks?

Proposed elevated railroad, 1833

Early proposals, such as this unrealized project for a stone viaduct, considered elevated rails as extensions of buildings rather than as stand-alone infrastructure. These early designs attempted to separate rapid transit from existing street activity. Though the designs of these early systems were in many cases flawed, the idea of separation was not. Indeed, the separation of our subway infrastructure has been critical for the enduring success of rapid transit in the city, and explains why New York was never fully subsumed by automobiles.

Elevated railroad, Greenwich Street, 1868

Building streetcar routes above sidewalks helped protect the openness of the street, but placing the routes adjacent to the buildings was problematic. There were capacity constraints as well as noise and vibrations that affected neighboring buildings. These early experiments, some constructed but long forgotten to history, taught valuable lessons to the entrepreneurs building new systems. If the city was to grow around new rapid transit, then it needed more than a track with a single train going back and forth. The city's arteries would have to extend over or under the street itself.

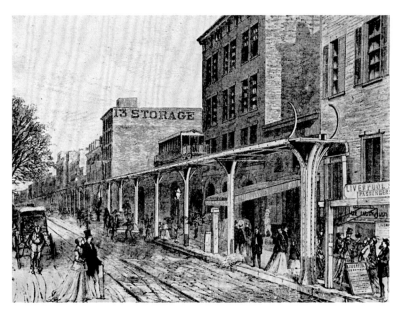

Richard P. Morgan's proposed elevated railroad on Broadway, 1869

Rufus H. Gilbert's proposed pneumatic elevated railway on Sixth Avenue, 1875

The city's first successful transit enterprise would be the network built above the street. The elevated tracks took advantage of open air, and avoided disrupting activities below. Nevertheless, constructing elevated rapid transit above the existing streets dramatically changed their look and use patterns. Long before they were used for automobiles and trucks, streets were a critical piece of city life where people gathered, merchants traded, and children played—all alongside horse-drawn carriages, which operated at leisurely speeds that allowed these activities. These images show how the elevated tracks were intended to act as a second story to the street and preserve the street itself for people to carry on their daily lives.

Alfred Ely Beach's proposed pneumatic underground railway, 1870

The first New York City subway was famously built under cover of darkness as a pneumatic tube. Constructed under a license to build a tunnel to transport small packages and freight, the luxury cars were propelled by a vacuum and delighted thousands of passengers brave enough to ride in them between Warren and Murray Streets under lower Broadway. The Panic of 1873 put an end to the demonstration project, though it is far from clear that the technology could have scaled to serve the whole city in any case. Other propulsion methods were considered for underground travel, but it was the development of electric-powered trains that allowed for rapid, reliable, and clean subway travel.

WARREN ST.

CURB STONE LINE

WAITING ROOM

CAR

AIR FLUE

VALVE

ENGINE

SHAFT

BLOWER

BOILERS

CURB LINE

SCALE OF FEET

PNEUMATIC

BROADWAY

CAR

TUNNEL

GENERAL PLAN, SHOWING THE ARRANGEMENT OF THE MA-
CHINERY, THE AIR-FLUE, THE TUNNEL, AND THE MODE
OF OPERATING THE PNEUMATIC PASSENGER-CAR.

on the wall of the tunnel; and before
gentle was the start, we were in mo-
om Warren street down Broadway.
nts the conductor opened the door,
Murray street!' with a business-like
ts all shout with laughter. The car
n the gentlest possible style, and im-
n to move back again to Warren
had no sooner arrived, than in the
d mysterious manner it moved back
r street; and thus it continued to go
for, I should think, twenty minutes,
d all ridden as long as we desired.
cy gave motion to the car, and the
we upon the inside could tell that we
red by atmospheric pressure was by
nds against the ventilators over the
hese were opened, strong currents of

wheels of the car touch
the wire at certain points,
and cause a bell to be
sounded in the main
building, where the æo-
lor, or blowing-engine,
is situated; and when the
engineer hears the bell,
he pulls a rope, which
operates an air-valve, so
as to let in or change
the air-current in the
tunnel. For example,
just before our car stop-
ped at Murray street,
the wheel of the car
sent the signal to the en-

Proposed arcade railway, 1886

Building beneath the street surface was another way to preserve rights of way and ensure speedy travel. Tunneling below grade, however, presented a number of technical and political challenges. Consistent movement of transit underground was also difficult. Steam engines, which were the dominant propulsion technology of the time, polluted the underground air. The idea also raised psychological issues. When the city began to investigate the idea of underground trains, it was not obvious that people would embrace subterranean transit.

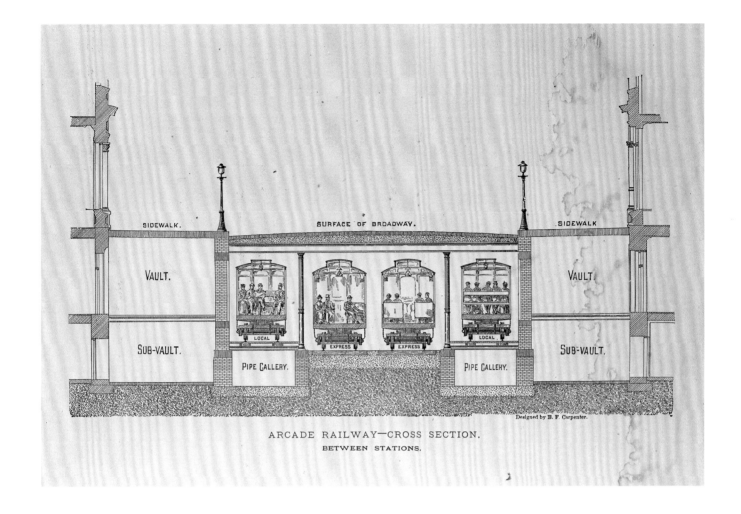

SIDEWALK.   SURFACE OF BROADWAY.   SIDEWALK

VAULT.   VAULT.

SUB-VAULT.   LOCAL   EXPRESS   EXPRESS   LOCAL   SUB-VAULT.

PIPE GALLERY.   PIPE GALLERY.

Designed by B. F. Carpenter.

ARCADE RAILWAY—CROSS SECTION.
BETWEEN STATIONS.

**Cross-section rendering of
arcade railway, 1886**

In addition to building and electrifying their new subway system, the subway franchisees in New York City ultimately did something that other cities had not done before: they built four-track systems that allowed for express and skip-stop service along busy routes. This was a boon for fast service over substantial distances. Yet the four-track systems had a related but unintended consequence—the extra tracks required very wide boulevards above. Broadway, which runs the length of Manhattan, turns into a divided road north of Columbus Circle where northbound and southbound traffic are separated. This layout is excellent for the efficient movement of cars but can result in an increased volume of traffic and make pedestrian crossing more difficult.

FIFTH AVENUE LOOKING NORTH FROM 42ND ST., NEW YORK.

**Fifth Avenue looking north from
42nd Street, 1920s**

Wide roads built to accommodate the subway underground, and the expansion in vehicular travel it facilitated, led to the development of traffic signals and rules of the road that had previously not existed. This was the start of a revolutionary shift to the modern view that streets should be designed to give priority to automobiles. As the trains were built above and below the city to maintain separation of travel modes, traffic signals did the same for surface streets. Traffic enforcement began with simple boxes, as seen above, where a police officer would mechanically operate signals to separate cars from crossing pedestrians. This period is also when mobility became a potentially criminal enterprise, as licenses and behaviors on the roads were now policed to conform with laws. The policing of movement changed the relationship of the street to the city, and forced many street activities to move elsewhere.

Taxis in front of the Hotel Marlborough, on the west side of Broadway between 36th and 37th Streets, 1920s

When automobiles were first mass-produced, it was not clear that they were destined to have near-universal ownership. Many entrepreneurs realized that cars were a chance to improve on surface transportation, which was still largely powered by horses, and a taxi industry quickly blossomed. The image above depicts French-built taxicabs. Note that all roads were not yet paved, but they were at least clear of manure.

As quickly as the taxi business took off, it was shut down. Taxicabs and multi-passenger jitneys were competing for passengers with the streetcar and transit companies, who lobbied successfully for regulation to limit the number of taxis on the streets and the elimination of jitney services. While taxicabs survived as a tightly regulated service—with very little growth in the number of cabs over the course of the century—jitneys were chased out of business completely. The era of experimentation and expansion of transit systems was coming to an end.

Demolition of 42nd Street elevated railway spur, 1935

By the 1920s, transit services at grade and on elevated tracks were in decline. Elevated trains were noisy and blocked the sun, while streetcars were not able to coexist with automobile and truck traffic on surface streets. A key factor for the permanent success of any particular transportation technology—bus, subway, ferry, or cars—was dedicated infrastructure that did not interfere with city life. Beginning in the 1920s, cities around the world began dismantling their surface rail networks. In New York, the elevated train tracks started to come down as well. The above photo shows the demolition of the 42nd Street elevated, a victim of the city's efforts to preserve the density of Manhattan by limiting proximity to noisy round-the-clock trains. With minor exceptions, the elevated tracks would ultimately survive only in the less densely populated outer boroughs.

Last run of the Third Avenue El, May 12, 1955

Though the elevated tracks were a nuisance for some, they were beloved by riders. The destruction of the elevated systems in Manhattan was orderly, occurring largely between the mid-1930s and the early 1950s. Periods of advance notice gave people a chance to ride their favorite trains before they were demolished forever.

BULKHEAD EARTH FILL

RETAINING WALL

CONCRETE
BULKHEAD
WALL

PRESENT
GROUND LEVEL

PRESENT
GROUND LE

Cross-section rendering of proposed expansion of Riverside Park, c. 1927

First Avenue tunnel looking north from 47th Street, c. 1947

By the 1950s, elevated trains and street-cars were nearly all gone, streets were designed for the flow of vehicles, and an underground subway system was the backbone of the city's transit system. The dawn of the modern era was the codification of dedicated space for each mode of travel. The image of Riverside Park on the left shows a proposal from the late 1920s that would have hidden commuter trains destined for Midtown. There were many benefits, including new parkland and access to the Hudson River, for instance, and the increased durability of hidden infrastructure. Delineating space to a particular technology, whether car or train, also allowed for speedier travel with less interference. This was ideal for mass transit.

However, once the city turned this approach to roadways problems arose. The image of Midtown Manhattan above looks like an elegant solution to auto traffic. Cars have ample space and ramps and tunnels ensure that they can move uninterrupted through town. Unlike the images shown at the beginning of this portfolio, where transportation innovations were designed to accommodate vibrant street life, by the mid-twentieth century, streets were no place for enjoying the city. People were to be safety tucked away. Cars had conquered the street.

5

The Evolution of the Skyscraper

1890–1930

The building is merely the machine that makes the land pay.
The more economical the machine both in construction and
operation, provided it fulfills the needs, the more profitable
the land. At the same time, one must not lose sight of the fact
that the machine is nonetheless a useful one because it has
a measure of beauty, and that architectural beauty, judged even
from the economic standpoint, has an income-bearing value.

—Cass Gilbert, 1900[1]

The idea of a dedicated office building was a new concept in the second
half of the nineteenth century. Purely commercial buildings had previously taken the forms of stores, warehouses, and, along the waterfronts,
counting houses. But the rise of manufacturing produced exponential
growth in the number of commercial transactions undertaken, and a parallel
rise in the number and types of people needed to carry them out. Legal,
financial, insurance, and a variety of other support services, many of them
born of maritime trade, matured as professions alongside manufacturing
and were drawn to central office locations, where proximity to a variety of
industries would allow them to support multiple clients simultaneously.

Many of the earliest office buildings, appearing in the 1850s and 1860s,
had arcades on the lower floors, in part as a way to announce themselves
to a passing public. Bank buildings were often particularly ornate, with
great banking halls that occupied much of the ground floor. Equally

substantial were the new, tall hotel buildings, some equipped with an early version of the elevator. Like the office buildings that they presaged, these hotels were designed to be modular, with uniform room dimensions making construction relatively easy. The same form would be repeated in the construction of speculative office buildings in the 1880s and 1890s.

Technological Innovation

To some extent, the evolution of the skyscraper is a classic example of the adage "necessity is the mother of invention." Various technological advances converged to allow construction of tall buildings. Foremost was the invention of the structural iron/steel frame. Load-bearing masonry walls traditionally used to support multistory structures needed to grow thicker as the height and weight of a building increased; as a masonry structure grew taller, more and more valuable space at lower levels of the building had to be sacrificed to supporting walls. These masonry walls offered limited opportunities for light to penetrate, further limiting the value of this ground-floor space.

The invention of the cast-iron frame, composed of carbon and iron, liberated the late nineteenth-century office building. By supporting the building from the inside, the internal metal frame eliminated the need for external load-bearing walls. Removing the masonry walls also reduced the weight of the overall structure, lowering the cost of building foundations and allowing additional windows to convey natural light to the interior. The benefits of structural frames were further extended by the use of lighter, steel frames in the latter part of the century, made affordable by the dramatic drop in steel prices that resulted from the Bessemer process.

First demonstrated by Elijah Otis in the New York Crystal Palace in 1853, the elevator quickly became a trusted method of accessing higher floors in tall buildings. The speed with which Otis's ambitious invention was accepted was unprecedented. As Montgomery Schuyler pointed out in his 1903 essay "The Skyscraper Problem," "no such innovation in the art of building

has been so swiftly accomplished since the development and expression of groined vaulting in masonry in the twelfth and thirteenth centuries and that took two generations."[2] Many of the early adopters were buildings on small, tight sites in Lower Manhattan, where value could only be realized by building tall.

The invention of incandescent lighting—electricity powering a filament bulb—further facilitated the rise of the commercial skyscraper. While gas lighting had been reasonably reliable, electric current proved safer, cheaper, and relatively easy to access. The first central power-generating plant, operated by Edison Electric, opened on Pearl Street in Lower Manhattan in 1882 and extended its reach to more than five hundred buildings downtown in the next three years. Although the lamps it supported were not powerful, they worked well in combination with natural light channeled into office floors through large windows.

Plumbing was as important as electricity in facilitating workplaces in the sky. The city's pressurized, municipal water network was put into service beginning in 1842 with the opening of the Croton Reservoir and delivery network. This new water supply supported a variety of plumbing-related interventions, including the flush toilet and the provision of hot and cold running water. First piloted in luxury hotels in Manhattan, by the end of the nineteenth century, flush toilets were standard in new commercial skyscrapers.

During the same period, new forms of centralized steam heating came of age, ensuring reliable temperature control in the winter. Similarly, techniques of forced-draft ventilation were sufficiently refined by the late 1880 to provide a reservoir of fresh air to large numbers of people. Newly invented telecommunication systems, primarily the telephone, were also significant.

The maturing of design and construction industries further nurtured the new skyscraper typology. Advances in material sciences led to the introduction of fireproof or fire-resistant materials to protect building occupants. The speed of construction accelerated as well, thanks to the introduction of power-operated equipment and compressed air to power machinery, as well as to the concept of the "general contractor" as a professional to coordinate the increasing complexity of building technology.

Early Chronology

These technological advances were not, of course, specific to New York; other cities, particularly Chicago, also looked to build tall. New York had several advantages, most notably its geology. Three separate formations of bedrock can be found under layers of gravel and sand; Manhattan schist is most prevalent, rising close to or piercing the surface in a number of locations, including Midtown and Lower Manhattan.

The earliest skyscrapers in New York very much reflected the footprint of the downtown lots available to developers: small parcels along irregularly shaped colonial streets that were not easily assembled. These small, valuable sites pushed developers to build tall, to create a sufficient amount of rentable square footage to justify construction costs. Early speculative buildings, such as the 10-story Tower Building completed in 1889 on a narrow site along lower Broadway, were more functional than fancy. Although decorative outside, the building floorplates were identical. As critic Ada Louise Huxtable noted, "The early skyscraper was an economic phenomenon in which business was the engine that drove innovation. The patron was the investment banker and the muse was cost-efficiency. Design was tied to the business equation, and style was secondary to the primary factors of investment and use."[3]

Many early skyscrapers in Manhattan were promotional vehicles for the corporations that funded them. Large and imposing, these corporate icons were rarely if ever filled with corporate staff; nearly all included speculative office space to be rented to others. Among many notable examples was the World Building, also known as the Pulitzer Building, which opened on Park Row in 1890 as the tallest building in the city. Home to Joseph Pulitzer's *The World* newspaper, its 18 stories provided speculative office space to a number of other companies and were served by 18 elevators. One of the survivors is the American Surety Building, opposite Trinity Church on lower Broadway, erected by a bond insurance company in 1894 following a design competition. Because of the high cost of the site, the company maximized the rentable space and constructed four separate facades so that it could be admired from all sides.

Coming of Age

By 1895 New York skyscrapers had reached 20 stories. However, the financing of these buildings changed in response to the increasing cost; many were syndicated commercial ventures, then known as "investment skyscrapers."

Architects struggled with the language and form of the skyscraper. Most New York designers adopted a three-part classical design composition including a street-facing "base," a "shaft" of varying heights, and a "capital" or "crown." In many cases, the incorporation of ornate classical references on the facades reflected the architects' training at the Ecole des Beaux-Arts in Paris and gave birth to the widespread use of the stylistic term "Beaux-Arts."

In many respects, these late 1890s towers remained focused on the bottom line. The office layouts were fairly standard, with private offices on the perimeter, administrative and lower-level staff offices toward the inside, and elevators in a central core. Small tenancies were encouraged: they paid more per square foot and were relatively easy to replace at a lease's end, ensuring low levels of vacancy for the developer. The 30-story Park Row Building, at Park Row and Ann Street, is a good example; built on spec, it contained around a thousand office tenants when it opened as the tallest building in the world in 1899.

The physical impact of these new towers on the historic fabric of Lower Manhattan was significant, with opinion divided as to the wisdom of economics driving building form. The British journalist George Warrington Steevens, first arriving in the city in 1896, noted: "Never have I seen a city more hideous and more splendid. Uncouth, formless, piebald, chaotic, it yet stamps itself upon you as the most magnificent embodiment of titanic energy and force. The very buildings cry aloud of struggling, almost savage, unregulated strength. It is the outward expression of the freest, fiercest, individualism."[4]

Over the next decade, skyscraper fever moved north. Ultimately, skyscrapers would come to dominate Downtown and Midtown more so than other areas, in part due to the relatively shallow depth of bedrock, but also because the neighborhoods between the two—including what would become SoHo, Greenwich Village, Union Square, and Gramercy—were already settled as manufacturing or residential areas.

Towers like the Met Life Building at Madison Square heralded the coming of new commercial districts in areas that had formerly been viewed as fringes of the city. Nowhere was this transformation more notable than in Times Square, which in 1904 celebrated both the opening of the Times Building and the debut of the city's first subway, the IRT. With rapid transit in place, development to the north of New York's original "downtown" would accelerate at a pace few could have envisioned. So too would the push for height, with notable buildings topping out at well over 30 stories by 1910.

Perhaps no commercial skyscraper was as much a testament to the aspirations of the developer who built it as the Woolworth Building, which rose on lower Broadway in 1913. Known as the "Cathedral of Commerce" in reference to its Gothic style, it was the brainchild of the company founder F. W. Woolworth. Its 36 stories were extravagant in design and far-sighted in functionality. The elevator system ran both express and local, and the building featured a swimming pool in the basement. Murals on the walls of the mezzanine over the lobby celebrate the rise of commerce, and both Woolworth and the building's architect, Cass Gilbert, are memorialized in sculpted relief in the lobby.

But the building was not even primarily corporate. Woolworth leased most of the building on a speculative basis to other tenants, keeping only one and one-half floors for his company.[5] Nor was Gilbert dreamy-eyed about its purpose: "In a business building . . . we cannot waste space for arches or colonnades or other architectural features, without sacrificing the rentable area, and we cannot project beyond the property line . . . It is these conditions that make the skyscraper problem so difficult of solution."[6]

Gilbert's efforts were successful in more than real estate terms. The advent of this spectacular building temporarily silenced the architectural critics of skyscrapers, who to this point had argued that the congestion in Lower Manhattan was an inevitable consequence of building tall. As critic Paul Goldberger has noted, "At its completion, the building was received with considerable acclaim. There was a general sense among architects and critics of the period that at last an architect had done it—had found a way to express height, to create a work that was stylistically appropriate to new forms."[7]

The Birth of Zoning

Though New York City grew almost religiously along the lines of the rectilinear street grid devised by the Commissioners in 1811, the speed and nature of that growth was largely unplanned. As industrialization took hold, factories located wherever they could find suitable real estate. So too did tenement housing, which sprouted up in undesirable locations, often on cheap land close to the docks or to sources of employment. Incompatible uses were often found adjacent to one another. Congestion on the streets grew with the city's population, and was made worse by the introduction of surface-level public transit.

The physical and social consequences of rapid growth, industrialization, and immigration fueled, both in Chicago and New York, the "City Beautiful" and "Progressive" movements, which would respectively call for governmental planning and oversight over private enterprise. Building regulation, still in its infancy and focused primarily on minimizing fire risk, gained steam and teeth as did tenement regulation, geared specifically at buildings housing more than three families. In 1892 the Department of Buildings began to regulate light, ventilation, and plumbing and formally approved skeletal-frame construction, legitimizing the new skyscraper typology.

With the formal support of government in hand, the push for tall buildings gained further momentum toward the end of the 1890s. By the turn of the century, the proliferation of towers in Lower Manhattan was beginning to take its toll on the infrastructure. Streets were increasingly congested. Underground water levels, lowered significantly by pumping associated with new tower and subway construction, left exposed pilings to rot and caused buildings to settle awkwardly, most noticeably in the poorer tenement areas atop the former Collect Pond.

Skyscrapers soon rose to the fore as a target for the "city reform" movement. To some architects, they represented crass speculation and commercialism. To others, towers posed a threat to public health and safety. Complaints ranged from inadequate light on the lower floors and concerns about street congestion to worries about earthquakes and the challenges of pumping water to high floors for fire-fighting. These fears underpinned calls for height limits throughout the 1890s.

These calls went unheeded, and the proliferation of tall buildings continued to gain pace: by 1913, fifty-one buildings of 21 to 60 stories had been constructed or were underway in the city, many on lots assembled from more than one plot.[8] So too did calls for height limits, but this time with reference to an area further north: lower Fifth Avenue. Here development had become a battleground between a variety of commercial real estate interests, primarily manufacturing and retail.

As loft buildings housing clothing manufacturers moved progressively north, high-end retailers on Fifth Avenue feared the impact of industrial neighbors on their clientele. Through an advocacy group known as the Fifth Avenue Association, retailers pushed for height limits, though in practice what they wanted was use limits along the Avenue. The Fifth Avenue Commission, established in 1912, recommended a 125-foot height on the avenue; the following year, the Height of Buildings Commission was set up to address the issue.

While the commission was doing its work, in January 1912, a huge fire ravaged the seven-story Equitable Building opposite Trinity Church on lower Broadway. The replacement was designed to be more than four times larger than the original. Configured in an H-shape, the tower would rise to 38 stories, with an unyielding and uniform facade along Broadway. In all, the building held 1.2 million square feet of speculative, rentable space, roughly 30 times the building's floor area.

This new Equitable Building would affect views of the harbor and cast shadows four blocks south. Ironically, the most vocal opposition to the new building came from real estate interests themselves. Some owners requested reductions in tax assessments because of impacts on their property; other owners worried about the effect of more office space on the market given vacancy rates above 12 percent in 1913.[9] Many were concerned that the surrounding area would be plunged into darkness as a result of the building's height and girth.

The remonstrations of the Fifth Avenue Association to the north and the real estate industry downtown led to the drafting of the Zoning Resolution of 1916. The bill's passage is attributed to the efforts of Edward Bassett, the law's architect. Knowing that government regulation of the real estate market would be construed by some as a "taking" and challenged in the courts, Bassett worked to construct a solid legal foundation for the new zoning regulations. He found the act's justification on the grounds of safety and health, arguing that regulating use and massing was important to minimize chances of fire and to preserve light and air essential to physical well-being.

Bassett defended the notion that use and massing should vary from place to place. He noted:

Some critics asserted that if zoning regulations were minimum standards of health and safety, it was illogical to have different standards of height and area in different parts of the city. The argument prevailed, however, that greater density always has existed and probably always will exist in the centers of a city where the need for speedy transaction of business causes people to be near together. Many workers desire to live near their work and avoid the expense of daily travel. On the other hand, suburban localities supply places for more roomy homes, where the supply of light and air is ample and space is not expensive. All these considerations of health and safety were held to justify making different standards of height and area at different distances from urban centers.[10]

New York was not the first American city to regulate physical aspects of its buildings, but its new statute was by far the most comprehensive. The Zoning Resolution of 1916 segregated uses by district, creating relatively distinct commercial and residential areas. It governed the height and bulk of buildings by promulgating a new concept called the "zoning envelope." To maximize sunlight in tall-building districts, the new law introduced the idea of a sky exposure plane: buildings would be required to set back from the edge of the sidewalk further as they grew higher, within an angle determined by a line from the building roof to the center of the street. This setback or "wedding cake" style resulted in smaller floors as the building grew taller. But there was no limit on the number of floors permitted: one-quarter of the site could be as high as the developer wanted.

While it did not ultimately espouse an absolute limit on height, the resolution did something more important: it cemented city government's role in regulating market-based development. The limitations it established on private development with respect to use types and building form continue to determine the parameters of real estate development and building design in New York City today. Perhaps most significantly, it also served as a precedent for zoning laws that now exist in most large cities in the nation.

The Growth of Midtown Tall: 1920–1930

It is hard to imagine an act of government, other than the Commissioners' Plan of 1811, that had a more

immediate and permanent impact on the physical evolution of New York than the Zoning Resolution of 1916. Monetization of small lots in high-demand areas by stacking one floor upon another was no longer feasible. From that point on, the only towers that "penciled out"—that it, seemed likely to produce a profit despite high projected costs—were those on substantial, assembled lots, where one-quarter of the lot could be built without a height limitation. Architects and developers embraced the "setback style" in ways that maximized floor area while minimizing construction costs.

The limitations imposed by the new zoning code did not dampen interest in the skyscraper form. On the contrary, land prices rose throughout the 1920s. Financing was relatively easy, allowing towers of 30 to 45 stories on large sites to take shape. By 1931 at least a dozen buildings topped 50 stories; four stretched to 70 stories, and one—the Empire State Building—was much taller. Most featured brick, terra-cotta, or stone facades, with offices laid out around a central core comprised of multiple banks of elevators.

The Empire State Building won the title of the city's tallest tower upon its completion in 1931. The building was the product of a failed venture to erect a retail complex on the former site of the Waldorf-Astoria Hotel; the investors who bought the site shifted the program to a speculative office scheme in 1929. Though enormous, the building did not use all of the floor area available; it proved impossible to do so while designing relatively small tenancies. Constructed after the Depression had begun, a large supply of available labor—as well as a simple and repetitive design—allowed the building to be constructed in a year. Speed would not save the project's investors however: dire economic conditions left much of the newly completed office space unleased—giving rise to the moniker "the Empty State Building."

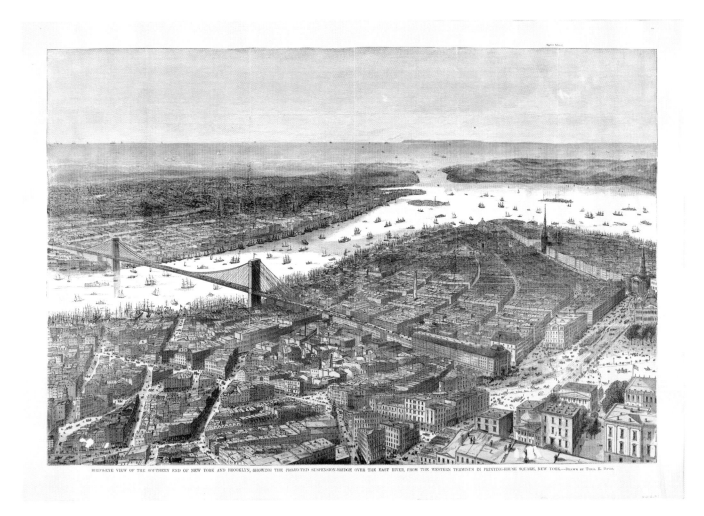

BIRDS-EYE VIEW OF THE SOUTHERN END OF NEW YORK AND BROOKLYN, SHOWING THE PROJECTED SUSPENSION-BRIDGE OVER THE EAST RIVER, FROM THE WESTERN TERMINUS IN PRINTING-HOUSE SQUARE, NEW YORK.—DRAWN BY THOS. R. DAVIS.

Theodore R. Davis, *Bird's-eye View of the Southern End of New York and Brooklyn, Showing the Projected Suspension-bridge over the East River, from the Western Terminus in Printing-House Square*, 1870

The bird's-eye view of Lower Manhattan, a hand-colored version of an engraving by Theodore R. Davis published as a supplement in *Harper's Weekly* for November 19, 1870, pictures New York in its last years as a low-rise city. Seen from just north of City Hall Park, the engraving describes a densely built metropolis, held level at a height of four-to six-stories by the absence of elevator technology. The only insistent verticals are the myriad ship masts that line the entire East River edge and the steeples of St. Paul's Chapel and Trinity Church that accent the diagonal cut of Broadway.

Overpowering the scale of the sprawling urban fabric is the prophetic image of the East River (Brooklyn) Bridge that had begun construction in 1869. By the time it was completed in 1883, the typical height for new commercial buildings was eight or nine stories as the pressures of development, driven by high demand for office and commercial space and resulting high rents, fueled the rise of the skyline. In its broad view, this print speaks to the importance of trade, in the gracious harbor and animated waterfront; to the prominence of major thoroughfares such as Broadway; and to the impact of the ambitious new infrastructure that would create a center of civic space and commercial activity in the expanding city.

THE WORLD BUILDING.   TRIBUNE BUILDING.   TIMES BUILDING.

SUN BUILDING.

New York.   CITY HALL AND NEWSPAPER ROW.

MADE IN GERMANY.

City Hall and Park Place, known as "Newspaper Row," c. 1893

This postcard view of Newspaper Row, on the eastern edge of City Hall Park, shows the skyscraper headquarters of three of the powerhouse papers that made New York the media capital of America. The earliest and shortest is the red-brick Tribune Building, which stretched its clock tower to 260 feet to become the city's tallest office building when it was completed in 1875. One block to the south (right) of the Tribune, in 1888, the New York Times Company commissioned architect George B. Post to design an imposing granite-faced thirteen-story high-rise to replace its five-story building on the same site. Behind the Times, and over-scaled, rises the top of the 288-foot American Tract Society Building of 1893.

The competing publisher Joseph Pulitzer, whose paper *The World* and its popular Sunday supplement boasted the highest circulation on the planet, hired Post to design his lavish monument, the World Building. Completed in 1890, the skyscraper, shown at the center, was surmounted by a drum and gilded dome that crested at 309 feet, to take the title of world's tallest office building. As with the other headquarters, the building served at once as a symbol of the success of the paper and a factory for its production, from the writing and editing of the articles in offices to the creation and composition of the lines of type and the printing presses in the basement.

Lower Broadway with the Tower Building at left, c. 1910

When historians debate the subject of the "first skyscraper," the partisans of New York versus Chicago stress different definitions of the building type: steel-frame construction is the key characteristic for champions of the Windy City, while advocates for Manhattan emphasize verticality and height. Both engineering innovation and the economic aspirations (or greed) to stack up many stories are important to the evolution of the skyscraper. Nevertheless, the idea of technology driving the rise of the skyscraper has generally prevailed. Many twentieth-century textbooks describe Chicago's Home Insurance Building as the "first skyscaper." Completed in 1884, it was the first office building in the world to employ a steel frame that carried most of the weight of both the interior and exterior walls.

The first high-rise in New York to use metal-cage construction was the Tower Building at 50 Broadway, designed by architect Bradford Lee Gilbert and completed in 1889. At 11 stories and 145 feet tall, the building gave the impression of a tower only because of its extreme slenderness. The frontage on Broadway was a mere 21.5 feet, so the use of a hybrid form of metal frame to reduce the thickness of the masonry wall was important to maximize rentable space. While New York's conservative building code did not explicitly allow for skeleton-frame construction until 1892, the Department of Buildings approved Gilbert's individual application and in doing so, initiated the era of steel structures.

This photograph of the Tower Building and its neighbors is an illustration from the book *Both Sides of Broadway* (1910) that documents, block-by-block, New York's dominant commercial artery.

Broad Street with curb brokers, c. 1907

This real-photo postcard view captures Broad Street sometime between 1903 and 1910, looking north toward the intersection of Wall Street, the epicenter of American capital. The stone-clad canyon of banks and brokers frame the temple front of the 1840s Custom House (now Federal Hall National Memorial), which at the turn of the century served as the U.S. Sub-Treasury Building. The other classical pediment at center left is the facade of the New York Stock Exchange, which, located on the same site since 1865, completed its new building in 1903. These financial institutions anchored the banks—with their vaults of gold and certificates—as well as related businesses and professions to the Wall Street area, which steadily rose in rents and heights of buildings, especially in the late 1890s. By 1910 the Gillender Building, a slender 18-story tower with an ornate cupola, erected just thirteen years earlier in 1897, was being demolished to make way for the Bankers Trust Tower, which would rise more than twice the height.

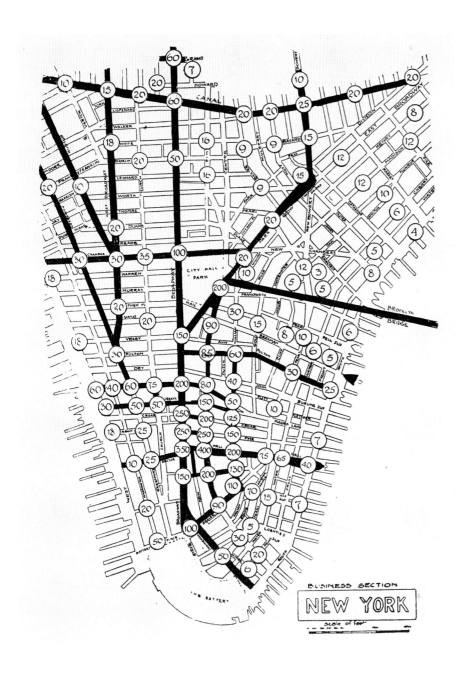

**Map of Lower Manhattan
showing real estate values per
square foot, 1903**

Richard M. Hurd, an early economist of real estate, wrote in his classic study of 1903, *Principles of City Land Values*: "In cities, economic rent is based on superiority of location only, the sole function of city land being to furnish area on which to erect buildings." One of Hurd's brilliantly informative maps shows land values by block across Lower Manhattan and helps us understand the value of key locations and the rise of the skyscraper.

At the turn of the twentieth century, New York's most expensive land, valued at $400 per square foot, was located at the intersection of Wall and Broad Streets, where the powerful financial institutions drove demand for the limited office space, producing high rents, high land values, and high-rise buildings. A few blocks north on Broadway, as well as near City Hall, values ranged around $200 per square foot. The map

also shows the great disparity between the high and low values just a short distance from the prime business arteries. Land values plummeted to $10 per square foot just three streets west of Broadway. The map of land values contradicts the assumption that Manhattan's buildings "grew upwards" because there was no room on the island to "expand out." Land values remained low where there was little demand for that location.

Looking Into Madison Square, New York.

**Madison Square Park with the
Metropolitan Life Tower on the left,
c. 1909**

By the 1880s high-rise development had spread continuously northward along the city's prime commercial corridor, Broadway. In the area known as Ladies Mile—the blocks of Broadway and Fifth Avenue from 14th Street to 23rd Street, as well as Madison Square Park, with its fashionable hotels—upscale emporia, office buildings, and lofts for light manufacturing, many ten or twelve stories or taller, began to replace older structures. Most of this construction was speculative, created to rent to multiple businesses by the room or the floor.

In 1903 Ladies Mile acquired a new center of attention, a 22-story, 285-foot skyscraper, officially named the Fuller Building for the firm that developed and built it, the George A. Fuller Company, one of the country's most successful builders and a pioneer of steel-frame construction. Better known as the Flatiron Building, the tower rose straight up on its small, triangular lot at the diagonal intersection of Broadway and Fifth Avenue. Although the slender form offered rentable floors of only 5,000 square feet, the building's extraordinary visibility made it famous. The great modernist photographer Alfred Stieglitz noted that the skyscraper appeared "like the bow of a monster steamer—a picture of a new America still in the making."

In 1909 the scale of Madison Square's skyscrapers more than doubled when the Metropolitan Life Insurance Tower topped out at 700 feet to claim the title of world's tallest office building. Modeled on the Renaissance campanile of San Marco in Venice, the 50-story tower was a triumphant addition to the company's headquarters, which had started on the square in 1893 with an 11-story building, then had expanded to nearly the full block as it grew to become the world's largest insurance company. While the lower-rise structures on the block were fully occupied by employees of Metropolitan Life, 40 percent of the signature tower was leased to outside tenants.

Cover of *New York Times* supplement showing Times Tower, January 1, 1905

In August 1896, the publisher Adolf S. Ochs purchased the *New York Times* and began a successful campaign to reinvent the paper and increase its circulation. Requiring space to grow his business, modernize his printing operations, and make clear the ascent of the paper under his leadership, in 1903 Ochs planned a new headquarters. His building was far from Newspaper Row, uptown on a tiny, but prominent, triangular lot on West 42nd Street where Broadway slices across Seventh Avenue, the area thereafter known as Times Square. A major attraction of the site was the new IRT subway tracks and station, then under construction. Connection to the subway allowed the *Times* to use the trains for the rapid distribution of papers, which could be transferred directly to the subway platforms from the basement pressroom.

Evoking the historical model of Giotto's campanile for the Florence Cathedral, the Times Tower was richly ornamented in glazed terra-cotta, a popular substitute for carved stone. The skyscraper, designed by Cyrus L. W. Eidlitz, served as both headquarters for the paper and an office building for tenants, although its tiny footprint afforded floors of only 4,100 square feet. Although the tower far exceeded its original $1.1 million budget, Ochs rationalized the extravagance as an advertisement of the paper's success and as an act of civic largesse. The *Times* proudly published its first issue in the new building on January 1, 1905, and commemorated its opening day with a lavish supplement that featured the colored rendering shown here.

French postcard of the Singer Tower, c. 1908

The 47-story Singer Tower was designed as a corporate headquarters for the Singer Manufacturing Company, a business founded in 1851, which by 1865 had become the world's largest manufacturer of sewing machines. When, in 1906, President Frederick Bourne undertook to unify and expand the hodgepodge of the company's buildings on Broadway at Liberty Street, he envisioned adding a tower "taller than all other existing buildings by from 200 to 300 feet." Completed in 1908, the Singer Tower rose 612 feet, surpassing the 1899 Park Row Building by 320 feet to become the tallest office building in the world.

The slender shaft, measuring only 65 feet square, expressed the conflicted motives behind the design of architect Ernest Flagg's Beaux-Arts or "modern French" tower. Its height was not necessary to house Singer's employees and executives: the company occupied only the space above the thirty-first floor, while the rest was rented to tenants. The extravagant tower advertised the success of the Singer Manufacturing Company and gained worldwide attention for its record-breaking height, as this French postcard shows. Flagg, a critic of the unbridled growth of skyscrapers, had tried to make his building an example for voluntary reform, setting his tower back from the street and filling only a quarter of the site. Other developers and architects were less idealistic. The same year the Singer Tower opened as the world's tallest building, the City Investing Company Building, a speculative structure on the same block, became the world's *largest* in terms of rental floor space.

BATIMENT SINGER
149, BROADWAY, NEW-YORK.
41 Étages.   186ᵐ de haut.

Lower Broadway, dominated by the Equitable Building, c. 1915

Dominating the center of this real-photo postcard of the view of Broadway just north of Wall Street is the massive Equitable Building at 120 Broadway. On its completion in 1915, the 542-foot flat-topped, classical block was the city's fifth tallest building: More significant, though, with 1.25 million square feet of rentable space, it was the world's largest office building in terms of rentable area.

Despite its corporate name, the Equitable was not a headquarters, but a savvy speculative project. Rising straight up for 38 stories above its full-block site (167 by 310 feet), split into an H-shaped plan with light wells cut in the main and rear facades. Its "economic height"—the number of stories that would provide the highest return on the investment—was determined by the formula of the efficiency of the elevator service (no wait longer than 30 seconds during peak usage).

The giant structure cast many of its neighbors into perpetual shadow, stealing their daylight and rents, and diminishing their property values. The negative reaction to its scale boosted the political support to pass the city's first zoning law, which in 1916 instituted a "setback" principle that ensured a measure of light and air at street level.

EQUITABLE BUILDING & SINGER TOWER, N.Y.

Sky Line, New York City.

Manhattan from Jersey City, c. 1915

The "skyline" of Lower Manhattan seen from the Hudson River, as shown in this postcard view of about 1915, reveals New York's skyscrapers to represent two formal types: tall and slender towers, which often rise above a wider base, like the Singer and Woolworth Buildings, and blocky behemoths such as the Equitable Building and the twinned Hudson Terminals above the Hudson and Manhattan Railroad commuter station, which later became the PATH train station of the World Trade Center.

Crowning the skyline—and taking the title of world's tallest building in 1913—was the "Cathedral of Commerce," the 792-foot Woolworth Building, designed by Cass Gilbert for the five-and-dime store king F. W. Woolworth. While the spire advertised the success of Woolworth's empire to the city and the world, his company occupied only one and one half floors of the tower, and the remainder of the space was leased to more than 1,000 tenants.

Fairchild Aerial Survey view of Manhattan from above New York Harbor, c. 1931

By the early 1930s, as this Fairchild Aerial Survey photograph shows, the ever-expanding city had developed two impressive skyscraper central business districts (CBDs): Downtown and Midtown. Through the 1920s, Lower Manhattan added many buildings of 40 to 70 stories to its already dense concentration, especially in the historic financial district and on Broadway from Bowling Green north to City Hall Park.

The main area of new commercial development in the booming economy of the 1920s, though, was in Midtown, where skyscrapers were replacing mostly low-rise residential rows. Tall buildings crowded around the transportation hub of Grand Central Terminal, and especially along the east–west axis of 42nd Street, Madison and Lexington Avenues, and northward on Fifth Avenue to 59th Street. On the West Side from 34th to 41st Streets, principally between Seventh to Ninth Avenues, a new, centralized Garment District added more than 125 speculative loft and showroom buildings, all erected in the 1920s.

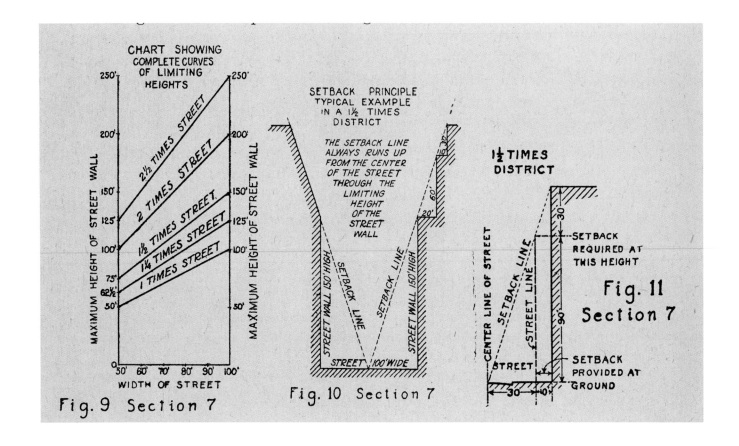

CHART SHOWING
COMPLETE CURVES
OF LIMITING
HEIGHTS

Fig. 9 Section 7

SETBACK PRINCIPLE
TYPICAL EXAMPLE
IN A 1½ TIMES
DISTRICT

THE SETBACK LINE
ALWAYS RUNS UP
FROM THE CENTER
OF THE STREET
THROUGH THE
LIMITING
HEIGHT
OF THE
STREET
WALL

Fig. 10 Section 7

1½ TIMES
DISTRICT

Fig. 11
Section 7

**Diagrams illustrating setback
principles from New York Commission
on Building Districts and Resolutions,
Final Report, 1916**

Until 1916, the owner of a parcel of land in Manhattan could erect a building of any shape, height, or use over the full area of the lot, as long as it conformed to the structural requirements of the building code, or for residential buildings, to the New York State's Tenement House Act of 1901. This laissez-faire environment changed on July 23, 1916, when the New York City Board of Estimate and Approval adopted the first comprehensive zoning law in the country.

The Zoning Resolution had two key features. It divided land into districts according to "use" in three broad categories: commercial, residential, and unrestricted (generally industrial). In order to preserve a measure of light and air on the streets and sidewalks, it also regulated the shapes of tall buildings by requiring setbacks at certain heights. There were five different "height" zones and setback formulas that specified a maximum vertical above the sidewalk before the first setback and set a diagonal within which the building could rise. Because developers sought to exploit every square foot of rentable space allowed, this template for the maximum mass or "envelope" that a building could fill determined the characteristic stepped-pyramid shape of the city's skyscrapers.

Renderings by Hugh Ferriss based on work by Harvey Wiley Corbett, *Study for Maximum Mass Permitted by the 1916 New York City Building Resolution*, 1922

This series of drawings by the delineator Hugh Ferriss, known as the "Four Stages of the Zoning Envelope," were among the most influential architectural images of the 1920s. Drawn for exhibition and published in the *New York Times* on March 19, 1922, to accompany an article entitled "The New Architecture," they projected the ways the 1916 Zoning Resolution could change both the shape of the city's skyscrapers and the skyline.

Created in collaboration with architect Harvey Wiley Corbett, Ferriss's renderings illustrated how, step by step, the maximum mass allowed by the zoning law could be transformed into a profitable commercial structure. The imposing scale of a full-block building made clear the potential of very large sites to exploit a feature of the law that allowed a tower of unlimited height to rise over 25 percent of the lot. The series' fourth stage pictured a central tower around 1,000 feet high, 70 stories, flanked by setback wings of 40 stories. The power and monumentality of Ferriss's simple sculptural forms demonstrated both the logic of developing buildings with hefty towers on large lots, as well as an aesthetic of modernity for which American architects of the 1920s were searching.

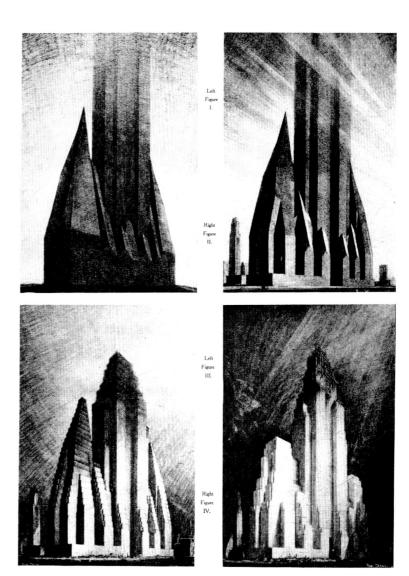

**Midtown with the Chanin Building
on the left and the Chrysler Building
on the right, c. 1930**

Located diagonally across 42nd Street
and Lexington Avenue, the Chrysler and
Chanin Buildings, designed by William
Van Alen and Sloan & Robertson respectively, illustrate the prescriptive power
of the 1916 zoning law in determining
the heights, setbacks, and proportions
of the city's skyscrapers. Occupying a
large lot (200 by 205 feet), the Chrysler
Building could develop a 25 percent
tower of substantial girth, with floor
plates of up to 8,800 square feet. The
56-story Chanin Building and the other
42nd Street towers visible in the background of this image rose over smaller
lots and offered floors of half the area
or less.

The height of a tower—i.e., the
number of rentable office floors—was
generally a function of what the real
estate industry called the "economic
height" of the building. This was a calculation that weighed the costs of land,
construction, and financing against the
revenues of anticipated rents in order
to find the most profitable return on the
money invested. A key factor in establishing the economic height was the
unproductive floor area required for the
additional banks of elevators necessary
to efficiently serve the upper stories:
empty shafts generated no rents, but
fast first-class service was essential for
Class-A buildings.

A premium for high floors was part of
the equation, but the decision to stretch
a tower to record-breaking height, as
with the Chrysler Building—where
a scalloped crown and 185-foot silver
needle were added to its functional
floors to reach 1,046 feet—took an extra
measure of ambition and ego.

The Empire State Building, 1931

The tallest building in the world when it opened on May 1, 1931, the Empire State Building broke every record in terms of both size and speed of construction. Six months after the setting of the first structural columns on April 7, 1930, the steel frame topped off on the 86th floor. The enclosed building—including the metal-clad mooring mast that raised its height to 1,250 feet or the equivalent of 102 stories—was finished in just eleven months, in March 1931.

Gigantic in every dimension, the Empire State Building surpassed the tip of the Chrysler Building's needle spire by 200 feet and the Manhattan Company Building at 40 Wall Street, the city's third tallest, by more than 300 feet. Even more impressive was its gross floor area, which at 2.1 million square feet exceeded that of the other two towers combined.

The masterminds of the construction schedule were the seasoned skyscraper builders Starrett Brothers and Eken, who won the contract in September 1929 and worked directly with the owners, with the architects Shreve, Lamb & Harmon, and with the engineers to design all the building's elements for speed of erection. At peak activity in the summer of 1930, there were 3,439 workers employed on the site, and the tower rose at the rate of a story a day.

The titanic scale of the Empire State Building was part of the development strategy of wealthy investors led by Pierre S. du Pont and John Jacob Raskob, and by former Governor Alfred E. Smith, who was hired as president of the Empire State Building Corporation. They believed the sheer size of their structure would create a new center of gravity for business on the intersection of Fifth Avenue and the retail crosstown axis of 34th Street.

However, the timing of its completion as the city and country slid into the Depression resulted in poor leasing. Fortunately, the popularity of the observation deck turned a profit in hard times and remains a significant revenue generator today.

Berenice Abbott, *Seventh Avenue Looking North from 35th Street, Manhattan*, December 6, 1935

Constructed almost entirely within the boom decade of the 1920s, New York's Garment District—occupying nearly eighteen blocks from 34th to 41st Streets between Seventh to Ninth Avenues—was the largest concentration of skyscraper factories in the world. More than 125 high-rise mixed-use structures for light manufacturing, offices, and showrooms housed an industry that employed more than 100,000 and produced nearly 75 percent of all women's and children's apparel in the United States.

The complex economy and hectic street life of the Garment District comprised myriad small manufacturers and employed tens of thousand of needle-trade workers, patternmakers, cutters, sewers, pressers, and finishers, as well as the executives, designers, and models who worked in the showrooms. Most of the high-rises were erected and owned by immigrant entrepreneurs who had begun their climb from clothing manufacturers, to builders, to real estate moguls.

No district in the city was more powerfully shaped by the formulas of the 1916 zoning law than the Garment District. A liberal "two-times" zone governed the area east of Eighth Avenue where the street wall could rise sheer to twice the width of the broad avenue.

View from Central Park showing, from left to right, the Pierre, Sherry-Netherland, and Savoy-Plaza hotels, c. 1930

Large hotels for transient, tourist, and long-term residence have been an important part of the urban landscape since the nineteenth century. Because of the long-distance train travel, many high-rise hotels clustered near Grand Central Terminal and Pennsylvania Station. In the mid-1920s, skyscraper hotels with moderately priced single rooms and apartments, sometimes for specialized populations such as single women, rose along Lexington Avenue.

At the top end of the market were the swank hotels on Fifth Avenue at the southeast corner of Central Park, which illustrate a characteristic form. Because hotels were considered commercial buildings under the 1916 zoning law, they were able to develop a 25 percent tower of unlimited height. Apartment buildings, no matter the class, were regulated by tenement laws, which capped height, so hotels were New York's only form of residential high-rise, at least until the reform of the Multiple Dwellings Law of 1929.

6

Housing the People

1930–1970

*Tear down the old, build up the new! Down with rotten
antiquated rat holes! Down with hovels! Down with disease!
A new day is dawning. A new life. A new America.*

—Mayor Fiorello LaGuardia, 1938[1]

Between 1935, when the low-rent First Houses on Manhattan's Lower
East Side became the first apartment complex in the nation to be built,
owned, and operated by a municipal government, and the 1970s, when
the U.S. government significantly curtailed its financial support of affordable housing nationwide, New York was the undisputed leader in the
field of affordable housing. Government, at the federal, state, and local
levels, made affordable housing (officially defined as costing a household
no more than 30 percent of its income) possible by providing direct or
indirect subsidies, including grants, loans, or tax breaks, which lowered
costs that would otherwise be borne by tenants, homeowners, landlords,
or developers.

   During the period, New York functioned as a kind of laboratory for subsidized housing. The city emerged not only with hundreds of thousands
of new affordable units housing serving a broad economic spectrum, from
some of the city's poorest citizens to members of the middle class, but also
with the provision and maintenance of low- and middle-income housing
as an industry in itself, combatting the city's ongoing, if unpredictable, real
estate market pressures. New York's assumption of a national leadership

role in the field, inspiring developments and programs in other cities, was perhaps not surprising given the city's long history of support for progressive social policies and its belief in activist government.

Those New York City–based individuals and groups who advocated for and supplied housing for New Yorkers of modest means had multiple motivations. Growing out of early social movements going back to the end of the nineteenth century and the beginning of the twentieth, including model or philanthropic tenements for the working class and the settlement house movement aimed at the educational and vocational needs of immigrants, the contribution of housing advocates was spurred on by a strong sense of social justice. Some advocates were also motivated by a desire to create a healthy and accessible labor pool.

New York City Housing Authority

The Depression years were a watershed for efforts within both the public and private sectors to build, own, and operate adequate housing for working-class and poor New Yorkers. Most importantly, in 1934, empowered by an amendment to the New York State 1926 housing law, Mayor Fiorello La Guardia and Senator Robert F. Wagner spearheaded the creation of the New York City Housing Authority (NYCHA), the nation's first public agency dedicated exclusively to housing.

For the first time in American history, government got directly into the business of building housing. Leveraging massive federal support from New Deal programs, La Guardia and his allies associated the pressing need for construction jobs for the city's unemployed with an ambitious housing reform agenda. Reflecting widespread public ambivalence toward direct government intervention into the residential real estate market, early efforts to publicize and promote public housing in New York stressed job creation, not housing per se. The authority's commitment to providing housing for the broadest swath of society was given further legal grounding in 1938 when the New York State Constitution was amended to say that "The aid, care and support of the needy are public concerns

and shall be provided by the state and by such of its subdivisions."[2]

To move forward with First Houses, the earliest NYCHA development, the land owner and pioneering real estate developer Vincent Astor sold much of the First Houses site between Second and Third Streets and First Avenue and Avenue A to the authority at a reduced price in exchange for favorable loan conditions on other transactions. The financier Bernard Baruch also helped to subsidize the land acquisition. Existing tenements were extensively renovated and every third building was torn down to increase the apartments' access to natural light and fresh air. Mayor LaGuardia and First Lady Eleanor Roosevelt were among the dignitaries who attended the First Houses opening festivities on December 3, 1935. LaGuardia boasted of the city's ability to utilize newly created federal funding sources for affordable housing, stating, "This is boondoggling exhibit A, and we're proud of it."[3] So effective did La Guardia prove at garnering federal support that a year into his mayoralty New York was claiming around 14 percent of the federal government's total relief outlay.

New York's efforts to construct quality affordable housing set an example for the nation during the interwar period, as the city took the initiative in the emerging field. A generation of outspoken New York housing leaders lobbied Washington, including Mary K. Simkhovitch, who as early as 1901 had co-founded the Association of Neighborhood Workers and the following year became the first director of the groundbreaking social services provider Greenwich House. In 1934 Simkhovitch became NYCHA's first vice-chairman, a position she held until 1948, and helped to persuade President Franklin D. Roosevelt to use federal funds for public housing. Under her leadership, social services, including child and health care, were inextricably linked to the city's housing programs.

Proponents of public housing did not envision the developments serving as long-term residences. They believed that affordable rents would result in more disposable income, enabling access to better educational and vocational opportunities and improving the lives of residents who would use public housing as a rung in a ladder of upward mobility.

New York lawyer Charles Abrams set the stage for one of the more controversial aspects of government intervention in housing markets nationwide: the taking of private property. As New York City Housing Authority's first counsel, Abrams convinced the city to turn to eminent domain, a bold but risky legal strategy that ultimately allowed NYCHA to seize land from landlords who had been unwilling to sell. He successfully defended this broad definition of housing as "public use" before the Supreme Court in 1936. The following year, Senator Wagner exercised a national reach in terms of government support of affordable housing, co-sponsoring the United States Housing Act of 1937. The legislation established the United States Housing Authority and allowed the federal government to directly fund municipal housing authority.

Immediately after World War II, NYCHA sought to meet the demand for affordable housing and avoid the arduous aspects of slum clearance by locating new developments on empty sites, often in more remote parts of the city. Nonetheless, in contrast to other cities nationwide, where subsidized housing was commonly located "on the other side of the tracks," new developments in New York often had easy access to public transportation and parks.

In 1944, a decade after NYCHA's founding, the Citizens' Housing Council, a non-profit educational and research organization established in 1937, organized "Housing Week," featuring "farewell-to-slums" parties held in NYCHA developments and a documentary film on public housing shown prior to feature films in theaters across the city. But opposition to public housing was extant and growing, some opponents arguing that public housing was a burden on taxpayers and that it had failed to either eradicate slums or deliver adequate low-income housing at the same cost as equivalent private-sector housing. Private landlords asserted that publicly subsidized apartments created unfair competition: some even contended that it "smacked of Socialist Vienna [and] Red Moscow." Perhaps the most vocal opposition

was voiced by those individuals and families in danger of being displaced by the construction of new developments.

Widespread slum clearance, despite some efforts to avoid the complex and often controversial process, was nonetheless often a hallmark of most urban renewal efforts. Nearly all civic groups were supportive of the process. Preservation and rehabilitation were proposed as urban renewal strategies as early as the late 1940s, but a truly multifaceted approach was not widely adopted in New York until the 1970s. Slash-and-burn demolition, replaced by towers-in-the-park developments, would predominate for decades.

In 1955 NYCHA was the nation's largest landlord, with 90,000 apartments in 78 developments; by the early 1960s, one out of fourteen New Yorkers lived in public housing. Despite its staggering rate of growth, NYCHA struggled to keep up with demand: in 1965, at the end of the agency's building boom, there were 135,000 NYCHA units, but 100,000 people were still on waiting lists. Managing and maintaining this swelling portfolio of properties required significant infrastructure. In the 1950s and 1960s, to combat increasing problems of crime and vandalism, NYCHA mobilized the largest public housing police program in the nation. By 1966 NYCHA had hired 1,070 officers, and by the end of the 1970s, the agency employed a staff of 12,000, including architects and planners, in addition to administrative, security, and maintenance staffs.

In its early years, NYCHA handpicked its tenants through a finely crafted system. Inspired by the English model of "council housing," NYCHA used a point system with seven categories that included not only financial circumstances, but factors such as rent payment record and "social background," which favored working people with stable incomes. Between 1934 and 1939, 174,000 New Yorkers applied for NYCHA apartments, but only around 14,000 qualified. In the 1960s, tenant selection procedures were changed to serve a broader spectrum of New Yorkers. Though NYCHA officially adopted a racially non-discriminatory policy from the outset, the number of non-white tenants was initially low, and it rose slowly: as late as 1960, African Americans were still under-represented in NYCHA developments.

Public housing was built on a massive scale, ultimately housing an estimated 600,000 people. But numbers housed did not always ensure success. By the 1950s, there was widespread criticism of public housing developments' isolation from the surrounding urban fabric, leading some to charge that they constituted a new form of ghettoization. Worse were accusations that the presence of high crime and poor maintenance in some developments rendered the red-brick towers little more than vertical slums. Still, the city's enduring commitment was reflected in the fact that, in stark contrast to other major American cities, including Chicago and St. Louis, where by the 1970s large amounts of public housing was been demolished, New York retained virtually all of its public housing stock and demand for it remained high.

Housing for the Middle Class

Although the establishment and growth of NYCHA were unquestionably the public sector's most direct involvement in the city's residential real estate market, New York State's reinstatement of rent-control laws in 1943 was impactful. In 1920, the state had enacted Emergency Rent Laws, granting state courts power to review the "reasonableness" of rent increases; the laws expired in 1929, at the outset of the Depression. Rent-control programs affecting New York City, which limited what landlords could charge tenants, were subsequently administered by the federal, state, and city government, as well as jointly by the city and the state. In time the measures, initially intended as temporary, became a key feature of the city's residential housing market.

Simultaneously efforts were underway to encourage private developers to build affordable homes for the middle class. In the 1940s, that market was particularly stagnant and strong demand, including that exerted by returning GIs and their families, remained unmet. During the following decade, the city would incentivize privately developed middle-class housing

in part to preserve its own tax base at a moment when both public and private dollars were pouring into the expanding suburbs, which were luring away city residents in large numbers. But the earliest forays into support for this market were decades earlier, when a number of unusual public-private partnerships were structured to remake targeted areas of the city.

Collaboration between the government and private developers was essential to the provision of middle-class housing on a massive scale. As early as 1926, New York State Governor Alfred E. Smith's signing of the the Limited Dividend Housing Companies Law had given rise to a new affordable housing type: the limited dividend (or limited-equity) cooperative. In such developments, residents owned shares in the corporation owning the development, but a potential profit from the sale of an apartment was limited by the established regulations. This method of ensuring affordability by limiting profit had long been employed in New York by philanthropic individuals and organizations. The innovation of the 1920s was to institutionalize the methodology by having government directly facilitate the approach. Labor unions were quick to take advantage of the new regulations.

The Amalgamated Garment Workers' Union completed housing developments in the late 1920s and early 1930s. While successful in both aesthetic and economic terms, these developments were relatively small in number and fell far short of resolving the city's chronic shortage of affordable housing. In the post–World War II era, labor union leaders such as Sidney Hillman and Abraham Kazan spearheaded much larger scale efforts to build affordable housing, culminating in the establishment of United Housing Foundation, a real estate investment trust, in 1951. Much of the foundation's work was realized in the city's outer boroughs, but union-sponsored housing was also built in many areas of Manhattan.

New York's "master planner," Robert Moses, who was instrumental in postwar public housing construction, first got into the affordable housing business during World War II, when he paved the way for privately developed and managed housing for returning

GIs, including tax abatements for Met Life's Stuyvesant Town. In 1943, responding to changes in the existing Urban Redevelopment Companies Law and tax codes affecting insurance companies, the Metropolitan Life Insurance Company—with Moses' support—embarked on Stuyvesant Town. In exchange for limiting its profit to 6 percent, Metropolitan Life received significant tax breaks; for twenty-five years, the company's municipal taxes were to be based on the neighborhood's valuation as assessed at the time Stuyvesant Town was first proposed. The city also played a strong role in assembling the Stuyvesant Town site; indeed, the massive development on 72 acres in between 14th and 21st Streets and First Avenue and the East River, an area previously known as the Gashouse District, required the relocation of 10,000 residents. The development's 35 buildings, each 12 or 13 stories, ultimately occupied only a quarter of the site and focused inwardly toward a landscaped area named Stuyvesant Oval.

The development, which was restricted to white tenants, soon attracted controversy. In response to protests at Stuyvesant Town, Metropolitan Life built Riverton Houses in Harlem for African-American tenants in 1945. The development housed 1,232 units, in comparison to Stuyvesant Town's 8,875 units. While the development was intended to appease the black community, criticism of the effort was harsh. In 1948 two black veterans sued Metropolitan Life and the Stuyvesant Town Corporation for racial discrimination. The initial court decision ruled in favor of the defendants. Subsequently, the Appellate Division of the New York State Court upheld the decision. Opposition to these court rulings and continuing protests ultimately led to the passage of the Brown-Isaacs Bill in 1957, which established the city's Fair Housing Practices Law. The legislation made racially discriminatory rental policies illegal in all private housing developments that received municipal tax breaks or subsidies.

Moses went on to work extensively with private developers building affordable housing under the federally administered Title I program, which had been set in motion by the United States Housing Act of 1949, a part of President Harry Truman's progressive domestic policies, collectively known as the Fair Deal. By 1960, under Moses's leadership, New York had been allocated more Title I money than any other American city—$65.8 million, which was twice as much as that received by the second-place city, Chicago. Despite his accomplishments—Moses is credited with the construction of 150,000 affordable units—his contributions were controversial. He was widely criticized for the large-scale tenant dislocation and the community disruption caused by the construction of new housing.

An important facet of the postwar effort to build government-subsidized housing for middle-class New Yorkers came in the form of the state's Limited Profit Housing Companies Act of 1955 (widely known as "Mitchell-Lama" after its chief sponsors). This program utilized eminent domain to offer building sites to private developers who received tax abatements in exchange for limiting their profits. Under the program, 101 rental developments with roughly 46,000 apartments were constructed, as were as more than thirty limited-equity cooperatives containing some 60,000 occupant-owned apartments. Projects were required to stay in the program for twenty or thirty years. By 2015, fewer than half of these developments retained their market-protected status.

In the late 1960s, responding to the city's legacies of racially discriminatory housing practices and urban decay, New York Governor Nelson A. Rockefeller called for the creation of a nonprofit, public-private initiative to build new housing in impoverished neighborhoods. The Urban Development Corporation (UDC—today Empire State Development) became the main vehicle for creating new subsidized housing in the state. The UDC exercised broad political and economic powers: it could issue bonds, use eminent domain, grant tax abatements to private developers, and overrule existing zoning regulations. As president of the New York State Urban Development Corporation from 1968 to 1975, Ed Logue focused the agency's efforts on Harlem, East Harlem, the South Bronx, and central Brooklyn, hiring young architects who pursued innovative design directions. Logue also oversaw the development of Roosevelt Island as a

5,000-unit development mixing low-income, middle-income, elderly, and market-rate residents.

In 1933, the year before NYCHA was established, the cost of housing in New York was not government regulated, with the exception of enterprises (involving both the leasing of apartments and homeownership) established under New York State's Limited Dividend Housing Companies Law of 1926. By the 1970s, it was estimated that more than 2 million New Yorkers benefited from some form of regulated real estate market, in addition to those homeowners who received a mortgage interest deducation. The economic landscape of the city's housing had been radically transformed by the establishment of rent control and rent stabilization programs, a hugely ambitious public housing system, and a wide variety of public-private partnerships involving government, developers, and sometimes non-profit groups. Despite the persistently high cost of much of the city's housing stock, efforts by both the public and private sectors had succeeded in allowing, at least to some extent, for the provision of decent housing across a broad economic spectrum.

COPR. DETROIT PHOTOGRAPHIC CO.

5464   YARD OF A TENEMENT, NEW YORK.

Tenement yard, c. 1900

The daily, densely filled interior life of a turn-of-the-century block enclosed with tenement buildings is depicted in this colored, Phostint postcard. These postcards were produced by the Detroit Publishing Company using a lithographic process originally developed in Switzerland.

Bracketed by red-brick residential buildings, colorful laundry in pinks, yellows, blues, and crisp whites are suspended on lines running "back to back" from tenement to tenement across a courtyard. As was typical for the time, the dimensions of the rear yard were compressed by buildings taking up as much land as possible. Only after the New York State Housing Act of 1901, in combination with the New York City 1916 Zoning Resolution, were building limits placed on development by restricting individual lot coverage; these new laws required building plans to allow for additional light and air to enter the interiors.

The Durst Collection includes a large group of postcards, typically scenes of street life—people on the sidewalks, entering shops, exchanging goods, or riding new streetcars. This image is a rare depiction of life at the interior of the block in the slightest of residential open spaces.

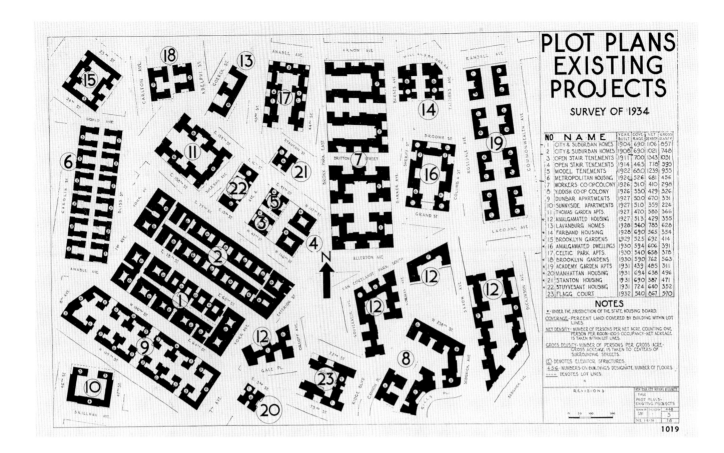

Frederick Ackerman and the New York City Housing Authority technical staff, Variations of the garden apartment type, 1934

This drawing documents the development of the garden apartment as a new housing type in New York City between 1904 and 1932. Richard Plunz, in his book A *History of Housing in New York City*, credits the drawing to Frederick Ackerman and the technical staff at the newly formed New York City Housing Authority (NYCHA). Twenty-three different plans are shown in random relation to one another, yet presented along the same adjacent street. The plans progressively depict a decrease in building footprint size in relation to open space, particularly at the interior of the block, thus producing increasingly large garden spaces. Prior to the 1901 Tenement Act, it was common to find blocks with more than 70 percent lot coverage; one such block was recorded at greater than 90 percent coverage, producing the type of windowless rooms captured by the photographer Jacob Riis in his book *How the Other Half Lives* of 1890. A detailed chart lists each building's lot coverage, net density, and gross density.

HISTORY
IN CAPSULE FORM

4 HOUSING STAGES IN 4 BLOCKS

Within only a moderately hefty stone's throw of one another in the blocks adjacent to Harlem River Houses stand typical representatives of the four stages which epitomize a century of New York Housing history.

1 Old-Law

Construction of this type of low-rent housing was forbidden in 1901, yet New York still treasures 67,000 such buildings with 524,000 apartments. Rooms with windows open on slot-like courts, with all that means in scarcity of light and foulness of air; but more than half the rooms have no windows at all. Old-law tenements have a much higher death rate than better houses. Fires in old-law tenements brought 33 fatalities in 1 year, with none in new-law tenements.

2 New-Law

These tenements are much better. They possess inner courts not less than 12 by 24 feet, and yards at the rear of all lots to provide better ventilation. Every room has a window, and every apartment running water and a toilet. About 53,000 tenements, containing 904,000 apartments, have been erected under the 36-year-old new law in New York. But they are generally too expensive for low-income families; and only 1¼ percent of those built in Manhattan for 5 years prior to 1933 rent for less than $12.50 per room per month.

3 Dunbar Apartments

With excellent ventilation because they are only two rooms deep, the buildings are grouped about garden courts which occupy one-half the block area. Club-rooms and other community features make this development highly desirable. A privately sponsored development, it is so far ahead of new-law tenements as to be in a different class. Unfortunately the costs are too great for average low-income families.

4 Harlem River Houses

Typical of the low-rent housing erected by the Housing Division of the Public Works Administration, this new completely fireproof community is constructed on extremely simple yet substantial lines. Here tenants will enjoy that standard of living of which America, often unjustifiably, boasts. But with all the economies of large-scale construction, and the benefits of low-cost financing which PWA enjoys, Harlem River Houses is only further proof that even modest low-rent housing for low-income families requires assistance in some form from Government.

Aerial view of Harlem River Houses and environs, 1936

Taken in 1936, this aerial photograph is overlaid with large black arrows and white text graphically recording shifts in New York City residential buildings constructed during the late nineteenth and early twentieth centuries. More specifically, this photographic montage illustrates three distinct housing types: Old-Law (pre-1901) tenements that came to be known as "black holes of Calcutta" due to their poor, even dangerous living conditions; New-Law (post-1901) tenements, which incorporated interior courtyards no less than 12 by 24 feet; and the garden apartment, as exemplified by the Dunbar Apartments (1927), and the Harlem River Houses (1936).

View of Gardens in Paul Laurence Dunbar Apartments, New York City
looking toward Seventh Avenue entrance

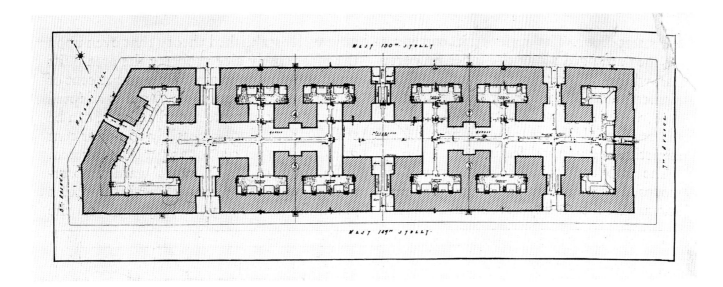

Dunbar Apartments, 1928

Completed between 1926 and 1928, and named for African-American poet Paul Laurence Dunbar, Dunbar Apartments occupy a full city block in northeast Harlem, between 149th and 150th Streets and Seventh and Eighth Avenues. Commissioned by John D. Rockefeller Jr., the development was part of a New York City tradition going back to the 1870s of what were first called "philanthropic tenements" sponsored by wealthy, socially concerned individuals. Built to the legal edges of its site, the development's solid, "Holland face brick" facade and terra-cotta parapet detailing enclose a series of open, interior courts and gardens. The six buildings are arranged around a series of interconnected interior courtyards running east–west,

with entrances through breaks in the streetwalls on the north and south and through two narrow, arched entrances at either avenue. Most of the development's construction features and materials, building systems, and interior finishes largely matched those found in contemporaneous middle-income apartments on the Upper West Side.

Covering nearly half of Dunbar's 150,000-square-foot lot, this landscaped interior space, including a playground, was designed to provide maximum fresh air and light to court-facing apartments. In addition to 514 apartments, Dunbar originally contained offices (including a doctor's), nine stores, and Dunbar National Bank. Providing a bank to its residents was of historic

significance, particularly since by 1935, with the release of the Federal Housing Administration's Home Owner's Loan Corporation (HOLC) maps of Manhattan, the majority of Harlem would become a redlined neighborhood, and Dunbar Apartments fell within the D grade, making loans impossible. This unethical practice only reinforced the importance of Dunbar as the first affordable, cooperative housing project for African Americans built in Manhattan. Notable residents included author, civil rights activist, and editor of the magazine *Crisis* W. E. B. Du Bois; poet Countee Cullen; entertainer Paul Robeson; labor leader A. Philip Randolph; and numerous other African-American artists and intellectuals.

FIRST·FLOOR·PLAN

"A"—SIMPLE PERIMETER, SUNNYSIDE PLAN.

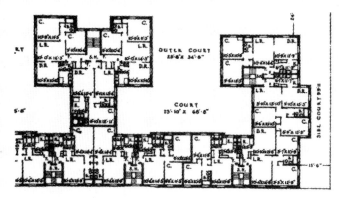

PLAN OF 2ᴺᴰ 3ᴿᴰ 4ᵀᴴ & 5ᵀᴴ FLOORS

"B"—DOUBLE PERIMETER. DUNBAR PLAN.

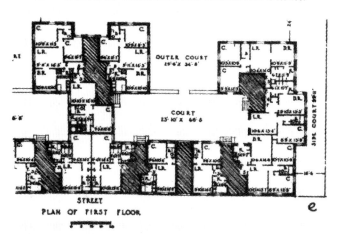

PLAN OF FIRST FLOOR

"C"—DOUBLE PERIMETER, DUNBAR PLAN.

Henry Wright, Comparison of Sunnyside Gardens and Dunbar Apartments plans, 1929

Published in 1929 by architect and planner Henry Wright, this comparative analysis was intended to show the increased spatial efficiency of Sunnyside Gardens' (1924–28) simple-perimeter plan over Dunbar's double-perimeter plan. As co-architect (along with Clarence Stein) of the City Housing Corporation, Wright was by no means impartial in his analysis. Here illustrated through selected portions of the first-floor plan, designated as "simple perimeter," the typical Sunnyside unit consisted of a living room, kitchen, dining room, and two bedrooms.

The comparison of the first floors of Sunnyside Gardens (Plan A) and the Dunbar Apartments (Plan C) fails to acknowledge the program differences between the two buildings. Dunbar features retail and social amenities and a permeable street wall offering residents easy access to wider Harlem, neither of which are part of the Sunnyside residential first floor plan

Similarly, Dunbar Apartments and Sunnyside Apartments present two differing approaches to the treatment of coverage, density, and open space. The Dunbar Apartments introduced a continuous internal courtyard to be shared by all tenants. By contrast, Sunnyside Apartments left open much of its lot-edge space for individual tenants to develop as they wished.

HARLEM RIVER HOUSES

FEDERAL EMERGENCY ADMINISTRATION OF PUBLIC WORKS

The cover of *Harlem River Houses*, an informational brochure, depicts the residential project to be located within the limits of 153rd Street to the north, 151st Street to the south, Harlem River Drive to the east, and Macombs Place to the west. The first federally funded public housing project, Harlem River Houses was notable for the mere fact of its construction in 1934–35 at the height of the City of New York's Slum Clearance program—a period during which, according to a banner displayed as part of a January 1935 NYCHA exhibition, more than five miles of slums were demolished.

Harlem River Houses increased the open spaces of the garden apartment type more than any previous project. Sited on nine acres, effectively taking up several city blocks, the development contained more space dedicated to open, natural and garden space, than buildings. Unlike the tower-in-the-park, soon to follow as the dominant new housing paradigm, Harlem River Houses maintained a strong street presence. By the opening of the Harlem River Houses, the neighborhood of Harlem was more of a city unto itself than the typical Manhattan neighborhood, housing a growing population in what would come to constitute the cultural and intellectual capital of black America. Yet despite the celebratory years of the Harlem Renaissance (1918–35), the neighborhood was increasingly a site of turmoil and neglect with respect to housing.

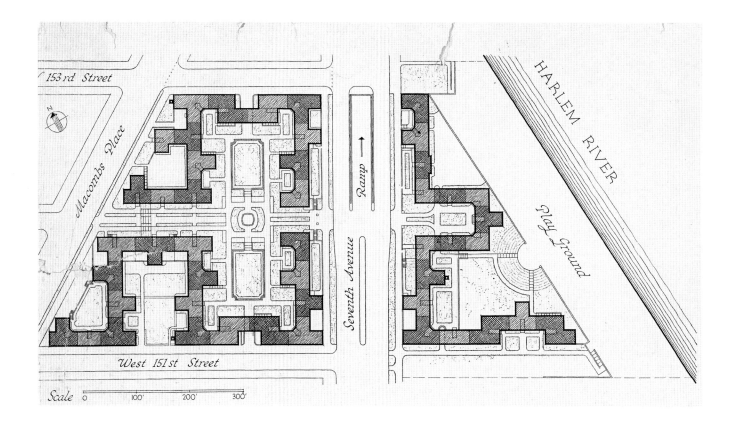

Site plan, Harlem River Houses, 1937

On March 19 and 20, 1935, the Harlem Race Riots erupted as a result of the combined effects of the Depression, red-lining practices, and racial discrimination. Despite a postwar increase in population and cultural flowering, Harlem had been largely overlooked by the city in terms of its physical development and maintenance. Harlem River Houses, designed by Archibald Manning Brown with John Louis Wilson and Horace Ginsbern, was, in this sense, a vision meant to offer hope to the area residents. One of two Public Works Administration (PWA) experimental pilot programs for residential buildings in the city, Harlem River Houses was designed specifically for African Americans. The other, Williamsburg Houses in Brooklyn, was for white tenants only.

The brochure does not use the term "public housing." John Louis Wilson, the first African American to graduate from Columbia University's School of Architecture, as well as the first to become a licensed architect in New York State, was a part of the development's team.

WHAT YOU WILL FIND

All apartments in the four- and five-story buildings of Harlem River Houses are of fireproof construction. Dwelling units consist of two, three, four, and five rooms, each with bath and kitchen. Every room is an outside room, and every unit has through or cross ventilation. Many of them face courts wider than the usual street.

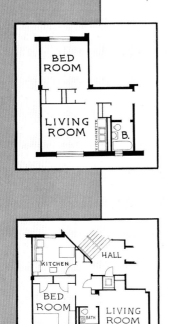

TWO ROOMS

A typical two-room apartment consists of a living room and a bedroom, with full-sized bath. A compact strip kitchen or kitchenette, with the same equipment as in full kitchens, makes it a complete and convenient housekeeping unit.

THREE ROOMS

Three-room apartments consist of living room, bedroom, and kitchen, plus bath. A feature which housekeepers will appreciate is the number of closets provided in this, as in all, Harlem River Houses apartments. Other arrangements of three-room apartments occur.

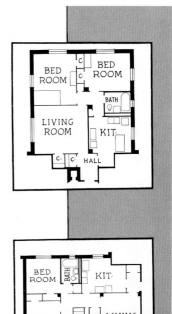

FOUR ROOMS

Four-room apartments are similarly simple in plan, with the addition of a second bedroom. Permissible families for this size of unit are no larger than five persons, two for each bedroom and one to sleep in the living room. Children under 2 years of age are not counted.

FIVE ROOMS

Five-room units are the largest in the community, having three bedrooms in addition to the living room. Families as large as seven, not including children under 2 years, may live in this suite.

NURSERY SCHOOL

In many housing communities the most popular feature is the nursery school. In Harlem River Houses it is anticipated that mothers will organize such a play school for young children. Not only will the children be safe from dangers of street life, but their play can be supervised and their health watched.

HEALTH CLINIC

Tenants of Harlem River Houses and other residents of the neighborhood make use of this city-maintained clinic. Ounces of prevention weigh heavily in the scales of health; and this clinic is counted on to reinforce the vastly improved living conditions in the new community.

U. S. GOVERNMENT PRINTING OFFICE   145299

Apartment floorplans, Harlem River Houses, 1937

All of the apartments in the Harlem River Houses were contained within four- and five-story fireproof buildings. Dwelling units consisted of two, three, four, and five rooms, and each apartment had its own bath and kitchen. Every room was located on an exterior wall with an operable window to ensure cross- or through-ventilation. The typical two-room apartment consisted of a bedroom and a living room, as well as a kitchenette, with the same equipment found in a full kitchen, and a bathroom, an arrangement touted as "a complete and convenient housekeeping unit." The three-room apartment boasted five closets. Four-room apartments, containing two bedrooms, were restricted to a maximum of five residents, with one person sleeping in the living room; children under two were not counted. The five-room apartment, with three bedrooms, could accommodate up to seven, again excluding children under two. The development contained a nursery school where children would "be safe from dangers of street life, but their play can be supervised and their health watched." In addition, New York City maintained an on-site health clinic, asserting that "ounces of prevention weigh heavily in the scale of health; and this clinic is counted on to reinforce the vastly improved living conditions in the new community."

MANHATTANVILLE RESIDENTS
EARN DIVERSE INCOMES:-

The Evolving Plans. The preliminary plans for the Morningside area had envisaged a public housing project from 123rd to 125th Streets between Broadway and Morningside Avenue. At its June 23rd, 1950, meeting, the Executive Committee agreed that two blocks of the proposed public housing site might be used for private or institutional housing development. These blocks would be from 123rd to LaSalle Streets, Amsterdam to Broadway.

The Executive Committee agreed to explore the possibilities of enlisting private capital to finance a housing project sponsored by member institutions for these two blocks. They suggested an investigation be made to determine the legal and financial possibilities under State and Federal legislation, as well as to explore the interest of cooperative housing groups in plans for the Morningside-Manhattanville area.

By the October, 1950, Executive Committee meeting, the Morningside-Manhattanville redevelopment survey had been completed. Based on its findings,

More than one-fourth of the entire sample had lived in the area at least fifteen years.

Organizational ties to the community were not many. The principal affiliation was with some church.

From the beginning of preparations for the survey, local residents and community groups showed great concern over the final outcome of the redevelopment projects. Some feared exorbitant rents; others felt that the plans implied a "lily white" development. To help allay such fears, the Board of Directors on May 18th, 1950, unanimously passed a statement of principles which said unequivocally that the Board "is opposed to discrimination in housing because of race, creed, color or national origin, and pledges itself to do everything in its power to see that the principle is honored in any redevelopment project undertaken in the Morningside-Manhattanville area".

These rumblings were only the first reactions. As redevelopment plans became more specific, community tensions increased. The Community Advisory Committee had succeeded in calming fears during the survey period, the phase for which it had actually been organized. After the survey was completed this main motivation for the Community Advisory Committee disappeared. Attempts to shift its emphasis to that of a community council interested in the broader aspects of community planning were unsuccessful.

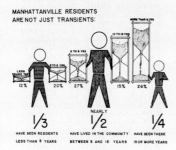

the staff began to prepare a report to be presented to the Mayor's Committee on Slum Clearance Plans. Particular emphasis was to be given to the ten-acre plot for private middle-income housing adjacent to the public housing project.

9

Diagrams illustrating local income diversity, *Morningside-Manhattanville Rebuilds*, 1955

In January 1949, reflecting an approach to urban renewal that stood at the heart of the U.S. Housing Act of 1949, Robert Moses and David Rockefeller discussed developing affordable housing, on the sole condition that construction occurred on "honest to goodness slum land." One means of confirming that these sites were in fact in decay—and, ultimately, could be considered slum lands—was the distribution of English- and Spanish-language surveys; nearly 3,400 were completed and compiled from thirty-six surrounding residential blocks. The survey included a line drawing of a hand, pointing to a single-line map with accompanying text reading:

"This is Manhattanville. You already know that it has . . . overcrowding, few playgrounds, run-down buildings . . . but did you know that the United States Government wants to help New York City to build . . . better housing, more parks and playgrounds, cleaner neighborhoods?"

Responses revealed that 23 percent of residents lived with a roomer or extra tenant, and that 49 percent of residents who worked did so either within walking distance of their homes or used "buses or direct subway lines." In an attempt to better understand residents, the Community Advisory Committee staff of Morningside Heights, Inc. also surveyed residents on their weekly

income and length of time living in the area. Diagrams tabulating questionnaire findings under the heading "Manhattanville Residents Earn Diverse Incomes" present 38 percent of residents as earning less than $40, twenty-seven percent earning $40 to $60, 18 percent earning $60 to $80, and 17 percent earning more than $80 per week. Comparable diagrams under the heading "Manhattanville Residents Are Not Just Transients" confirm more permanent ties to Manhattanville: only 12 percent of those surveyed had resided in the area for less than two years, with more than 26 percent having been in Manhattanville for more than fifteen years.

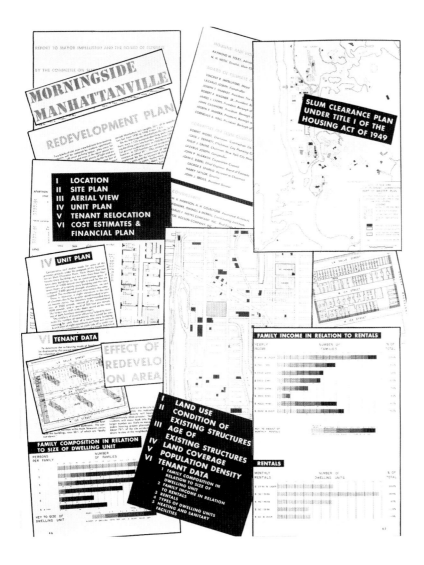

Collage of redevelopment reports from *Morningside-Manhattanville Rebuilds*, 1955

In May 1951, proof sheets and drawings of the official report were shown at the meeting of the Morningside Committee on Cooperative Housing. Black-and-white drawings, charts, lists, graphs, and bold-faced text and titles attested to the thoroughness of the report. Titles such as Slum Clearance Plan Under Title I of the Housing Act of 1949, Unit Plan, Tenant Data, Family Composition in Relation to Size of Dwelling Unit, Family Income in Relation to Rentals, were among the highlighted points. One point of the report was to note a $30 month per room per month rental versus the $25 per room per month, which would have still excluded some institutional personnel as well as the

majority of the people already living on the site. A plan drawing shows the density of the buildings with some of the lots being built to nearly 90 percent coverage.

The proposed $19 per room per month rental fee was only possible with tax concessions. Moses required that there be "sponsorship." Despite this plan, the tax exemption was deemed too difficult to achieve and so two alternate rental structures were established: one for a privately financed rental project of $31 per room per month and the other a cooperative project with charges of $23 to $25 per room per month in place of the $19 rental fee. This proposal was met with "furor" by the neighborhood residents, and an

initial hearing scheduled for October was postponed for a month to work on community relationships. At the November hearings, opposition speakers noted that not only was $31 and $25 too high, but also that local residents would be hard pressed to afford the $9 or $10 rental cost of public housing let alone $19. A new proposal was written with rental fees between $15 and $20 a month per room for this middle-income cooperative, and prominent organizations, such as the Urban League of Greater New York, Citizens Union of the City of New York, Citizens Housing and Planning Council, Regional Plan Association, Inc., and the Negro Labor Committee, advocated for the project.

RESIDENTIAL FLOOR SPACE

1940

250 sq. ft./PERSON X 3.6 PERSONS/FAMILY = 900 sq. ft./FAMILY

900 sq. ft./FAMILY X 2.0 MILLION FAMILIES = 1,800,000,000 sq.ft.

RESIDENTIAL
F L O O R
S   P   A   C   E

1970 (ESTIMATED)

285 sq. ft./PERSON X 3.1 PERSONS/FAMILY = 885 sq. ft./FAMILY

885 sq. ft./FAMILY X 2.8 MILLION FAMILIES = 2,478,000,000 sq.ft.

RESIDENTIAL
F L O O R
S   P   A   C   E

Diagram illustrating floor-space requirements in affordable housing from Harrison, Ballard & Allen, *Plan for the Rezoning of New York City; A Report Submitted to the City Planning Commission*, 1950

In 1940, at a time when average family size in New York was 3.6 persons, roughly 250 square feet of floor area was dedicated to an individual, and the average family apartment measured 900 square feet. Approximately 2 million families would require 1.8 billion square feet of residential floor space, all of which the city would have to provide in order to accommodate its residents. By 1970, dedicated floor area per individual would increase to 285 square feet while the average family size would decrease to 3.1 persons; in order to house nearly 2.8 million families in 885-square-foot apartments, the city would have to provide almost 2.5 billion square feet of residential space.

In 1942 the New York City Planning Commission eliminated the floor-area standard as a fixed requirement in affordable housing. The standard was used, however, as a general guide in determining bulk and population densities as applied to developments realized through public subsidy of private developers, including those built under the Redevelopment Companies Law, enacted in 1942, to "enlist the support of business entities such as insurance companies."

HOW MANY FAMILIES?

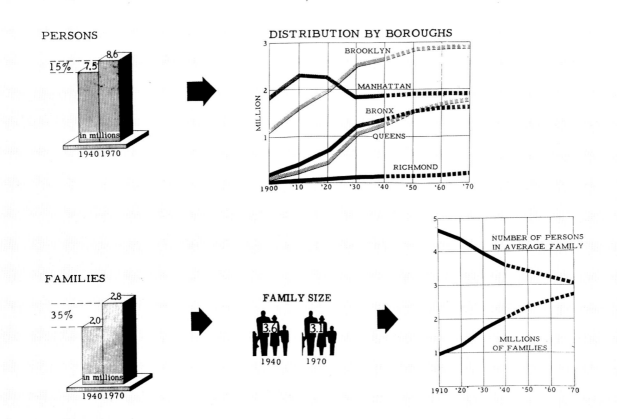

Diagram illustrating demographic shifts in New York, *Plan for the Rezoning of New York City*, **1950**

Under the title "How Many Families?" this set of diagrams and charts reflects the shifting nature of the five-borough population and its family makeup. Excepting Manhattan, whose population peaked around 1930, New York boroughs saw an increase in their populations from 1900 until the 1950s, when growth seemed to reach its height and then flatline. While Manhattan declined to its pre-1910 population of just under 2 million, the Bronx and Queens would each approach 2 million, and Brooklyn would grow toward the 3-million mark. However, the development of affordable housing across the city over this period had seemingly less to do with responding to increased or decreased population density, and more to do with placing these developments in neighborhoods already hosting lower-income populations.

MORNINGSIDE-
MANHATTANVILLE
REBUILDS . . .

The Morningside Gardens Cooperative

Elizabeth R. Hepner, *Morningside-Manhattanville Rebuilds—A Chronological Account of Redevelopment in the Morningside-Manhattanville area, with Special Reference to the Development of Morningside Gardens*, 1955

The founding of Morningside Heights Inc. and the redevelopment of the Morningside-Manhattanville area is detailed in a step-by-step account in this report. The cover presents a hand-drawn aerial perspective looking over the rooftops of the six proposed residential towers of Morningside Gardens and includes views of the Hudson River, Grant's Tomb, and the Morningside Heights neighborhood. It seems to purposefully exclude the site of the neighboring "related" public housing projects to the north and the deteriorating conditions in the adjacent blocks. It is possible to read into the cover illustration that this area was vulnerable to the problem of relocating residents due to the "high cost of housing and shortage of housing."

Founded in July 1947, Morningside

Heights Inc., the non-profit corporation responsible for the area's redevelopment, included Barnard College, Columbia University, Home for Old Men and Aged Couples, St. Luke's Home for Aged Women, Women's Hospital Division St. Luke's Hospital, Riverside Church, and Julliard School of Music. The corporation's aim was "to foster, plan, develop and promote the improvement, development and advancement of the Morningside Heights district of the Borough of Manhattan, City and State of New York, as an attractive residential, and educational and cultural area." In its first year, the group focused largely on existing conditions, undertaking statistical research, mapping, and graphic presentations. In addition to providing basic information about demographics,

land use, and population density, an "extensive door-to-door survey" revealed the need for additional school facilities.

By January 1949, David Rockefeller, president of Morningside Heights Inc., discussed the possibility of an affordable housing development for the northern end of Morningside Heights with Robert Moses. The Rockefeller family had been stakeholders in Morningside Heights' fate since International House, a student-oriented service organization that John D Rockefeller Jr. had co-founded, built its first facility in the neighborhood in 1924. By June 1951, member institutions had addressed a letter to Moses stating that there was an "interest in developing a cooperative housing project whose monthly charges would not exceed approximately $19 per room per month."

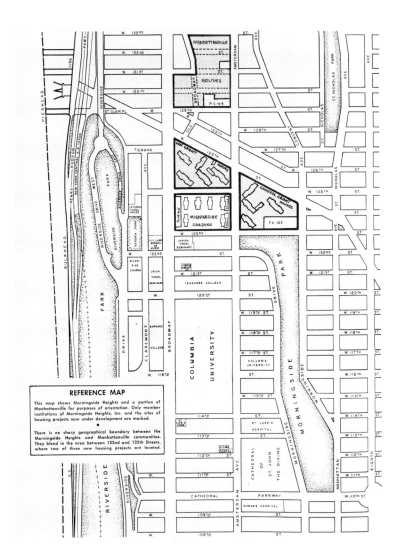

Map of Morningside Heights and Manhattanville neighborhoods showing proposed housing developments, *Morningside-Manhattanville Rebuilds,* **1955**

This map shows the proposed residential buildings of Morningside Gardens as well the NYCHA developments, General Grant Houses and Manhattanville Houses, all located between 123rd and 129th Streets and along Amsterdam Avenue in proximity to one another. The map's accompanying text notes, "There is no sharp geographical boundary between the Morningside Heights and Manhattanville communities." The site plans of Morningside Gardens and General Grant Houses did, however, encompass large amounts of open space and thus stood in marked contrast to the surrounding area on both sides of 125th Street. Additionally, the developments' comparatively low population density of roughly 300–500 persons per acre was markedly lower than that of either Morningside Heights or Manhattanville.

These projects collectively reflect and represent Moses's affinity for the tower-in-the-park—that is, European-modernism-influenced forms for housing people in urban settings, like Le Corbusier's Ville Radieuse. The Morningside Committee on Cooperative Housing met on January 11, 1951 and on February 17, 1951, after the presentation of three proposals to Robert Moses, a proposal located at Morningside Gardens was approved with the firm of Harrison & Abramovitz as the architects.

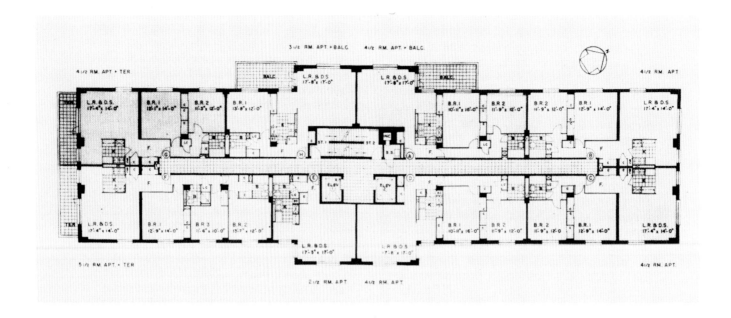

**Morningside Gardens,
typical floor plans, 1957**

Architects Wallace K. Harrison and Max Abramovitz designed the complex's six twenty-one story buildings using red-brick bonded masonry walls bearing on a cast-concrete structural frame. The typical floor plan for Morningside Gardens included in the report shows a double-loaded corridor running in the north–south direction with two elevators and a scissor stair in the middle of the plan. Apartments had two or three bedrooms. Those on the south side had accessible terraces from their living/ dining room, while units on the westerly side had balconies adjacent to the living/dining rooms and large bedroom. Typical bedroom sizes ranged from 11.75 by 12 feet to 12.75 by 14 feet. An interior corridor ran parallel to the main corridor, leading to bedrooms and the only bathroom. A fully enclosed kitchen sat relatively close to the entrance with a limited view of the living room. Apartments on the east and north side of the buildings had neither a terrace nor a balcony. The units were to be served by elevators that were faster and could support more weight than those in many contemporaneous developments.

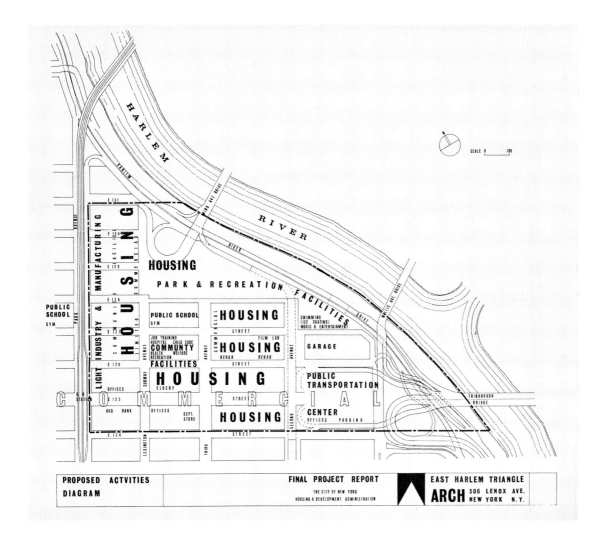

HARLEM RIVER

SCALE 0   /00

E 131
HOUSING
MANUFACTURING
COMMERCIAL
PARK AVE DRIVE
RIVER
PARK & RECREATION FACILITIES
DRIVE
WILLIS AVE BRIDGE

PUBLIC
SCHOOL
GYM.
PARK AVENUE
INDUSTRY & LIGHT
COMMUNITY LIMITED
HOUSING
PUBLIC SCHOOL
GYM
HOUSING
STREET
SWIMMING
(ICE SKATING)
MUSIC & ENTERTAINMENT

JOB TRAINING CHILD CARE
HOSPITAL
HEALTH WELFARE
RECREATION
COMMUNITY
FACILITIES
COMMERCIAL
AVENUE
HOUSING
FILM LAB
REHAB   REHAB
STREET
GARAGE

OFFICES
SUBWAY
HOUSING
ELDERLY
PUBLIC
TRANSPORTATION

COMMERCIAL
R.R. STATION
AUD.   BANK
OFFICES
DEPT.
STORE
E 123
STREET
SECOND AVENUE
CENTER
OFFICES   PARKING
TRIBOROUGH
BRIDGE

E.124
HOUSING
STREET
LEXINGTON
THIRD

PROPOSED ACTVITIES
DIAGRAM

FINAL PROJECT REPORT
THE CITY OF NEW YORK
HOUSING & DEVELOPMENT ADMINISTRATION

ARCH
EAST HARLEM TRIANGLE
306 LENOX AVE.
NEW YORK N.Y.

**Diagram illustrating site usages in East Harlem from Architects'
Renewal Committee in Harlem, *East Harlem Triangle Plan*, 1968**

Originally proposed as part of the City Planning Commission's recommendation for New York City's 1961–62 middle-income housing and renewal program, the East Harlem Industrial Triangle site was outlined by Mayor Robert F. Wagner as part of the Harlem-East Harlem area for "developing middle income housing, maintaining and upgrading existing housing and strengthening the City's industrial base." At the time, the area, taking its name from the loose triangle formed by the bounding streets of Park Avenue, 125th Street, Harlem River Drive, and 131st Street, was one of the most blighted neighborhoods in Manhattan. Working toward renewal as a "tool" to stabilize and protect neighborhoods, the CPC noted the isolation of the East Harlem Triangle due to infrastructural and natural barriers that rendered it unsuitable for housing. Declining in population by 50 percent since 1920 and seeing no new construction since the 1930s, by the time of this report the site held roughly 1,800 dwelling units with mostly overcrowded, slum conditions. More ethnically and racially diverse than most Harlem neighborhoods, in 1960, 60 percent of East Harlem Triangle residents were black, 20 percent were Puerto Rican, and 20 percent were white.

The Housing and Redevelopment board sought federal assistance in creating a comprehensive study, in order to make the site a significant location for light industry and manufacturing. In 1968 a project report was issued by the Architects' Renewal Committee in Harlem, headed by the African-American architect J. Max Bond. The final report included this diagrammatic map listing the proposed activities on site. Only through months of negotiations were neighborhood self-study groups able to persuade city officials to permit "housing on the periphery" of an area that had been zoned "M1-2," a classification permitting a wide variety of uses.

7

The Making of Midtown

1930—1980

Perhaps Commercialism is a new God, only too powerful and too appealing, to whom men are building today their highest, costliest structures.

—Sheldon Cheney, 1920[1]

By the early 1930s, Midtown was home to numerous skyscraping office and mixed-use buildings (some, like the Daily News and McGraw-Hill Buildings, combined offices and industrial loft space), rendered in a wide variety of architectural vocabularies that collectively established the area as a commercial rival to Lower Manhattan. These buildings, among many others, captured the imagination of the city—and the world—and fueled a much-publicized "race for height," as corporations and their selected architects vied for the title of the world's tallest building.

Participants in this contest brought into focus another rivalry that had already been going on for decades. In 1909 the Singer Building on lower Broadway had been the world's tallest building for only a year, when it was surpassed by the Metropolitan Life Building on Madison Square, which four years later was bested by the Woolworth Building opposite City Hall. The status of the Woolworth Building, was threatened in 1926, when the architect and engineer John A. Larkin, together with his brother Edward, planned to develop a 110-story tower on 42nd Street between Eighth and Ninth Avenues. Dismissed by many as impractical and never built, the proposal was nonetheless a harbinger of things to come in Midtown.

The race for height reached a fever pitch in 1929, when the Bank of the Manhattan Company Building, on Wall Street, and the Chrysler Building, on Lexington Avenue, went head to head. The battle was intensified by the fact that the two architects, H. Craig Severance and William van Alen, had recently dissolved a professional partnership, giving the heavily documented race a personal dimension. Walter Chrysler, head of the eponymous automobile company, who craved a New York headquarters despite the fact that none of his cars was manufactured in the city, had requested that Van Alen add floors during the building's construction. Severance increased the height of his building and even added a 50-foot-tall flagpole as insurance. Van Alen, in turn, hid a 185-foot-tall spire, which he dubbed the "vertex," within the core until the Bank of Manhattan building was finished. Van Alen then had the final element of his building installed to grab the coveted title of the world's tallest building.

The building's significance, however, was not limited to its height. It reified the notion of the skyscraper as corporate advertisement, eschewing a historicist architectural vocabulary for a design that drew inspiration from Chrysler's cars, with gargoyles resembling radiator caps, a frieze decorated with forms evoking running boards and hub caps, and a pinnacle that some saw as looking like a series of spoked wheels superimposed on each other.

Despite the fiercely waged battle for height, the Chrysler Building victory proved meaningless, as both it and its competitor were soon surpassed by the Empire State Building, which rose dramatically on 34th Street in the valley of low-rise buildings between the skyscraping ensembles to the north and south. The developer, John Raskob, knew how to fully exploit the property's advertising potential. Raskob, who had run New York Governor Al Smith's 1928 presidential campaign, hired the colorful Smith to run the Empire State Company and even sitting President Herbert Hoover got involved, marking the building's official opening by remotely turning on its lights from the White House.

Among Midtown's notable projects of the period was Rockefeller Center, a development undertaken by the Rockefeller family on a site between Fifth and Sixth Avenues then owned by Columbia University. Rockefeller Center was unique on a number of counts. It was unusually situated on a "mega-block" spanning multiple streets and connecting two major avenues. In addition, the slab-like rectangular form of several buildings rose vertically from the plaza area, largely rejecting the setback style completely, yet conforming to the new zoning code. Open space between the buildings, bordered by high-end retail, was designed as a series of civic plazas and promenades.

Three separate architectural firms were employed as a consortium to produce the ultimate design for Rockefeller Center. Despite the large number of chefs in the kitchen, and despite the vastness of its size, the complex proved a success with the critics. As critic Paul Goldberger later noted in his history of skyscrapers, "What emerged was a brilliant blend of Beaux-Arts and modern leanings, a set of towers and plazas and theaters and shops that seem at once to possess a strong, classicizing order and a sense of lively, almost spontaneous urban vitality."[2] Indeed, the completion of Rockefeller Center proved not only that the skyscraper could surpass its function as an isolated architectural icon to become an effective building block of the city, but also, and perhaps most importantly in terms of real estate, that Midtown had become the city's most sought-after corporate address.

Postwar Development

The advent of World War II brought construction in New York to a virtual halt, but when activity resumed, much of the action moved to the surrounding metropolitan region, as many returning GIs and their families left New York—principally the outer boroughs—and headed to the suburbs. As commuters fled the city for so-called bedroom communities, Midtown experienced an office building boom such as the city had never seen before, with the existing low- and mid-rise masonry buildings in whole swaths of the district torn down and replaced with glass-and-steel towers. As rebuilt, Midtown came to epitomize corporate

America's wholehearted embrace of International Style aesthetics, becoming a modernist mecca for large-scale, high-rise office buildings.

Among the areas most dramatically affected during the 1950s was Park Avenue between 46th and 59th Streets. The foundations of that transformation were established in 1945 when the real estate development firm Webb & Knapp, Inc., led by William Zeckendorf, announced that the 12-story Marguery Hotel, a courtyard-type apartment building leased from the New York Central Corporation, the area's most important landowner, would be replaced by a taller office building. The decision reflected the economic reality that the area's apartment buildings were no longer profitable, in part, some argued, as a result of New York State rent control regulations.[3]

In Midtown, the rental rate of residential properties had dropped to 25 percent during the Depression. The owners of unprofitable apartment buildings on sites zoned for non-residential purposes often sold to developers who replaced the structures with office buildings. On Park Avenue in Midtown, where zoning law revisions instituted in 1929 had allowed for office and retail development, this phenomenon was widespread.

The first new postwar office buildings to arrive on Park Avenue were not the glass-and-steel boxes that would become synonymous with the avenue in the postwar period, but rather brick-clad buildings of the "wedding cake" type that conformed to the setback paradigm encouraged by the Zoning Resolution of 1916. Some of the International Style buildings that soon followed also adopted the setback form, while others occupying larger sites sometimes conformed to the tower-and-base type. The sweeping changes to the city's zoning regulations instituted in 1961 allowed for towers that, if restricted in footprint to not more than 25 percent of the site, could rise without any height limitations. Regardless of the massing, most new or significantly remodeled buildings along Park Avenue, many of which were designed with Emery Roth & Sons, received, at best, a mix of positive and negative responses from critics. The public, however, seemed to quickly grow more dominantly negative in its reactions.

Two Park Avenue office buildings were striking exceptions to what was widely considered to be a trend toward architectural banality: Lever House and the Seagram Building. Both reflected creative responses to the city's zoning regulations and the advances of modern air-handling technology as represented in glass curtain wall. Together, they firmly established Midtown as a site for the most up-to-date modernist architecture.

Lever House, designed by Gordon Bunshaft of Skidmore, Owings & Merrill and completed in 1952, consisted of a one-story horizontal form lifted above the ground on columns and an 18-story vertical slab turned perpendicular to the avenue, breaking with the thoroughfare's building wall. Both elements were entirely clad in curtain walls of blue-green glass. The design of the corporate building surprisingly sacrificed space for aesthetics; if the building had been massed in a standard fashion, all of its interior space could have been contained within an eight-story building— far smaller than the site's zoning allowed.

The Seagram Building raised the aesthetic bar for corporate office buildings even higher. In 1954, in what would become a legendary story within architectural circles, the Seagram Company hired Charles Luckman, an architect who had served as the president of the Lever Brothers Company, and under whose tenure the company's Park Avenue headquarters had been built before he returned to architectural practice. Upon seeing a picture of the Luckman's proposed scheme in the *Herald Tribune*'s international edition, Phyllis Bronfman Lambert, the 27-year-old daughter of Seagram Company president Charles Bronfman, implored her father not to go ahead with the design. Bronfman agreed and put Lambert in charge of finding a new architect. Lambert set out for New York from Paris, where she had been living, to start the search.

On the advice of Philip Johnson, who was heading up the architecture and design department at the Museum of Modern Art, Lambert considered some of the world's leading modernist practitioners, including Le Corbusier, Walter Gropius, Louis Kahn, Ludwig Mies van der Rohe, and Frank Lloyd Wright, among others. Mies was selected, but although he was internationally famous, the émigré architect was not licensed in New York State, and Johnson was hired to work with him. The building was strongly distinguished by its placement far back from the avenue, decisively breaking with the surrounding building wall. While the radical revisions to the city's zoning laws made in 1961 encouraged the creation of plazas, and such open spaces subsequently sprouted up all over the city, rarely were they as successful as the Seagram Building's elegantly detailed public space.

The story of Park Avenue's post–World War II transformation can be said to have ended with the completion of the Pan Am Building in 1963. The development of the building, designed by Emery Roth & Sons, Pietro Belluschi, and Walter Gropius, was controversial. Early proposals had called for a narrow slab oriented north–south, retaining views up and down the avenue, on either side of the New York Central Building of 1929. Gropius called for the slab to be turned east–west, blocking the vista, in a decision that was widely criticized.

Another section of Midtown to be thoroughly reimagined and rebuilt in the postwar period was the stretch of Sixth Avenue that ran through the district. In 1939, just as Rockefeller Center was being completed, the elevated train line that ran up and down Sixth Avenue was demolished, an event that triggered large-scale redevelopment. Six years later, in a move intended to give the avenue more cachet, it was renamed the Avenue of the Americas, but the street continued to be known as Sixth Avenue. Sleek towers rose along the avenue in the early 1950s, but it was not until the end of the decade that its distinctly new urbanism, with large buildings rising without setbacks and set back on plazas, began to emerge.

Paradoxically, the rebuilding of Sixth Avenue, which provided conveniently located sites for corporations that had considered abandoning the city in favor of sprawling facilities in idyllic suburbs, itself reflected a process of suburbanization, at least in aesthetic terms. The rebuilt avenue's ubiquitous plazas were intended to "open up" block fronts in a reflection of a growing desire on the part of leading architects and urban planners to counter the density of a traditional cityscape with a sense of spaciousness associated with significantly less urban places.

In 1963 in a move that would lead to the further decreasing of street-level density along Sixth Avenue, Rockefeller Center announced that it would develop a coordinated scheme known as the XYZ plan on the west side of Sixth Avenue between 47th and 50th Streets. The plan called for a campus-like arrangement of three office buildings set amongst extensive open spaces. In the end, the site plan was developed as three massive office towers that were far more conventionally arranged in relation to the surrounding street grid. Nonetheless, the buildings, as well as others to the north and south, fulfilled, to some extent, the urban vision of "towers-in-the-park" championed by Le Corbusier in the 1920s, albeit with the "park" space limited to plazas, some below grade.

Third Avenue as it ran through Midtown, once well known for the preponderance of small bars and antique shops, underwent massive changes as well, particularly after the incremental demolition of the elevated train line that finally ceased operation in 1955. A few office buildings were completed soon after the demolition of the el, but it was not until the 1960s that perception of the avenue changed and it became a magnet for first-class office development. By the 1970s, the avenue had been thoroughly transformed and was home to the headquarters of numerous nationally significant corporations and financial institutions. The construction of the mixed-use Citicorp Center in 1977, only two years after the city had teetered on the brink of default, seemed to be not only a confirmation that the once dilapidated avenue had become a prestigious address, but also a reflection of the city's economic resilience.

**Paul Manship, *Prometheus Fountain*,
Lower Plaza, Rockefeller Center, 1933**

Prometheus was the Titan who defied Zeus and, so goes the myth, taught humans the art of architecture. Atlas was his brother, condemned eternally to lift the celestial sphere. Here is the inscription, adapted from Aeschylus, that forms a backdrop to the sculpture depicting Prometheus caught in the act, holding fire in his outstretched hand, mounted at the very heart of Rockefeller Center: "Prometheus teacher in every art brought the fire that hath proved to mortals a means to mighty ends." These words summarize the conventional modern understanding of Prometheus as, essentially, the god of technology. Behind the sculpture, completed in 1934 by the artist Paul Manship, rises the RCA Building, behind which nestles Radio City Music Hall. RCA, Radio City: these names suggest the conversion of

Promethean fire into electricity which, in turn, gave rise to the radio and television signals to which the center was and remains symbolically dedicated. Digitized, such signals still emanate from the NBC studios in one of New York's first modernist skyscrapers. Each week those signals scream: "Live from New York, it's Saturday Night!" Prometheus refigured then, as the god of television.

Unsatisfied with Sigmund Freud's "Oedipus complex" as a proper interpretation of Sophocles's Oedipus the King, the literary critic Harold Bloom has suggested the "Prometheus complex" as a possible substitute. Though outright defiance brings unconscious burdens of its own, such a complex would presumably be characterized less by parent-child relations than by those conflicts that govern the relation

of humanity to nature. Following the Rockefeller Center inscription, we can therefore understand Prometheus's titanic defiance as a kind of technology transfer. Aeschylus's hero, chained and impaled on a cliff-like rock, boasts to the daughters of Ocean: "All human arts derive from Prometheus." How? Through teaching. This is technology as tutelage, a sort of mechanized, eventually digitized training in how to live like humans. It will be our guide to Midtown Manhattan's Promethean feats. That this tutelage entails a power struggle (Prometheus vs. Zeus, humans vs. nature, humans vs. humans) locates our brief tour squarely in the polis, or the city, understood as an agonistic, technologically mediated realm.

PHOTO WENDELL MC RAE

5A-H382

RCA Building at night, Rockefeller Center, 1933

Lee Lawrie and Rene Chambellan, *Atlas*, in front of the International Building, Rockefeller Center, 1937

View south from the observation deck of the RCA Building, Rockefeller Center, c. 1940

View north from the observation deck of the RCA Building, Rockefeller Center, c. 1940

The RCA Building is the centerpiece of the Rockefeller Center complex. It was designed by a team known as the Associated Architects led by Raymond Hood and opened in 1937. At night, its looming, luminous presence threatens the fire-stealing Titan with his fate. A sheer, rocky cliff fashioned from limestone, quartz, and metallic ores, a "motherland of iron" (Aeschylus) awaits the hammer of Hephaistos, the blacksmith, who will secure the wayward technologist to the stone. Guarding Rockefeller Center's threshold on Fifth Avenue is Lee Lawrie and Rene Paul Chambellan's *Atlas* (1937). Prometheus laments: "I'm already worn with grief over what has happened to my brother Atlas, who stands in the west and carries on his shoulders the pillars of heaven and earth, no easy burden."

The RCA Building, recently renamed 30 Rock, has an observation deck on its uppermost roofs (now the "Top of the Rock"). Looking south at night, the spires of the Chrysler Building (William Van Alen, 1930) and the Empire State Building (Shreve, Lamb & Harmon, 1931) stand out. Their verticality recalls Gothic cathedrals, but the technology with which it was achieved, which combines the dynamics of the elevator with the statics of the steel frame, again recalls Prometheus, who "led mortals to this unmapped art, clearing the sight for fire's once clouded signs." The fiery electric light burning in the windows of each building suggests lives lived inside. Looking at the windows immediately to the east, on Madison Avenue, we imagine televisual "(m)ad men" and stereotype-defying "office girls;" just outside the frame, immediately south and west, are no doubt seamstresses working nights in the garment district, among others.

Prometheus was fated with fore-knowledge of the future, including his own. Perched atop a cliff-like tower, looking backwards at history's post-cards, we see New York's future. From the RCA Building's observation deck, to the north this time, more luminous signs are burned into the landscape. Straight, perspectival lines trace Fifth Avenue and Central Park West, and in the distance, north of the park, Seventh Avenue (now Adam Clayton Powell Boulevard) and Sixth Avenue (now Malcolm X Boulevard). Between and below them run the meandering, curvilinear roadways and pathways of Central Park. By the time

the undated photograph was taken, Adam Clayton Powell Jr., Representative from Harlem, may well have become New York's first African-American congressman. But the assassination of Malcolm X had not yet turned those lights into fault lines along which the civil rights movement would cleave.

Lower Manhattan, visible to the south, began its electrification in 1882. In the beginning, New Yorkers had to learn how to live with and use the enchanted, dangerous current. Later, Midtown Manhattan became a beacon of the electric age. Like the Empire State Building, the crowns of many towers, upheld by fireproofed steel frames, were lit ablaze at night. The towers themselves were unthinkable without the electricity that drove the motors powering their elevators. But New Yorkers had not yet learned to live and work entirely in electric light, or breathe entirely conditioned air. The stepped profile of the RCA Building reflects the falling away of elevator banks as they climb toward the top, such that no interior office is more than twenty-seven feet from a window.

PHOTO BY KEYSTONE

Manhattan entrance to the Lincoln Tunnel, 1937

In the early 1980s, onstage at studio 8H on the eighth and ninth floors of the RCA Building, the "Saturday Night Live" bit player Joe Piscopo, as Paulie Herman from Piscataway, immortalized the line "You from Jersey? What exit?" The joke referred to the great north–south axis of the New Jersey Turnpike (Interstate 95), which by that time had become as much of a geographical reference point in the region's megalopolitan sprawl as were Midtown Manhattan's towers. Interstate 95 connects to those towers via the NY-495 spur, which runs through the Lincoln Tunnel and emerges in a tangle of ramps between 34th and 42nd Streets. Piscopo's earnest, all-too-human character was recognizable as a member of the "bridge and tunnel" population that passed daily through the infrastructure that connected the island to the suburbs to the east and west. Some in this population worked in what regional jargon still calls "the city." Others only frequented its nightspots, like Studio 54 at 254 West 54th Street where, in the 1970s, they might have met that glamorous representative of the postindustrial working class, Andy Warhol.

The Lincoln Tunnel's first, central tube was completed in 1937, the same year the RCA Building opened. The other two tubes were completed in 1945 and 1957, respectively. Designed by the civil engineer Ole Singstad, the brick-and-stone clad entrances and exits, as well as the sleekly tiled tubes, spoke the monumental, streamlined language of interwar public works. In an evocative speech delivered at the opening ceremony, New Jersey Governor Harold G. Hoffman credited the tunnel, "a magnificent machine of mass transportation," with unbinding drivers from the "shackles of time and distance." The suburban Prometheus, released from his chains by this "great servant of individual liberty," was now free to drive his or her "swift machine" into the urban future. On the other side, in a photograph probably dating close to the tunnel's opening, a small, carefully placed sign reads: "Slow."

East Side Airlines Terminal, 1953

In 1953 the Triborough Bridge and Tunnel Authority opened another interface with Midtown, the East Side Airlines Terminal. Until then, passengers not wishing to drive or ride taxis across tunnels or through bridges to the region's three airports could check in at a small facility on Park Avenue and 42nd Street and take a bus from there. In the new terminal, which spanned an entire block on First Avenue between 37th and 38th Streets and was designed by John B. Peterkin, 10,000 passengers could now do so daily in a grand, air-conditioned hall configured like the massive bus depot that it actually was. Carey Transportation, Inc. would later transport some of those passengers to Eero Saarinen's new terminal building for Trans World Airlines (TWA) at Idlewild Airport (now JFK), which opened in 1962. While the East Side Terminal's architecture was not as literal in its dynamism as Saarinen's soaring concrete wings at TWA, its rounded corners and streamlined surfaces, inside and out, were closely allied with the architecture of the tunnels and the design of the buses streaming through them. These infrastructures belong to the same social and technological order as the hundreds of elevators transporting passengers up and down Midtown's skyscraper-cliffs, daily and in awkward silence. Unlike demonstrative works of architecture such as Saarinen's terminal, it is said that infrastructure becomes most visible only when it fails. As background to a city that "never sleeps," their relative anonymity thus marks New York's tunnels, bridges, terminals, and ports as true heirs to the Promethean fire.

East 34th Street looking toward the Empire State Building, c. 1931

Aerial view of Midtown looking northeast from above Times Square, 1974

For the better part of the twentieth century, the city's subway and elevated train lines were anything but background. Before the noisy elevated lines on Second, Third, and Sixth Avenues were phased out from 1940 to 1970, the trains operated by the Interboro Rapid Transit Company (IRT) and its precursors rattled and shook their way across New York. The 34th Street Shuttle, which in this postcard frames a view of the newly completed Empire State Building, was a branch of the IRT's Third Avenue line that connected Midtown to the First Avenue Ferry Terminal on the far East Side. From there, passengers could travel to and from Hunter's Point in Long Island City, Queens. Made redundant by newer tunnels and bridges, the last Queens ferry departed on the evening of March 3, 1925. The elevated shuttle would operate for only five more years. As subways gradually replaced other elevated lines, the Third Avenue elevated remained in operation as a placeholder of sorts for the Second Avenue subway, plans for which were shelved by the city's fiscal crisis in the 1970s, revived in 2007, and partially realized when the first spur opened in 2017. The last piece of Manhattan's last "el," the Third Avenue elevated line, was demolished in 1956. Two decades earlier, as Rockefeller Center was built, the Sixth Avenue elevated line running directly behind it was demolished, paving the way for a modular series of office buildings that the architectural critic Peter Blake would dub a "Slaughter on Sixth Avenue."

View of Midtown showing Hotel Royalton, 1939

New York has never been only for New Yorkers. A postcard dated August 30, 1939, and mailed from Times Square from an anonymous Pete to a certain M. W. "Poddy" Myers in Pendleton, Oregon, advertises the Royalton Hotel at 44 West 44th Street. "Ever seen this place?" writes Pete, presuming Oregonian familiarity with the New York cityscape.

Built in 1897 as a residential hotel, with provisions for bourgeois bachelors and their servants, the Royalton was designed by the firm of Rossiter & Wright. Well known in the first half of the century as a temporary domicile for young men of means, during the postwar years it housed figures from Midtown's theater world. In 1988 the Royalton's pedigree was renewed once more when the French designer Philippe Starck renovated it on behalf of former Studio 54 proprietor Ian Schrager. The Royalton was the first of a series of stylish, neo-Surrealist hotel renovations undertaken by the Schrager-Starck partnership, which also included the Paramount (1990) on West 46th Street, and the Hudson (1998) on West 57th Street.

In a certain symmetry with the Royalton, the Hudson had been built in 1929 as a 1,250-room residence and clubhouse for working women for the American Women's Association, under the patronage of Anne Morgan and to the designs of Benjamin Wistar Morris. In 1946, having been previously converted into a facility for both sexes and rechristened the Henry Hudson Hotel, the future Schrager-Starck set-piece hosted a meeting of the United Nations Security Council, whose new headquarters were soon to rise on the East River.

44 W. 44th Street   THE ROYALTON   47 W. 43rd Street

United Nations Headquarters from across the East River, c. 1952

General Assembly Hall, United Nations Headquarters, c. 1952

The fact that the United Nations Security Council once met in the Henry Hudson Hotel reminds us of New York's many, enfolded histories: regional, national, and international. Seen from Queens, perched on the river's edge at First Avenue and East 42nd Street, the United Nations Headquarters challenges the Empire State Building for command of the eastern skyline. Concealed but also revealed in this juxtaposition of a skyscraping, stripped-down Art Deco tower and the "new monumentality" of international modernism facing broadside toward an imaginary public, is the additional fact that the United Nations is not in New York. Geographically it may be, but jurisdictionally, the land on which the headquarters complex stands is extraterritorial with respect to both New York City and the United States. The unanswerable question as to where, exactly, the United Nations is located is the basis for that institution's claims on "universal jurisdiction," or the applicability of its statutes and agreements regardless of national or territorial borders. In principle, only by answering the question "Where are you?" with a definitive "Nowhere!" can the United Nations credibly claim jurisdiction everywhere.

This spatial paradox cannot be explained entirely by the resistance of national sovereignty to the incursions of international law. Another name for the UN's juridical "nowhere" is Utopia, a "non-place" traditionally associated with islands. But the closest the United Nations comes to Utopia is not as an island-like precinct on the island's edge, but inside, in the "heterotopia," or "other space," of the General Assembly. Unlike the Security Council, where the superpowers, their surrogates, and a few others have played the "great game" of geopolitics ever since that meeting at the Hudson Hotel, the General Assembly has been known on occasion to give voice to the "wretched of the earth," or at least to some of their designated representatives. Countless televised speeches have been delivered from its marble rostrum. A consortium of internationally prominent architects led by Wallace K. Harrison designed the complex, which opened in 1952 after surviving a series of bitter rivalries, to emerge as an elegant enigma inconceivable to the architects involved yet born of their disputes and compromises. Compositionally, but also in daily ritual, the theater of the General Assembly and the Security Council finds its counterweight in the Secretariat Building, a shimmering, flattened monument to paperwork that celebrates the bureaucratic procedures that make anything like "universal jurisdiction" thinkable in the first place.

FELLHEIMER & WAGNER, ARCHITECTS

Fellheimer & Wagner, proposal for Grand Central Terminal office complex, 1954

Grand Central Terminal with Pan Am Building under construction, c. 1961

In 1954 the firm of Fellheimer & Wagner unveiled a proposal to demolish Warren & Wetmore's Grand Central Terminal and replace it with a 50-story tower atop a three-block base, with parking for 2,400 cars, to connect New York's two horizontal transport machines, the automobile and the train. As in all other towers, the city's third, vertical machine-type, the elevator, was a silent centerpiece of Fellheimer & Wagner's chunky, neutral glass tower. It was even more silently present in a mysterious rival scheme allegedly designed by I. M. Pei, when the developer William Zeckendorf announced plans for an 80-story tower on the site, which, although it was never published, contributed to the public and professional outcry in defense of the old terminal building.

Along with similar, failed protests to prevent the demolition of McKim, Mead & White's Pennsylvania Station on the West Side, this resistance to altering the monumental streetscape is often credited with inaugurating the historic preservation movement. At Grand Central, preservationists successfully protected the terminal building. But work on the skyline proceeded apace, and in 1960 construction began on the Pan Am Building, which looms precariously above the preserved terminal, in a jarring exposure of archaeological strata.

Like the United Nations complex, the Pan Am Building was designed collaboratively, this time by the former Bauhaus director Walter Gropius and his firm, The Architects Collaborative, together with his former student Marcel Breuer. Its architecture, which could be called brutalist, was a marked departure from the metal and glass prisms that punctuated the Midtown skyline during the 1950s and early 1960s: Lever House (Gordon Bunshaft, Skidmore, Owings & Merrill, 1952), the Seagram Building (Ludwig Mies van der Rohe and Philip Johnson, 1958), and the Union Carbide Building (Bunshaft, SOM, 1960), among others. In their collective debt to the modernity of the United Nations Secretariat, all of these corporate headquarters transposed the utopian universalism of the UN onto the interests of multinational capital. In the architectural idiom of the time, this symbolic and technological sleight-of-hand replaced one "international style," and one internationalist project, with another. Atlas shrugged, and Prometheus wept.

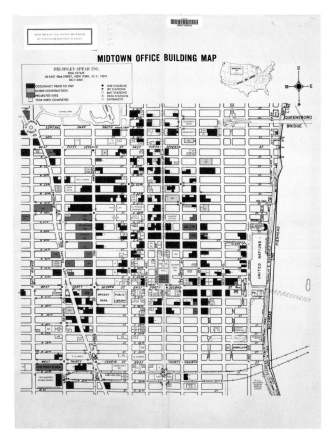

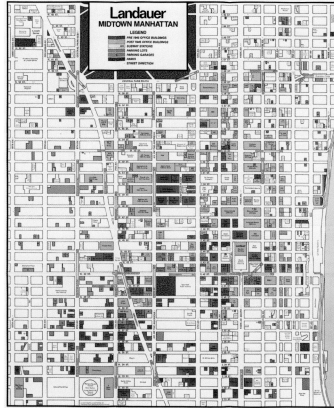

Helmsley-Spear, Inc., Midtown Office Building Map, c. 1970

Landauer Associates, Midtown Manhattan Map, 1979

Cross & Brown Company, Midtown Manhattan Map, 1986

A series of three maps reveal the allegedly universal laws that govern this new, multinational jurisdiction: the "laws" of real estate development. Each describes Midtown Manhattan's office landscape differently, at a different moment. The first is from Helmsley-Spear, Inc., the owners of the Empire State Building and an innovator in real estate syndication, a precursor to the Real Estate Investment Trust (REIT). It shows clusters of office buildings in use prior to 1969 along Third, Lexington,

Fifth, Park, and Sixth Avenues, with a large swath of Sixth Avenue behind Rockefeller Center and below West 50th Street coded as "Projected Sites," including the future Esso (Exxon), McGraw-Hill, and Celanese Buildings, all designed by Wallace K. Harrison. When completed, these three would become known as the XYZ Buildings. Their vertically lined facades, echoing but also clarifying the vertically striped RCA Building, testify straightforwardly to the underlying quantification: a maximum extrusion of the buildable site, with enhanced zoning allowances provided by a Publically Owned Private Space (POPS), or a plaza, located at the base of each extrusion. The pioneer of such a strategy was Eero Saarinen's CBS Building, nicknamed "Black Rock" (1965) just up the avenue, which combined vertical extrusion with a stepped,

sunken plaza where a "lonely crowd" of office workers could gather.

A second map, published in 1979 by Landauer Associates, differentiates Midtown office space according to the real estate broker's convention of "prewar" (pre-1945) and "postwar" (post-1945) listings. Landauer was a real estate consulting firm founded in 1946 and specializing in valuation. At one point the firm assessed the land under Rockefeller Center, and, during the planning of the Pan Am Building, it assessed that tower's marketability. The Landauer map shows the XYZ Buildings completed, along with other monuments to multinational capital such as the Chemical Bank Building (Park Avenue between East 47th and 48th Streets, Emery Roth & Sons, 1964), the Citicorp Tower (Lexington Avenue between East 53rd and East 54th Streets Hugh Stubbins, 1977), and the AT&T

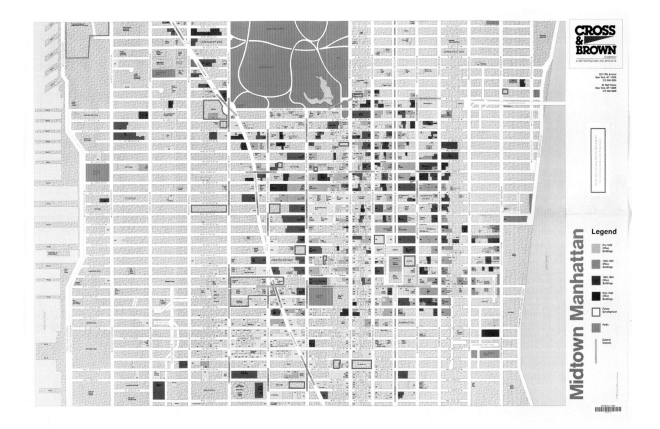

Building (Madison Avenue between East 55th and 56th Streets, Johnson Burgee, 1984). The map shows a proliferation of new office buildings in Midtown further north on Park, Lexington, and Third Avenues. Just as tellingly, it also shows a higher concentration of parking lots and parking garages on the far West Side, where land had begun to turn over in the area formerly known as Hell's Kitchen and now renamed the more real-estate friendly "Clinton."

The third map, published in 1986 by the Cross & Brown Company, real estate brokers and property managers, refocuses attention eastward. Now the color-coded distinction is between office buildings built before 1945, from 1945 to 1965, from 1966 to 1984, after 1984, and sites identified for future development. For the first time in these three maps we see a new office building (in fact a

mixed-use tower) marked at 725 Fifth Avenue at East 56th Street, adjacent to the Tiffany Building. There, in the lobby of the Trump Tower (TT), completed in 1983 and designed by Der Scutt and Swanke Hayden Connell, visitors were once greeted by a pair of menacing, brassy "T's" reminiscent of the ubiquitous, theological "T" (as in the Model T) in Aldous Huxley's *Brave New World*, where Ford is Lord. The capital that set the stage for the TT had derived, in part, from profits on low-income housing inherited by its builder-developer from his father. Around 1950, one of the elder Trump's tenants, Woody Guthrie, wrote angrily of the "color line" that excluded black residents from Beach Haven, a federally subsidized housing project in Brooklyn. In the tower's meretricious lobby, informed visitors could glimpse that color line shining through.

Model of the World Trade Center, 1964

The prelude to all of this, as well as its eventual climax, is visible in a model of another office complex descended from Rockefeller Center and the XYZ Buildings but located downtown, on the former site of Radio Row, adjacent to Little Syria, where the components of the electric talking machines that gave Radio City its name were bought and sold. There, plans were afoot to demolish those neighborhoods to build a new World Trade Center (WTC), with twin towers and a cluster of smaller buildings at its base, all designed by Minoru Yamasaki. The model dates from 1964. The WTC would open in 1972. Its towers, square in plan and ringed with twenty-two inch windows extruded into vertical slits 110 stories high, were to sit astride a windswept plaza. That plaza would complete a string of such spaces begun on the eastern edge of Manhattan's southern tip with Gordon Bunshaft's One Chase Manhattan Bank, running westward to Bunshaft's Marine Midland Bank, then through the POPS later known as Zuccotti Park (ground zero for Occupy Wall Street in 2011), and on to the site that would, after 2001, be known as Ground Zero. At the center of the World Trade Center's plaza was a split-open spheroid cast in bronze by the sculptor Fritz Koenig, the celestial sphere fallen from Atlas's shoulders.

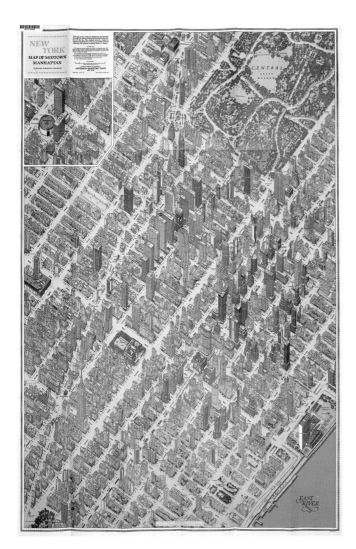

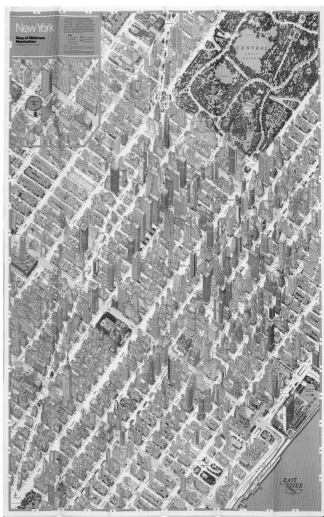

Map of Midtown Manhattan in detailed axonometric projection, 1980

Map of Midtown Manhattan in detailed axonometric projection, 1985

Back in Midtown, two maps drawn in isometric projection track the Prometheus complex to its destination. Not to the WTC's supertall skyscrapers downtown, or even to its supertall residential offspring in Midtown (432 Park Avenue, Raphael Viñoly, 2016), but into the air-conditioned atrium. An isometric map from 1981 shows two towers, the AT&T Building (Johnson Burgee) and the IBM Building (Edward Larrabee Barnes) under construction on adjacent blocks between East 55th Street and East 57th Street, flanked by Fifth and Madison Avenues. By 1985 as shown in a subsequent map, an office worker-shopper could pass between the IBM Building and the newer Trump Tower without breathing outdoor air. If she held her breath long enough as she crossed 56th Street, she could breathe conditioned air again inside the AT&T Building's vaulted glass atrium. This turning inward of urban space, born of new zoning provisions and a certain grasping for psycho-spatial security, dimly recalled the nineteenth-century European arcades, but filled with loyal subjects in place of defiant flâneurs.

In the Trump Tower atrium, the shining brass, glass, and marble surfaces speak of televisual, bridge-and-tunnel glamour. But, like a lord only renting the manor, they also evince a profound insecurity, a nervous self-regard, a generalized, unnamed phobia. In the months after September 11, 2001, defensive barriers surrounded many of Midtown's skyscrapers, as prudence met target envy. On Fifth Avenue in front of Trump Tower, the border wall of potted plants that appeared on the sidewalk echoed the forest of potted trees climbing the building's facades, nourished by the tears of Prometheus. Fifteen years later, the tower's builder-developer imagined a street scene there that still circulates on fiery screens: "I could stand in the middle of Fifth Avenue and shoot somebody and I wouldn't lose voters." Several blocks away at Rockefeller Center, Prometheus, the gilded god of television, reached for the remote.

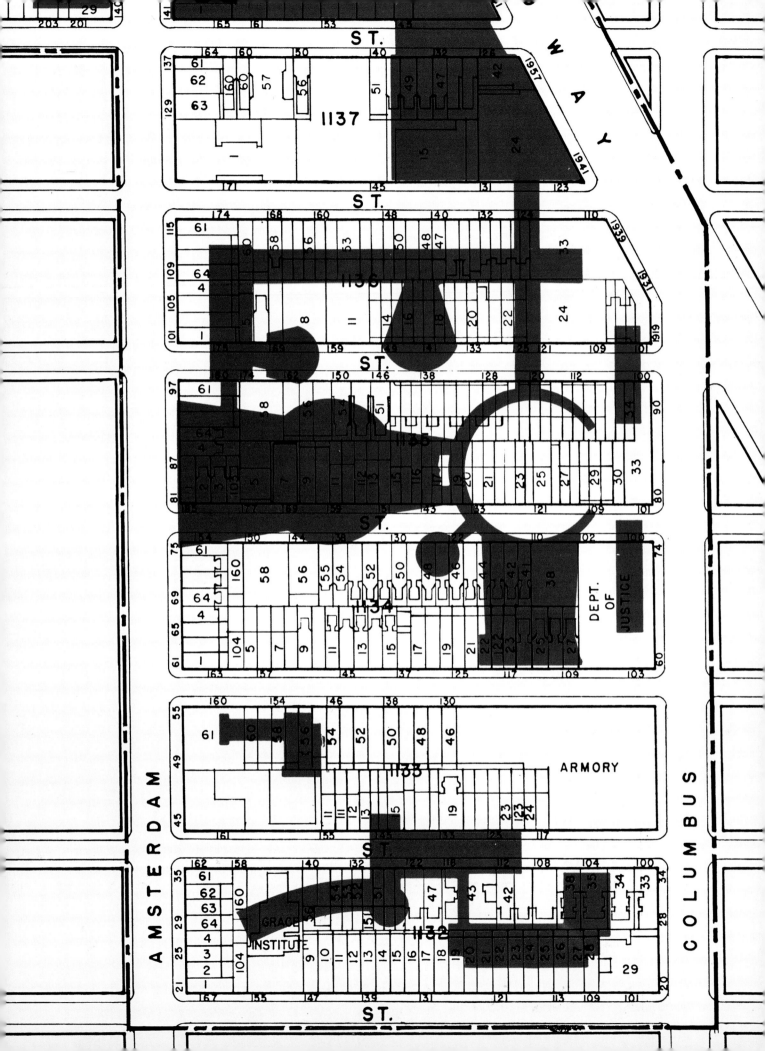

8

Urban Renewal

1950–1980

I raise my stein to the builder who can remove ghettos without removing people as I hail the chef who can make omelets without breaking eggs.

—Robert Moses, 1974[1]

City planners are always saying you can't make an omelet without breaking eggs. But they are talking about people, not eggs! If planning helps people, they ought to be better off as a result, not worse off.

—Jane Jacobs, 2005[2]

The period following the end of World War II was challenging for New York City. Postwar economic doldrums lingered for years, with both unemployment and the cost of conducting business high in New York compared to other parts of the country. Yet by the time the city celebrated the fiftieth anniversary of municipal consolidation in 1948, the design of new Midtown office buildings was underway, encouraging the city to reimagine itself as the national epicenter of corporate headquarters. The city's great skyscraping set pieces, many erected during the boom years of the 1920s, still dominated the skyline, but the cityscape was rapidly changing and the streets bustled with economic activity, energy, and self-confidence. New York seemed ready to assume the title of the greatest city in the world.

As new corporate headquarters were being planned, however, the shift from urban to suburban living gained momentum. Demand for suburban development in areas easily reached by railways and increasingly by an expanding highway system would make the daily commute a reality for myriad New Yorkers. Long-established towns on Long Island, and in Westchester, Connecticut, and New Jersey, grew rapidly as vacant lots were filled in; at the same time, new developments sprung up seemingly overnight, replacing woods and farmland. Expanding suburban communities put the American dream of a single-family home on its own plot of land within the reach of hundreds of thousands of New Yorkers who had previously lived in apartments and row houses in the city, particularly in the outer boroughs. Typically, residents of the Bronx moved to Westchester and residents of Brooklyn and Queens resettled further out on Long Island.

So strong was the lure of suburbia that the notion of the city as a discrete entity came to be questioned by scholars of urbanism. Many New Yorkers began to feel that the city was governable only with support well beyond the local level, especially from the federal government. At the same time, private citizens increasingly demanded localized control of what they considered to be a series of small villages whose ability to self-govern offered the only chance that the city would remain livable and a viable alternative to suburban and exurban life. A struggle for the city's future between those favoring a top-down approach and those advocating bottom-up development emerged as a key issue in the postwar period.

Robert Moses and Jane Jacobs

A central figure in that story was Robert Moses, whose career in public service had begun in 1919 when he was appointed chief of staff of the New York State Reconstruction Commission. Five years later, Governor Alfred E. Smith appointed Moses president of the newly established Long Island State Park Commission, and in 1927 he became Secretary of State for New York. Throughout the 1930s, Moses masterminded

and completed a vast and complex network of parkways that provided access to Westchester and to Long Island's public parks and, perhaps ironically, served as the foundation for a rapid expansion of the city's commuter suburbs that both reflected and anticipated the automobile's enormous influence on the city.

In the postwar era, Moses's construction of highways continued, but it was rivaled in impact by his focus on large-scale public and affordable housing projects, often realized as part of broader urban renewal efforts. Moses was most effective, and controversial, in his targeted attempts to use federal money to transform the physical landscape of what he felt were parts of the city demanding renewal. In his twin roles as New York's construction coordinator and chairman of the city's Committee on Slum Clearance, he was able to harness an outsize share of available federal funding to rebuild large swaths of the city, often without the direct participation of the City Planning Commission.

The lion's share of the construction Moses oversaw was powered by the Title I program of the United States Housing Act of 1949. New Yorkers, and Robert Moses in particular, were among the first to recognize the opportunity that federal funding for urban renewal offered; other cities, less aggressive in pursuing Title I funding, would benefit less from Washington's increasing role in financing urban projects. In large-scale Title I housing developments throughout the city, Moses became a major proponent of the towers-in-the-park schemes formerly adopted by the New York City Housing Authority, themselves inspired by the early twentieth-century urban proposals of European modernist architects.

Typical of Moses's Title I undertakings was an attempt to remake a central portion of Greenwich Village. In January 1951, he announced the complete rebuilding of an approximately forty-acre site south of Washington Square Park as two towers-in-the-park developments, one a government-subsidized, privately developed enclave for middle-income residents and the other a New York City Housing Authority public housing project. The undertaking was financially ambitious, with land acquisition costs averaging between an estimated $14 and $20 per square foot, nearly $10 more than three contemporaneous Moses-backed projects in other New York City neighborhoods.

Neighborhood opposition to Moses's Greenwich Village proposal soon mounted. Among the organized responses was the creation of the *Village Voice*, a local newspaper that became an important vehicle for sustained critiques of urban renewal proposals throughout the city. Though Moses's plans evolved and over time diminished in scope, opposition intensified. After three years of court battles, with a case ultimately heard by the U.S. Court of Appeals, the project was finally realized in 1960 as Washington Square Village.

While the new towers-in-the-park housing stood in dramatic contrast to the low-rise housing it had replaced, Moses's vision for the area was never fully realized. Community advocates blocked his proposal for a major, four-lane roadway running through Washington Square Park, a central component of his plans to expedite car passage between Fifth Avenue and the new housing development south of the square. Design concessions by Moses failed to appease the activists, whose protests would prove unexpectedly fruitful: by 1963 Washington Square Park was closed to all traffic and remains so today.

Even stronger opposition to urban renewal was mounting in the West Village. In 1961 the city announced plans to explore the redevelopment of a fourteen-block section of the far West Village. Renewal efforts, by the early 1960s, were structured and intended to minimize tenant relocation challenges. However, Jane Jacobs, an architectural journalist and a resident of the targeted area, helped create and became co-chairman of the Save the West Village Committee once she heard word of the redevelopment study. By the end of the year, opposition had succeeded not only in forcing the City Planning Commission to halt any area study, but also in having the city remove the area from the municipal slum-clearance map. Two years later, the committee, headed by Jacobs, issued its own plan for a middle-income cooperative housing development in the area.

Both a keen observer of urbanism and a sophisticated activist, Jacobs championed many of the same qualities that urban renewal had promised to eradicate: small-scale, walk-up residential development, density, and disorder. At the same time, Jacobs adamantly opposed the prevailing approach to eradicating slums; instead she advocated knitting existing towers-in-the park developments back into the surrounding neighborhoods by reestablishing de-mapped streets and redesigning ground floors to permit new uses, particularly those conducive to street activity. Old buildings were seen as central to the fabric of a neighborhood, rather than visual pollution to be replaced or upgraded.

Jacobs's landmark work, *The Death and Life of Great American Cities,* was published in 1961.[3] Though the book had a national scope, it focused on Manhattan and unabashedly celebrated her own neighborhood, Greenwich Village. In some ways, its timing could not have been better for her purposes. It followed the completion, in 1960, of Park West Village on the Upper West Side, a project long mired in corruption that for some symbolized the shortcomings of broad urban renewal strategies as practiced by Moses. It also followed on the heels of the groundbreaking for Lincoln Center, a landmark in the ongoing debate regarding the goals and methods of urban renewal.

Like Moses's Washington Square Village project in Greenwich Village, initiatives within the Lincoln Square Urban Renewal Area relied on Title I funds (ostensibly for "predominantly residential" projects), but incorporated a variety of new uses, including homes for cultural, non-profit, and educational institutions. Conceived by Moses and the Zeckendorf and Rockefeller families to celebrate a "free and democratic culture" in the face of an increasing Soviet threat, the vision for Lincoln Center paired culture and housing in a way that was intended to both make a statement about the values of American society and simultaneously keep the middle class in the city.

What distinguished the Lincoln Square project from countless urban renewal efforts nationwide was the inclusion of a cultural agenda; for the first time, the arts, and not just housing, were seen as a key component of government-supported urban strategies. The campuslike plan of Lincoln Center, a megablock development stretching between 62nd and 65th Streets and Columbus and Amsterdam Avenues, was intended to emulate in form the great plazas of Europe. At the same time, the elevation of the plaza above street level to accommodate parking was a sign that the cultural institutions expected many of their patrons to be automobile-driving suburbanites, not strap-hanging New Yorkers.

Opposition to the project was swift, with criticism of the overall renewal plan leveled by many voices. Homeowners and local businesses resented their homes and livelihoods being wiped out, and challenged the project in court. Many saw an ethnic overtone to the project, given the high percentage of Puerto Ricans residing in the area and the intention to replace existing homes there with "middle-class housing" nearby. Others saw the fact that Fordham University, a Catholic institution, stood to gain a new Midtown campus as a violation of the separation of church and state.

However, unlike Jacobs's success in opposing renewal efforts in Greenwich Village, opposition to the Lincoln Square renewal plan served only to delay rather than stop it. Federal dollars were initially withheld as criticism of the project got stronger in 1957. Court cases challenging the legality of the use of eminent domain played out throughout 1958 and 1959, but were ultimately unsuccessful. Groundbreaking proceeded in 1959, and the center's first completed building, Philharmonic Hall, opened in 1962.[4]

The rising tide of opposition to top-down planning in the late 1950s went far beyond Lincoln Square. Some of the biggest battles between Robert Moses and community activists involved proposals for roads and highways across Manhattan. In 1956, following the passage of the Interstate and Defense Highways Act allocating federal funds for interstate highways, Moses proposed several elevated highways, including the Mid-Manhattan Expressway, reaching across Midtown near 30th St and the Lower Manhattan Expressway, stretching across Broome Street, just south of Canal Street. Though the highways had been mooted by the Regional Plan Association as far back as 1929, Moses's proposals came in the middle of construction of the Cross-Bronx Expressway, a controversial project that cut across densely built neighborhoods of the South Bronx and forever severed the borough. Within a dramatically shifting political landscape, Moses's Mid- and Lower-Manhattan highway projects would never be realized.

The defeat of Moses's proposed highway connecting the Manhattan Bridge and Holland Tunnel at Broome Street was particularly notable. The proposal for a Lower Manhattan Expressway, or "LOMEX," had significant momentum and government support at the outset. Because of its connections to the Holland Tunnel, the elevated ten-lane roadway would have been considered an "interstate" and therefore funded primarily by the federal government. Moses and Mayor Wagner, claiming "blight" as a justification for the project, received City Planning Commission approval in 1960 and began condemning buildings standing along the highway's proposed path three years later.

Artists who had begun to colonize the area, transforming industrial lofts in nineteenth-century cast-iron buildings into live/work spaces, challenged the plan. Numerous alternative designs were devised to address their concerns: an open-cut, a cut-and-cover tunnel, a higher roadway, and a circumferential expressway were put forward for consideration. None would ultimately pass muster and the city's Board of Estimate rejected the project in 1969. Many saw this defeat both as a turning point in the reach of Moses's hegemonic power as well as a sea-change from a top-down government-led approach to one reflecting bottom-up community involvement and self-determination.[5]

Frederick Kelly, _Musicians in Washington Square_, 1962

Listen, Robert Moses, listen if you can,
It's all about our neighborhood that you're
_   trying to condemn_
We aren't going to sit back and see our
_   homes torn down_
So take your superhighway and keep it out
_   of town._
—Bob Dylan, 1962[1]

The Age of Moses removed all innocence about urban futures in America. It was a period of national cultural and spatial dislocation unique in modern urban history. For New York City, perhaps this moment can be capsulized in the statistic that between 1950 and 1960, 10 million of 15 million residents in the region changed homes.[2] This displacement was as much about internal urban displacement as suburban exodus. Robert Moses, more than any other figure,

was the mastermind of implementation of the de-urbanist strategy, characterized by his infamous advice that "when you operate in an overbuilt metropolis, you have to hack your way through with a meat ax."[3] In New York City, it is variously estimated that primary and secondary effects of Moses projects directly displaced 500,000 persons,[4] and indirectly several times that number depending on criteria applied including cultural fallout.

New York became a refuge from emerging suburban culture, especially for estranged youth who sought alternatives. What they found in New York was the fossilization of older "official" cultural institutions as well as opportunities to claim new "alternative" cultural territory. By the 1970s, at one end of this spectrum was the making of Lincoln

Center; at the other, the enclave for new culture that was SoHo. The Moses putsch touched both. Robert Caro's monumental and critical biography, _The Power Broker: Robert Moses and the Fall of New York_ (1974), was a key moment in understanding the egregious nature of his project. In recent years, revisionist history has attempted to revisit his legacy following an argument that there was no other way. What remains least explored are the long-term cultural effects over several generations so eloquently characterized by Marshall Berman, who had suffered construction of the Cross-Bronx Expressway. Moses was his personal Moloch, who "helped bring my childhood to an end."[5] And Moses was such for many of us.

West Side Story filming on West
68th Street between Amsterdam
and West End Avenues, c. 1961

The musical *West Side Story* opened
in 1957 at the Winter Garden Theater
and was followed by the film in 1961.
The script was by Stephen Sondheim,
adapted from the book by Arthur Laurents, with music by Leonard Bernstein
and produced by Jerome Robbins. The
story was said to be a modern interpretation of Shakespeare's *Romeo and
Juliet*.[6] The set for the film was San
Juan Hill, already ravaged by the "slum
clearance" process underway for the
Moses "Upper West Side Renewal Plan,"
and including the "Lincoln Square Slum
Clearance" plan. The script of *West
Side Story* aestheticized this history of
ethnic differences in San Juan Hill while
removing the earlier African Americans
and substituting a white and Hispanic
divide. By 1957 more than 5,000 families had been removed from this poor
but still vibrant neighborhood,[7] and the
remaining buildings were in a state of
ruin. Total site clearance was completed
within a year of the city's acquisition

of the site in 1958. Rehearsal photos
for the film show something of the San
Juan Hill pathology and contribute to
the musical's aura of social resiliency
within a degraded environment that was
central to the film script.[8]

Brooks Atkinson, in his review of the
original theater production, headlined
that the "material was horrifying," and I
suppose that in 1957 it was such for the
white middle class already ensconced
in their new suburbs and lifestyle. That
the film sets were actually what was left
of San Juan Hill could only reinforce
the perversity of this "horror" given its
state of semi-destroyed abandonment.
No artificial set could have produced the
same effect and succeed in moving the
narrative beyond Shakespearian tragedy.
Perhaps most perverse of all was the
1968 *West Side Story* revival at the New
York State Theater, as the audience and
stage were literally above the original
San Juan Hill. As students, we could

not avoid noticing the drastic change
in social milieu during the intervening
eleven years between the original production and the revival. A romantic view
of urban poverty had been supplanted by
the social fallout from de-urbanization
and "urban renewal," especially with the
urban insurrection that engulfed Los
Angeles in 1965 and Detroit and Newark
in 1967. Dan Sullivan, theater critic for
the *New York Times*, put it succinctly:
"The rumbles of the nineteen-fifties
have been replaced by the even more
frightening riots of the nineteen-sixties
and the animosity of Puerto Rican and
Italian kids on the West Side seems mild
compared with the black-white confron-
tation staring us in the face today."[9] Over
the years, perhaps not much changed
from that prognosis, although in the
2009 *West Side Story* revival some lyrics
were finally sung in Spanish.[10]

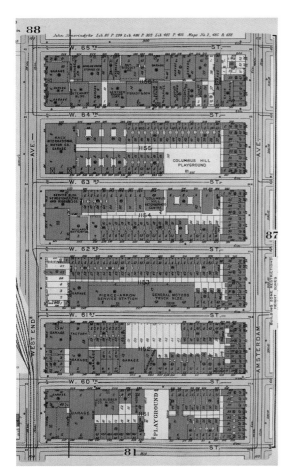
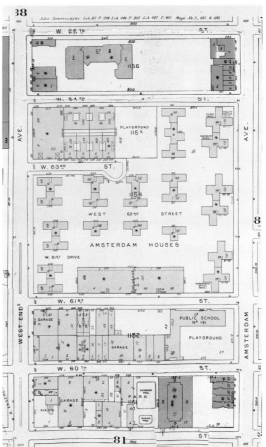

G.W. Bromley & Co., maps of San Juan Hill area, Upper West Side, 1934 and 1970

By the turn of the twentieth century, San Juan Hill in the West 60s had become the largest African-American community in New York City, having reached a population of more than 60,000.[11] Allegedly named for an largely African-American regiment that fought in the Spanish-American War, it harbored a sustained history of violence against its black residents from the adjacent Irish neighborhood and widespread abuse by the police.[12] In 1941 San Juan Hill was officially established as a "slum clearance" priority by Moses, with the proposed NYCHA Amsterdam Houses project.[13] Following considerable protest from residents, they were finally cleared by 1942. Promises were made to residents, predominantly African Americans, that they would be able to return but such did not transpire and many had difficulty finding new homes, given racial barriers in the city. Many ended up in Harlem, and some in adjacent areas on the Upper West Side. The new NYCHA residents were almost all white.[14] Much was made of the innovative urbanism of "towers-in-the-park" that would obliterate the dense footprint of the old neighborhood. In total, 1,048 larger apartments replaced 1,121 smaller ones. No commercial activity was permitted under the Federal Public Housing program.

As architecture students, my peers and I saw the contradictions. NYCHA projects were not the pristine Ville Radieuse of Le Corbusier, and while we were seduced by his images of slabs, pilotis, and dense flowing nature, there was no way to correlate that fantasy against the public housing being built in New York.

Modernist ideals were failing us. Already in 1957, Catherine Bauer, an advocate for "modern housing" in the 1930s and for public housing in the 1940s, had written about the "Dreary Deadlock of Public Housing."[15] Walking along the remnants of West 61st or 62nd Streets, we were forced to confront the limitations of the "tower-in-the-park," but without exactly understanding why a project like Amsterdam Houses had to be the way it was. In architecture school, public housing was a topic to be avoided, but Jane Jacobs resonated with her Lower Manhattan struggles reported in the *Village Voice* and especially her *Death and Life of Great American Cities*. It would be another decade before Robert Caro's *The Power Broker* dissected the deep politics. Meanwhile, in New York City the "meat ax" kept swinging.

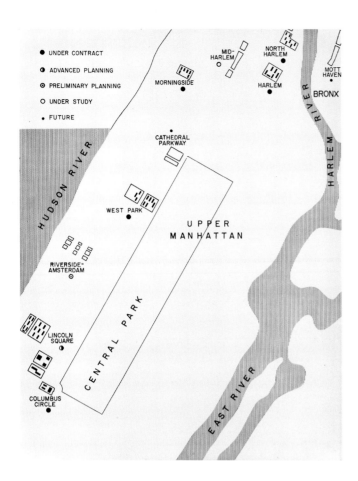

**New York Committee on Slum
Clearance, slum clearance map
of the Upper West Side, 1956**

Amsterdam Houses was incorporated into the larger scheme of Upper West Side "slum clearance" operations that ultimately displaced 60,000 families. Moses's strategy was conceived with the precision of a military campaign and tainted by an aura of corruption around tenant removal of increasing public concern by the mid-1960s. On the Upper West Side there was intensifying resistance from both the Lincoln Square clearance and from Manhattantown, a smaller but more egregious project adjacent to Central Park West on the Upper West Side, with scandal leading to Moses's resignation from the Mayor's Committee on Slum Clearance by 1960.[16] Learning from Manhattantown, today known as Park West Village and shown as West Park on the map above, Lincoln Square was more nuanced; William Zeckendorf argued that the clearance

for Lincoln Towers was handled with "dispatch and fairness."[17] The same was represented for Lincoln Center. Edgar Young, John D. Rockefeller 3rd's chief advisor for the Lincoln Center project, was even more effusive about the relocation "thanks to the cooperation of tenants."[18]

As students in upstate New York, we found the same destruction in our own backyards. The 430-mile-long "Empire State" megalopolitan corridor, stretching from Manhattan to Buffalo, was de-urbanizing before our eyes. That string of rich and urbane cities was being devastated by highways, suburbs, and the flight of money and industry to elsewhere. In Albany, the Rockefellers could practice their craft at its extreme, with the South Mall project, reputedly sketched by Governor Nelson

A. Rockefeller on a napkin.[19] From his Capitol offices, Rockefeller saw a "slum" and an "anthill." We watched in disbelief as the homes and businesses of some 9,000 persons were destroyed in what would be a billion-dollar project, including an expansive highway system that would bypass the old city of Albany while servicing the new Mall. It was a powerful confirmation of our worst suspicions about urbanism under siege.[20] Included was the passenger rail system: the elegant Boston and Maine station in Troy was destroyed in 1958 and in 1971 the remarkably urbane Schenectady station would suffer the same fate. In Albany, the Union Depot was spared only to become a shopping mall. Station replacements were tin shacks in the suburbs. For us, it was all part of the same package. We knew that it was an endgame for "urbanism as a way of life."[21]

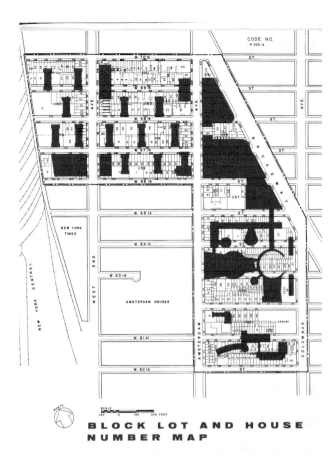

BLOCK LOT AND HOUSE
NUMBER MAP

**Map showing proposed Lincoln
Square project in red, 1956**

Lincoln Center, including a new house for the Metropolitan Opera, would be the crowning achievement of the Lincoln Square project, providing the final impetus for raising the private investment needed for the housing component. In this Moses had the crucial support of the Rockefeller family, which was heavily invested in the project. In October 1956 at a real estate luncheon, Moses asserted that the "scythe of progress must move north" even as Lincoln Square tenants picketed outside. His response to their protests over the removal of more than 20,000 families was that "the hardships of tenant removal have been exaggerated."[22] A day-long hearing held in September 1957 by the Department of City Planning presented stark contrasts in power. Moses didn't bother to show up, and the statements of the project advocates, including Rockefeller and Harrison, embodied a calm that reflected their knowledge that the project was assured no matter what. The pleas of

Lincoln Square residents only served to magnify the futility of their battle. Aramis Gomez was particularly articulate in pointing to the fundamental distortion of the mandate of Title I Program to provide low-income housing, given that it was being used to benefit elite cultural institutions and luxury housing: "As you can tell, I am a Puerto Rican. When I first heard of Title I, I said to myself, 'This is a blessing for my people. Now we can get good and decent housing at prices that we can afford.' But the way New York is using this law, it is more of a curse than a blessing."[23] Five years later demolition was complete. Moses was ecstatic: "It has been a long time happening, this realization of a reborn West Side, marching north from Columbus Circle, and eventually spreading over the entire dismal and decayed West Side."[24]

It is amazing how, in 1957, those Lincoln Square community voices from the real *West Side Story* could be silenced

so quickly, together with erasure of their homes and livelihoods. *West Side Story*, the musical, made certain that the focus on community was redirected. One could easily imagine an alternative script to Stephen Sondheim's, reflecting the desperate testimony heard on that Wednesday in September in 1957, only fifteen days before the musical opened at the Winter Garden. By the mid-1960s the cacophony was growing, not just about the community removal but about its replacement. The voices amplified such that we students could not avoid hearing the noise of the entire Lincoln Square project. The September 1962 opening of Philharmonic Hall set the stage for questions. By 1965 the book *New York City in Crisis* published by the *Herald Tribune* put things succinctly: "In the place of the low-rent housing that formerly stood there, a string of expensive apartment houses has been built, far out of the price range of the people who have been dispossessed."[25]

Hugh Ferriss, Rendering of proposed Metropolitan Opera House at Lincoln Center, 1955

As the Rockefeller family architect, Wallace K. Harrison had pursued schemes for a new Metropolitan Opera house at several Manhattan locations, including at Rockefeller Center and at the United Nations.[26] His early Lincoln Center design appeared to bear a curious relationship to Etienne-Louis Boulleé's design for an opera house, and the contemporary interpretation in Novosibirsk, Russia, by Sergey Poligalin. Opened in 1945, it was, and still is, the largest opera house in Russia, seemingly only adjusted from the original design by a neoclassical facade.[27] Harrison's design, and especially the renderings by Hugh Ferriss, were central to Moses's public campaign for the Lincoln Square renewal. And much was made about the promise for Lincoln Center, as the *New York Times* put it, to be "the boldest and most exciting artistic project ever attempted in the United States."[28] Even more succinctly, Howard Taubman, *Times* music critic, wrote that Lincoln Center would "show that democracy has the determination and power to devote itself to the things of the mind and heart as well as to creature comforts."[29] And the *Times* itself was indebted to Moses, as the Lincoln Square scheme included its new printing facility.

It was the Cold War, and Lincoln Center was undoubtedly strategic in the minds of our cold warriors. But by the 1970s, it was obvious to many that Lincoln Center had little to do with the burgeoning arts scene that was mushrooming downtown. The design itself was lacking "artistic" interest, even to the clients. Early on, Harrison's sketches did not convince Lincoln Kirstein, founder of the New York City Ballet. Already in 1956, he complained to Rockefeller that Harrison had not yet put anything "on paper for us which gives me any confidence in an ultimate masterpiece. For whatever I can judge of his talents, they are in the realm of organization, not design."[30] As students we agreed, and nothing about this assessment changed in the project as built.

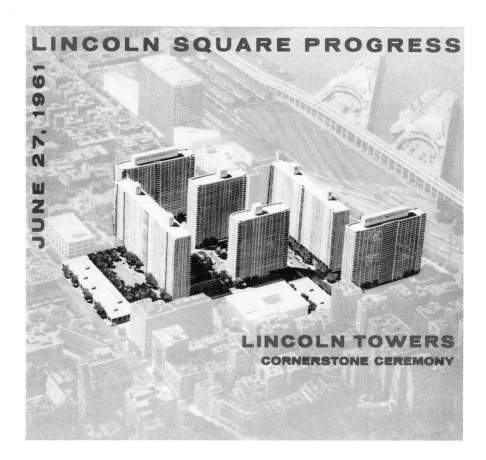

Webb & Knapp, Lincoln Square Progress: Lincoln Square Cornerstone Ceremony, 1961

While Title I was intended to benefit low-income families, Moses's "New York System" had distorted this intention such that at Lincoln Square, the beneficiaries were cultural institutions and middle-income citizens. Lincoln Towers represented the principal housing initiative within the Lincoln Square Urban Renewal area. It replaced 7,000 low-income families with 4,400 new families, which included only 400 with low incomes.[31] By 1961 the new families had been located within a primitive landscape of six large slab-blocks with some commercial development, a school, and underground parking. The design was generally seen as mediocre, even by the developer, William Zeckendorf of Webb & Knapp. He called it "pseudo-luxury," blaming the project's financial backers for the poor design, and asserting: "I

am not proud of the final product; I am ashamed of it."[32] Still Lincoln Towers stood in significant contrast to the neighboring Amsterdam Houses, both in terms of lives and livelihoods. Linda Ocasio grew up in Amsterdam Houses when the remaining San Juan Hill neighborhood was still intact. It was not a slum, and she saw her neighbors as "not largely poor, not mostly white, but working families who were getting so close to the security of the middle class that they could almost touch and taste it." With Lincoln Towers and Lincoln Center all of that disappeared, not to be replaced. At Amsterdam Houses "suddenly there was the smell of urine in the elevator. Something began to fray about the place, and the connections that made us feel strong seemed thinner."[33]

In spite of the design mediocrity of Lincoln Towers, just a casual walk along West End Avenue would reveal that it was not NYCHA. It was not Amsterdam Houses. The design poverty of the NYCHA slabs and site planning was obvious, but most obvious was the color of the brick. NYCHA was exclusively red. Lincoln Towers was white, with balconies, commercial amenities, and indoor parking, all strictly forbidden for NYCHA developments. And this was enough to make it "middle-class," which is what it was. It was a major domino in the Moses Lincoln Square strategy. And so was the nearby *New York Times* printing plant that had opened two years earlier, assuring continuing support for the Lincoln Square Urban Renewal by that crucial news outlet.[34]

**Interior of the Old Metropolitan
Opera on Broadway at 39th Street,
early twentieth century**

The Old Met came down in 1967, victim of the arcane politics of the Rockefeller family, Moses, and the Metropolitan Opera Association, in response to their fear that a competing opera company might eventually take it over and make competition for Lincoln Center.[35] A long battle was waged to save it, engaging cultural icons including Leonard Bernstein, but to no avail. The newly formed Landmarks Preservation Commission was prevailed upon to let demolition proceed. In 1966 the Met moved to Lincoln Center, where it was crucial to completion of the Lincoln Square Urban Renewal Project and to Robert Moses's larger plans for all of the Upper West Side. But the Met was also crucial to John D. Rockefeller 3rd's fixation with

establishing the global cultural dominance of New York City, and for Lincoln Center to be "the one and only."[36] Without the opera, this strategy would have been empty.

So it came to pass that the Old Met's demise was imminent, as the last performance was to be on April 16, 1966. Fresh in our minds was the shameful destruction of Penn Station in 1963, as the ultimate disrespect for a city and its institutions that was unfolding before our eyes. During spring break in March 1966, I went with friends from the Yale School of Music for a final moment in that remarkable old hall on Broadway at 39th Street. It was *Manon Lescaut* with Richard Tucker as Des Grieux. Of

course, for us it was standing room with almost no view of the stage, but there was that auditorium with its extraordinary acoustics and the patrons to be seen and remembered.

The roof came off the house on January 18, 1967, with total destruction completed in only several days.[37] We all read Nathan Silver's *Lost New York*, the first book on destruction of the city's landmarks. He wrote that the Met's demise was "the archetype of unjustified destruction in cities—a great public building at the disposal solely of its owner." And he joined numerous critics who disagreed with the strategy for a Lincoln Center monopoly on high culture, pointing to the need for something to remain "below Times Square."[38]

Fountain and Plaza, Lincoln Center, 1964

The fountain and plaza were the finishing touch for the Lincoln Center complex, designed by Philip Johnson and dedicated in 1964. The Opera, Philharmonic, and State Theater halls faced the plaza that opened to Broadway. The highly classicized paving consisted of concentric circles and radii emanating from the elaborately programmed central fountain that dominated the composition. Donated by the Revlon family, the fountain was notable for its *jet d'eau* performance, forty feet high. A second phase of development, never realized, would have created an axis across Broadway culminating in Central Park. [39]

We laughed when that fountain first erupted in April 1964 and at what we saw as a proto-fascist backdrop for the Opera, Philharmonic, and State Theater. The whole Lincoln Center composition seemed reminiscent of Mussolini's EUR in Rome, and with the axis would have seemed even more so. It was surely akin to what we understood of Philip Johnson's political sensibilities. Our little joke was that the fountain was the latest in "cosmetic" architecture (via Revlon), or better yet, a breakthrough as "orgasmic" architecture. Of course, there was no way to equate the new Met auditorium with the old Met by Carrère & Hastings; underneath was the parking garage providing "easy-in easy-out" convenience for the new suburban patronage that Lincoln Center so desperately needed, such that even so venerable an urban institution as the Met could be "suburbanized."

**Grand foyer of Philharmonic Hall
with Richard Lippold's *Orpheus
and Apollo*, 1962**

From the beginning, Philharmonic Hall was seen as a symptom of certain problems associated with culture-driven urban renewal. To get Lincoln Center underway, the relocation of the Met was essential in legitimizing the entire scheme. So was the Philharmonic, however. Relocation of the Philharmonic was easier to accomplish because it would be evicted from its home in Carnegie Hall. In turn, with the loss of the Philharmonic, Carnegie would lose revenue to the point that, like the old Met, it was threatened with demolition. In the end, however, Carnegie Hall was

salvaged, with a successful preservation effort spearheaded by Isaac Stern and Leonard Bernstein to save the building and its remarkable acoustics. By contrast, the extremely poor acoustics at Philharmonic Hall were apparent from its opening in 1962, with several attempts made to remedy the problem until today.[40]

But, of course, we didn't like Philharmonic Hall from any point of view—the architecture, the urban design, the acoustics, or the politics. Apart from the fountain, the "cosmetics" seemed

to infiltrate everything, including the potted plants in the lobby. In July 1966 there was Stravinsky's last New York performance as conductor. My Yale friends were experts at moving potted plants around a bit for covert attendance purposes. Stravinsky was last on the podium so things worked well for the timing. It was "Symphony of Psalms," and the orchestra gave a tribute that was far more than one could have ever imagined with the third movement still to be remembered today. And the poor acoustics were overwhelmed by the moment.

— all the finest in dignified, cosmopolitan living is embodied in this magnificent 30 story tower. Its unique architectural concept beautifully compliments the overall design of the Lincoln Center Performing Arts complex.

**Promotional brochure for
Lincoln Center Tower, c. 1971**

Offering "the finest in dignified cosmopolitan living," Lincoln Center Tower was the first definitive luxury statement in Lincoln Square, with a quick succession of others. With the new luxury of the Lincoln Square Tower and the displaced poor from the Lincoln Square Urban Renewal, the Upper West Side was quickly becoming a "tale of two cities." Horace Ginsbern, who had died in 1969, was a Russian émigré who was among the first of his generation to attend Columbia Architecture School; much earlier in his career his production of solid middle-class housing, especially in the Bronx, had been prodigious. He was one of the team of architects who designed Harlem River Houses in the 1930s, NYCHA's first project and generally accepted as its finest. Grosvenor

Atterbury, also a Columbia graduate and one of the important innovators in social housing in the early twentieth century, similarly closed his long career with Amsterdam Houses.[41] It was been a long step from Ginsbern's Harlem River Houses or Atterbury's Roger's Model Dwellings to the reductivism of Amsterdam Houses or the pretentions of the Lincoln Center Tower.

By 1973 I had ended up on West 89th Street just in from Central Park West, in a tiny apartment in a converted brownstone. It was an inexpensive and interesting neighborhood; not much left of the old gentry and with an apparent influx of many of those displaced from the Lincoln Square Urban Renewal Area to the south or from Manhattantown

Urban Renewal Area to the north. The census figures tell the story. There were hard times. Drug traffic was everywhere. A university classmate had just bought a brownstone several blocks south for around $80,000, considered to be a "pioneer" venture, involving considerable risk. And the New York City "financial crisis" was unfolding. Down the way, Philharmonic Hall was renamed "Avery Fisher Hall" in honor of the benefactor who contributed to the first large renovation expense.[42] Neighborhood realities had not exactly matched Edgar Young's euphoric representation that Lincoln Square had accomplished a "long-range stimulation . . . on the West Side of Manhattan," and a transformation from an "impoverished and neglected, and degrading area."[43]

Looting on the Upper West Side during blackout, 1977

On the evening of July 13, 1977, a massive power failure darkened New York City and much of the region.[44] The power was not entirely restored until the next night, leaving the entire city in darkness throughout the night. Looting ensued on an unprecedented scale, especially in poor neighborhoods. Some 3,400 persons were arrested. Damage estimates vary, but there were at least $155 million in business losses and possibly double that figure, mainly involving small merchants, at least 1,383 in number and possibly double that as well. In large part, blame was placed on the growing distance between rich and poor which had been heightened by the suburban flight of the middle class and urban renewal policies that decimated the cohesive neighborhoods and displaced large numbers of persons. The blackout was of particular concern in that it contributed to a loss of innocence. It joined several harbingers including the 1960s urban riots; the Vietnam War; a 1973–74 stock market crash; the oil crisis of 1973; and New York City's fiscal crisis of 1975–76.

Mercifully the Upper West Side had escaped Moses's 1958 plans for the "Riverside-Amsterdam Urban Renewal," halted due in large part to the troublesome reputation of Moses's choice for sponsor.[45] It was to be "spot clearance" of primarily low-income persons, and almost half "non-white." [46] With West Side real estate devastation and the fiscal crisis in full bloom, it was cheaper to try to buy something on the Upper West Side than to pay rent. I found a place for $14,500 on West End Avenue and 85th Street, but Columbia did not want to put up $7,000 for the mortgage as the neighborhood was considered "too risky." Columbia finally agreed, given our argument that it was hardly riskier than Morningside Heights at that time. It was clear that urban renewal had in fact spawned expansive poverty in the neighborhood, with the displacements from Lincoln Square, Manhattantown, and elsewhere. The lights went out around 9:30 PM on July 13, 1977. There was extensive looting in the poor neighborhoods in Central Brooklyn and the South Bronx, dramatically exposing the disenfranchisement of the growing numbers of those in poverty. But to the surprise of many, apart from the Bronx and Brooklyn, looting was also close-by on Broadway and on Amsterdam Avenue. By one estimate, 61 stores were looted on the Upper West Side between 63rd and 100th Streets.[47]

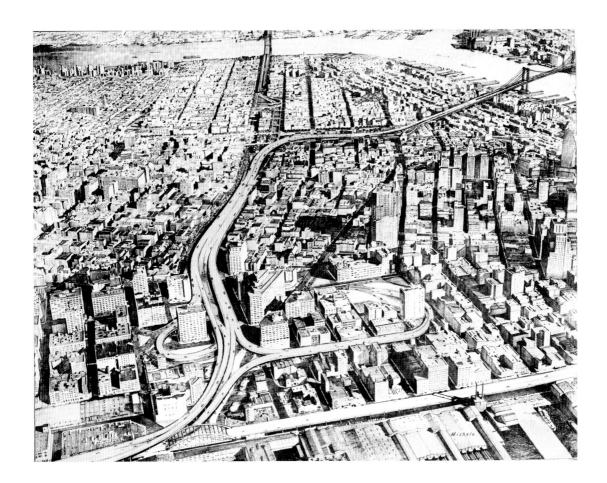

**Triborough Bridge and Tunnel
Authority, proposed Lower Manhattan
Elevated Expressway, 1965**

Three large Moses Downtown Urban Renewal projects were thwarted by community opposition: the extension of "Fifth Avenue South" through Washington Square Park and beyond; West Village clearance; and the Lower Manhattan Expressway. By the time of the West Village struggle, Jane Jacobs and the Committee to Save the West Village had learned well from the failures of the Lincoln Square community resistance.[48] Perhaps the most challenging and potentially most destructive project proposal was the elevated ten-lane roadway planned above Broome Street in SoHo and Little Italy, an idea that Moses had doggedly pursued since 1940. It would have removed fourteen blocks, displacing almost 2,000 families and more than 800 businesses, and decimated SoHo,

which Moses saw as worthless detritus of the industrial era.[49] In reality SoHo had become a cultural incubator as early as the 1960s and was growing rapidly. The Expressway project, often referred to as LOMEX was effectively killed with Jacobs's leadership in tumultuous 1968. Jacobs soon faced a potential prison sentence for her activity, as well as the possible draft of her sons for the Vietnam War, and left New York permanently for Toronto. In 1971 Governor Rockefeller removed what power Moses still enjoyed. By the early 1980s, SoHo had become a new cultural engine for the city.

By 1979 manifest destiny led to SoHo, which by then was a cultural scene more accessible, vibrant, and international

than Lincoln Center, albeit one of a different and distinctly more experimental nature. "Certifiable" artists numbered at least 64 percent of residents.[50] There were more than ninety galleries.[51] Apart from large cheap space, there was enormous energy within a few blocks: Gordon Matta-Clark's FOOD on Prince and Wooster; Richard Foreman's Hysteric Ontological Theatre just down Broadway; and the New Museum in its new space just up Broadway; Creative Time; Printed Matter on Lispenard; Don Judd's Saturday night loft gatherings on Spring Street; the Guerilla Girls on the walls. You name it. Storefront for Art and Architecture was born and blossomed as the first alternative exhibition space in New York City devoted to architecture. It was euphoria.

9

Remaking Lower Manhattan

1960–1980

*Thirty years ago, New York City's waterfront bustled with
the noise of tugs groaning under the weight of ships towed
to their berths, the horns of commercial and passenger
ships travelling to and from the Caribbean, South America,
Europe and Asia, the shouts of the longshoremen as they lifted
150-pound bags on and off ships, and the rumble of trucks
filled to the brim with cargo headed to all parts of the country.*

—New York City Council, 1989[1]

By the 1960s, Lower Manhattan, once the commercial heart of the great
port city of New York, was a shadow of its former self. The golden era of
the South Street docks was long gone. Freight traffic between New Jersey
and Manhattan had shifted from water to road and, thanks to the Holland
and Lincoln Tunnels, largely moved underground. As one observer noted,
"The area, with its banks, insurance companies, shipping offices and
investment houses, was known as the dullest place in New York to visit."[2]

While the docks of New York remained active, their fate was being
sealed by an experiment across the harbor. The first container ship, brainchild of a trucker named Malcom McLean, sailed from Port Newark in
1956, laden with fifty-eight metal containers for a destination in Texas. Its
success would transform working waterfronts around the world. Shipping
lines that had historically relied on large labor forces to load and unload
cargo saved enormous amounts of money and time by moving fully laden

containers between the back of a truck and the deck of a ship by crane, paving the way for an explosion in international trade.

The success of container technology, and the promise of Sea-Land, McLean's shipping company, encouraged the Port Authority of New York and New Jersey to invest heavily in transforming New Jersey swampland into the expanse of flat, paved land required for container handling (today known as Port Newark and Elizabeth Marine Terminals). In less than a generation, the bulk of the metropolitan area's maritime trade moved from the docks of Manhattan and Brooklyn to the container port in Newark Bay, hollowing out the once-vibrant markets and neighborhoods that adjoined the docks.

Even before the container fully took hold, the area around the piers of Lower Manhattan had become somewhat seedy. That situation, combined with the perceived drabness of the financial district, became known as the "Lower Manhattan problem," which some of the most powerful men of the day—among them David and Nelson Rockefeller—set out to solve. Starting in the late 1950s, they consulted with many of the city's leading figures in business and government to imagine a different future for Lower Manhattan, initially as a hub for white-collar trade businesses and subsequently as a mixed-use live-and-work community.

David Rockefeller's ideas about the future of Lower Manhattan were underpinned by action on his part. As president of Chase Manhattan Bank, he had committed the bank to build a new headquarters on a site at Broadway and Liberty Street, in part to stem the flight of financial service businesses to Midtown. Originally known as One Chase Manhattan Plaza, the 60-story, 1.8 million-square-foot tower was designed by Skidmore, Owings & Merrill (SOM) and opened in 1961—an unqualified commitment to the Downtown of the future.

Among the ideas embraced by the Rockefellers and Manhattan's other civic leaders was to concentrate maritime businesses in Lower Manhattan to cement the city's prominence as a center of international trade. A "world trade center" could serve as home to a variety of trade-related businesses, now separated by the Hudson River from the cargos they insured, financed, or delivered that increasingly moved through the new facilities at Port Newark and Elizabeth in New Jersey. As Austin J. Tobin, director of the Port Authority, noted in 1964, "The merchandising, financing, insuring and governmental clearing of our foreign commerce is scattered all over Manhattan. It is the objective of the World Trade Center to become not only the core of these activities but the very structure in which most of them are housed."[3]

The World Trade Center

The original plans for such a center were put together by SOM for the Downtown Lower Manhattan Association (DLMA), established in 1956 when a group organized by David Rockefeller combined forces with the extant Downtown Manhattan Association. The complex was to be located on a 16-acre site at the eastern end of Wall Street, not far from the city's earliest public dock at the foot of Broad Street. Included in the $250 million plan were a 6-story "world trade mart" and exhibition hall, a stock exchange, a marina and heliport, and a building rising up to 70 stories that would house both a hotel and office space.

The Port Authority was tapped to deliver the plan. The agency knew the maritime industry and had bonding capacity to deliver the funds to construct the new center, the condemnation powers to clear the site, and the engineering capacity to design and build it. But in securing internal approvals, the bi-state agency hit a snag. New Jersey saw the development of the trade complex as a "gift" to New York and demanded equal expenditure on the west side of the river. To balance the ledger, New Jersey requested that the Port Authority take over the ailing Hudson & Manhattan Railroad (today known as PATH) carrying New Jersey commuters to work in Manhattan. This would allow the new trade complex to be moved west along the Hudson River, replacing the Hudson & Manhattan Railroad terminal and two adjacent office towers on Church Street.

The decision to empower the Port Authority to construct office buildings on a 15-acre site in an area that served as the center of the city's electronics trade and was known as "Radio Row" immediately sparked controversy. Local merchants questioned whether the area was sufficiently "blighted" to justify its condemnation by the state for an unconvincing "public purpose." They found unusual allies among developers and owners of buildings, including some in Midtown, who argued that a public agency should not be competing for tenants with private landlords.[4] Responding to criticism from the real estate industry, the statutes giving birth to the initial World Trade Center (WTC) limited the Port Authority's reach in luring tenants by specifying that 75 percent of the businesses in the building had to be engaged in international trade. The vision, unrealistic as it may have been, incorporated the idea of "maritime floors," where brokers, forwarders, admiralty lawyers, shipping companies, and maritime financiers would co-exist and in doing so strengthen the industry as a whole in the New York region.

To cover the costs of operating PATH and developing the controversial site, and to ensure a market for tenants, the Port Authority announced plans to build the world's tallest office towers. Two 110-story skyscrapers would be accompanied by lower buildings arranged around a plaza above an underground retail mall. Some 50,000 workers and 80,000 visitors were expected to use the hotel, retail, office, parking, and restaurant space on a daily basis.

For the Port Authority, staffed by hundreds of engineers, the opportunity to build skyscrapers was one it savored. The complexity of the project was unprecedented: digging a deep foundation in what had been until recently riverbed, devising a structure that was light yet strong enough to reach higher than any other, and ensuring that the buildings' sway did not reach the level of human discomfort. The proposed building structure was unique. The project's architects, Minoru Yamasaki and Emery Roth & Sons, embraced a novel form of "framed-tube" construction. Rather than rely on traditional internal steel columns, the building load would be carried by a host of columns on the perimeter, thus increasing internal spans and freeing up floors

for maximum efficiency in office layout. The external tubes, closely spaced and made of high-strength steel, would help resist lateral wind pressure and allow for floor-to-ceiling glass panes providing dramatic views of the harbor. Not everyone loved the design. Critic Ada Louise Huxtable noted that Yamasaki's "choice of delicate detail on massive construction as a means of reconciling modern structural scale to the human scale of the viewer is often more disturbing than reassuring."[5]

Vertical circulation in such tall buildings presented a major challenge. To serve the large number of users, Port Authority engineers devised a system of express and local elevators. Express elevators that opened on two sides would carry fifty-five people at a time from the ground to two "skylobbies," located on the 44th and 78th floors, where passengers would change to local elevators to access their floors. By stacking the local elevators above one another, the shafts required less space in the building's core and helped to maximize rentable square footage.

While the technological challenges were significant, the most daunting aspect of the project was arguably the leasing of so much space in a Lower Manhattan real estate market that was already saturated. By 1973, when the buildings were officially dedicated, the towers were only half filled; six years later, 10 percent remained unfilled. The international trade "industry" would ultimately occupy only a fraction of the 75 percent of space earmarked for it originally; instead, much of the vacant space was turned over to public sector tenants, with 25 percent of it going to New York State, 10 percent to the Port Authority, and 5 percent to U.S. Customs.

Over time, the Twin Towers, as the skyscrapers were called, and the surrounding buildings —tenanted by U.S. Customs and other federal agencies—would fill up. The two towers served the anticipated number of workers each day, and many more people daily passed through the center's shopping concourse, hotel, and transit facilities. Numerous radio and television stations broadcast from the antenna on the north tower, and tourists flocked to its glamorous 107th-floor restaurant, Windows on the World, for unsurpassed views of Manhattan and the harbor.

Battery Park City

The World Trade Center was not the only plan conceived by David Rockefeller and the DLMA to reinvigorate Lower Manhattan. The idea of making the area a "live-work" community by constructing residential units on landfill had been proposed in the late 1950s. The dream would ultimately be realized with the construction of Battery Park City, but only after decades of delay, political infighting, and expense on the part of both city and state.

The original idea came from a handful of developers, who advocated creating land on the site of dilapidated West Side docks to Governor Nelson Rockefeller. Rockefeller again turned to architect Wallace K. Harrison to develop a plan for a mixed-use community that would be marketed as a "city within a city" with a wide range of residential development—apartment hotels, middle and low-income housing, townhouses, and luxury apartments. (Rockefeller was directly involved with the complex's design and many of the original plans, though Harrison signed the drawings.)

The governor's plan was not the only one for the site. The City Marine and Aviation department, the DLMA, and the City Planning Commission all developed their own plans. The city was in a particularly powerful position to push forward since it controlled both the land and its use through zoning and other regulatory powers, and the state could not move forward without it.

After two years of negotiations between city and state, the parameters of the new development were resolved, organizationally, by the creation of the Battery Park City Authority (BPCA) in 1968. Modeled on the Port Authority and the Metropolitan Transportation Authority, the BPCA was established as a public authority under New York State law and thus able to raise capital by selling bonds. New York City would assign the new land to the authority under a 70-year lease, with the proviso that affordable housing

be funded through the proceeds of sales and rentals of BPCA property.

Despite the new form of governance, none of the original plans for the 90-acre site ultimately moved forward. Architect Philip Johnson was brought in to mediate between various competing visions. Johnson, together with Harrison and William Conklin, as well as the planning firm of Alan M. Voorhees & Associates, devised a proposal for Battery Park City, publicly presented in 1966. The megaproject did justice to the idea of a "city within a city." The numbers were staggering: 5 million square feet of office space, 14,000 new apartments, 500,000 square feet of retail space, and 27 acres of new parkland. Hexagonal skyscrapers were to be connected to each other by pedestrian bridges, while a multilevel retail complex was to run north–south through the development and incorporate a monorail described as a "people mover."

The engineering involved in realizing any iteration of the new development was ambitious. When the project's underpinnings were ultimately realized in 1976, 1.2 million cubic yards of ground had been removed from the World Trade Center site and transferred by truck across West Street to fill the cells of steel cofferdams projecting 700 feet into the Hudson along a six-block run of waterfront. (This required approximately 100,000 hauls.) In addition to the roughly 25 acres created by these efforts, another 70 or so acres were constructed within cofferdams in the water—some of them over the PATH tubes that contained the trains connecting Lower Manhattan to New Jersey. Much of the fill for the additional acreage was brought in from other municipal projects, including the construction of a new water tunnel and the dredging of Ambrose Channel.

Few questioned the value of filling in land for new real estate development, particularly to help support low- and middle-income housing. However, by the time the solicitation went out to commercial developers in 1972, the Lower Manhattan real estate market was saturated with available commercial space, and a development deal, which would in part rely on commercial space to offset the cost of the residential develoments, proved elusive. By 1975 BPCA—like the city itself—was all but bankrupt and was placed under the oversight of the Financial Control Board, an end to an inglorious chapter in Battery Park City's evolution.

In 1979 the state moved forward with a new master plan devised by the urban designers Alexander Cooper and Stanton Eckstut that took a distinctly different approach from earlier proposals, imposing a street grid and building height limits, as well as introducing significant amounts of open space, particularly along the waterfront. Instead of focusing on building design, new guidelines emphasized the articulation of open space, giving developers greater flexibility in designing buildings. Commercial development was to be concentrated to the north, residential to the south, and a linear waterfront park would connect the two.

In response to the new master plan, the city formally transferred the property to the state, and the BPCA was reconstituted. All low-income housing was moved off the site, with a promise that funds from BPCA bond proceeds would be instead earmarked for construction of affordable housing in Harlem and the South Bronx. Although the city gave up control over the site, design parameters were established at the outset. The site would have a height limit set at half that of the original WTC, and be zoned to support roughly 6 million square feet of commercial office space. Importantly, the public sector recognized the need to incentivize developers and set about providing the civic infrastructure to attract them. Building parcels were delineated. Roughly one-third of the site was designated for open space and parklands, including a waterfront esplanade designed to run the length of the site. A street grid conceived to extend existing streets to the east of West Street, established view corridors open to the river.

This focus on the public realm was a significant factor in turning around the project's fortunes. As Paul Goldberger, architecture critic of the *New York Times,* noted in 1986:

> *The genius of Battery Park City is that it does not represent any single style vision at all. It represents a diversity of vision; like a real city, it encompasses many views. There is not only architectural diversity at Battery Park City—there is a much deeper kind of diversity, what we might call true balance of the public interest and the private interest. And far from frustrating the development of a coherent community, that balance enhanced it.*[6]

In 1980 Olympia & York (O&Y), a Canadian firm, won a public procurement to develop office and retail space in the middle of Battery Park City. O&Y soon hired architect Cesar Pelli to design the series of granite-faced buildings that would become known as "The World Financial Center" (now Brookfield Place) and quickly entered into leases with well-respected financial institutions including Merrill Lynch and American Express. The center comprised four commercial towers tied together by a series of retail-lined mezzanine-level corridors that led to a vast central atrium called the Winter Garden, which took on a civic function with extensive public programming.

Though the World Financial Center opened for business in 1988, the completion of Battery Park City took another twenty-four years. By the time it was completed in 2012, the area boasted a total of 47 new buildings, over 9 million square feet of commercial space, almost 14,000 new residents occupying 7 million square feet of residential space, 36 acres of open space, and two museums. Battery Park City's waterfront plaza and marina became destinations in their own right, and a new ferry service from Hoboken, New Jersey, brought large numbers of New Jersey commuters through the complex during peak hours. The West Side waterfront, once moribund and dying, had been transformed.

THE AQUARIUM, WITH PUBLIC BATHS AT SEA WALL, NEW YORK CITY   37

View of the Battery showing New York Aquarium (formerly Castle Clinton) and public baths at sea wall, 1939

Lower Manhattan, from its founding through the mid-1800s, was a live-work community. On the east side of the area, shops and stores combined with living spaces, were interspersed within an active port. Homes and business lined the lower Hudson, from the Battery to the lower end of what is now Battery Park City. By the early eighteenth century, the population—presumably with more free time—needed recreational space. The Battery, a battlement in the seventeenth century, was transformed into a promenade. This postcard image shows the outer pathways filled with strolling residents and visitors enjoying the vista at the water's edge. The city created a park on the upland, with successive additions of landfill.

A pair of dentists introduced a new recreational facility to the Battery in 1832: two floating baths. Here middle- and upper-class patrons paid to enjoy the allegedly healthful benefits of the sea air and enclosed salt water pools. The baths became the property of the Department of Public Works in 1880 and were repurposed as a facility for residents of the growing tenement community to cleanse themselves. In fact, they soon became favorite swimming holes. Sex-separated and watched over by paid attendants, the baths were considered a place to control the behavior of vagrant children and unemployed immigrants.

The Aquarium, the last piece of the recreational compound, opened in 1896. Here, in one scene, we see people promenading, lining up to use the middle bath, and entering the New York Aquarium, which the card reverse describes as containing "the most valuable and complete collection of marine life in the world."

Battery Park, c. 1914

In 1914 a committee of Trinity Church, a not-for profit religious institution with property on the Lower West Side, reported on the living and working conditions around Washington Street, then a poor, primarily immigrant, residential area that years later would become home to the World Trade Center. The Trinity group appears to have been part of the "tenement house" and "public park" reform movements of that period. Included in the report is a survey of recreational facilities within the district. Both Battery Park and the two floating baths are described as virtually unusable. A single playground inhabited by "idlers" and a few men playing baseball sat under the elevated railroad at the northern end of Battery Park. Neighborhood children played various games on the cross streets above Battery Place. The green areas between Battery Park's pathways, which might have been used by children, were empty, edged by signs warning "Keep off the Grass." However, the report did note that the two remaining floating baths were heavily used by local boys and girls. These facilities were not without their problems: sewage poured into their open wells, and health officials had to recommend against river bathing.

12744 THE DOCKS ALONG WEST STREET, NEW YORK.

**Hudson River docks along
West Street, c. 1905**

The mixed-use profile of the Lower Manhattan shoreline changed in the nineteenth century. Shipping and its associated facilities and trades, among them dry docks, iron foundries, and sail makers, had lined the East River waterfront since the colony's founding as New Amsterdam. The introduction of the steamboat in the nineteenth century opened the ice-prone waterfront on the West Side to ever larger commercial and passenger ships. By 1860 New York's tonnage exceeded that of both London and Liverpool, and the Hudson River waterfront was the center of the country's maritime trade. Immigrants from Ireland, England, and France found work and lived near these docks. By the 1830s, the residential city limits had moved northward from Duane Street to Washington Square.

The shoreline held a system of piers attached at right angles to a cement block bulkhead that formed a semi-circle around the lower half of Manhattan, from West 61st Street around the tip of the island to East 51st Street. Railroad lighters, trans-Atlantic steamers, warehouses, and a street laden with goods waiting to be loaded on vessels or trucks complete the picture. A block or two to the east, walk-up, multifamily housing sat among warehouses and manufacturing structures. Save for the occasional rowdy boys who jumped into the Hudson (much to the annoyance of well-dressed ferry riders), the Lower Manhattan waterfront was heavily used by industry and completely walled off from the public.

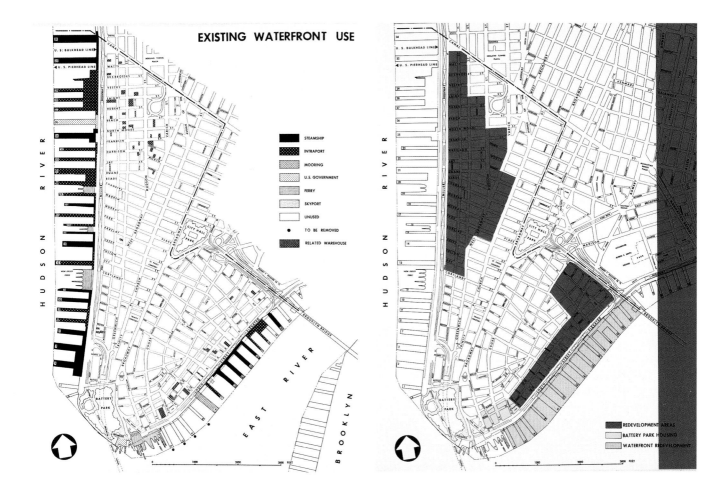

EXISTING WATERFRONT USE

STEAMSHIP
INTRAPORT
MOORING
U.S. GOVERNMENT
FERRY
SKYPORT
UNUSED
● TO BE REMOVED
RELATED WAREHOUSE

REDEVELOPMENT AREAS
BATTERY PARK HOUSING
WATERFRONT REDEVELOPMENT

**Downtown-Lower Manhattan
Association, maps indicating existing
and recommended waterfront uses,
1958**

Nearly a century later, Lower Manhattan was "decaying at the edges." In an attempt to return the area to its former excellence (and to shore up the financial district where its members had significant investments), the Downtown Lower Manhattan Association (DLMA) undertook an independent study. The private group, headed by David Rockefeller, hired Skidmore, Owings & Merrill to investigate and recommend traffic improvements, walk-to-work housing, and new commercial uses. Working with city agencies, the group intended to create a foundation for the eventual redevelopment of Lower Manhattan. The map in the report showing the Existing Waterfront Use in 1958 (above

left) is indicative of the importance at the time of maintaining and improving the many still active shipping and industrial facilities on the Hudson.

On the East Side, the DLMA report recommended the construction of new, moderate-income residences known as Battery Park Housing. This area bounded by Whitehall Street, Water Street, Coenties Slip, and South Street was part of an Urban Renewal Plan put forward by Robert Moses under the aegis of the Mayor's Committee on Slum Clearance in 1956, and was indicated on a map showing recommended development sites (right). Federal funds would be used to replace fifty- and one-hundred-year-old commercial

and industrial buildings with small, elevator buildings that could house middle-income residents. To the east, the empty East River Piers 4, 5, and 6 were noted for reuse.

The report recommended that these piers be demolished and replaced by transportation and recreational uses: a heliport and a small boat basin. Not shown on these maps is a plan put forth by the DLMA in 1960 that identified one of the new commercial ventures shown in red on the map: 13.5 acres along the East River between Old Slip and Fulton Street that would be the site for a World Trade Center, to be planned and constructed by the Port Authority of New York and New Jersey.

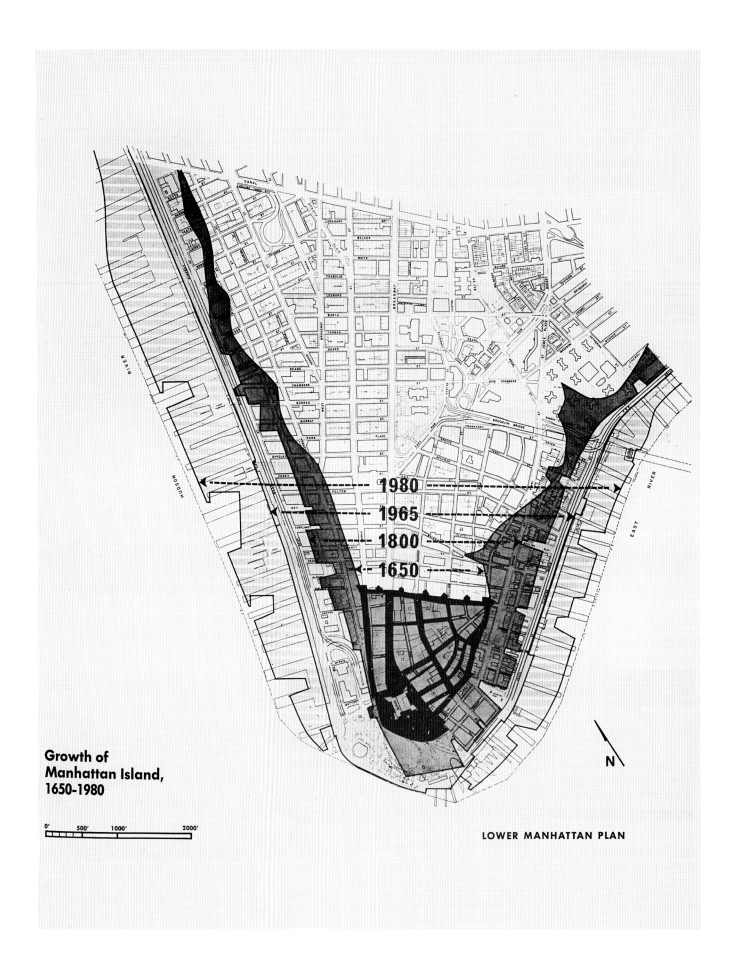

**Growth of
Manhattan Island,
1650-1980**

1980
1965
1800
1650

0'   500'   1000'   2000'

N

LOWER MANHATTAN PLAN

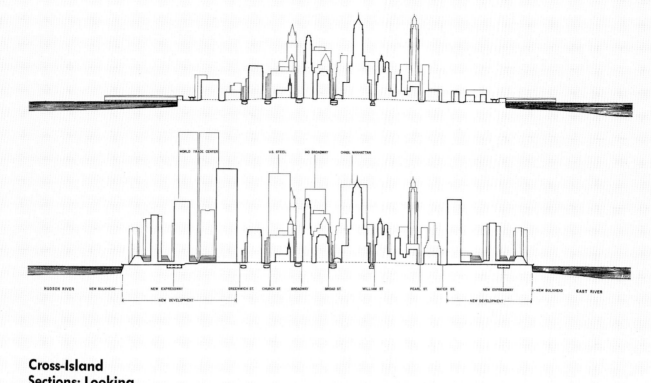

Cross-Island
Sections: Looking
North at Wall Street

1950-1980

0'   500'   1000'

New York City Planning Commission, map indicating physical growth of land mass in Lower Manhattan, 1966

The Lower Manhattan Plan, cross-island sectional drawings of Lower Manhattan looking north toward Wall Street, 1966

Because of city and state policies that historically encouraged expansion into the rivers, Lower Manhattan south of City Hall is 33 percent larger than when the Dutch arrived in the seventeenth century. By 1960, in order to reinvigo-

rate Lower Manhattan, it appeared to be time once again to expand outward. As can be seen on the map to the left, by mid-decade the physical area had expanded exponentially from its origins at Pearl Street and Greenwich Street to the East River Drive and Twelfth Avenue. By 1980 a new slate of high-rise developments was expected to fill the outer rims of Lower Manhattan. One complex shown on the cross-island section, above, is the World Trade Center, now moved to the West Side, between Church Street and Twelfth Avenue.

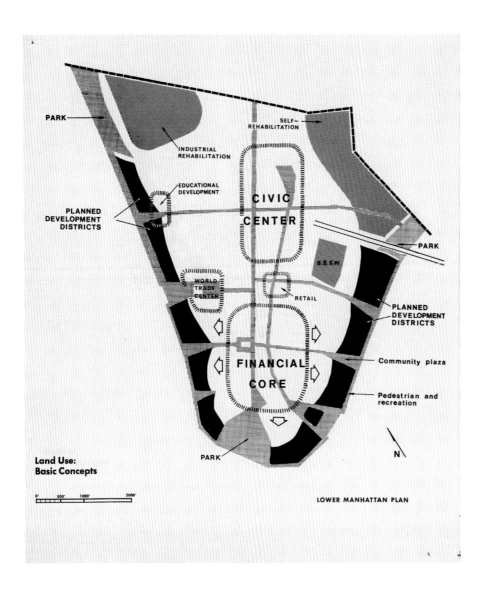

PARK

INDUSTRIAL
REHABILITATION

SELF–
REHABILITATION

EDUCATIONAL
DEVELOPMENT

PLANNED
DEVELOPMENT
DISTRICTS

CIVIC
CENTER

PARK

B.B.S.W.

WORLD
TRADE
CENTER

RETAIL

PLANNED
DEVELOPMENT
DISTRICTS

Community plaza

Pedestrian and
recreation

FINANCIAL
CORE

Land Use:
Basic Concepts

PARK

N

0'   500'   1000'   2000'

LOWER MANHATTAN PLAN

The Lower Manhattan Plan, map indicating basic land-use concepts, 1966

The Lower Manhattan Plan, map indicating future land use, 1966

In response to the DLMA Report sent to the Mayor eight years earlier, the City Planning Commission in 1966 commissioned a Plan for Lower Manhattan from a group of architecture, planning, and transportation consultants led by the firm of Wallace, McHarg, Roberts and Todd. The primary goals of the plan were to provide frameworks for strengthening the business core and to provide walk-to-work housing. A third goal was "to take "maximum advantage" of the "beauty" and "striking physical plant" of the downtown waterfront in order to serve the recreational needs of an expanding business and residential community.

These two images from the plan show a framework that would become visible in the actual redevelopment of the Lower Manhattan waterfront by 1990. In the Basic Concepts map (above) the piers would disappear, and be replaced by undefined office and residential structures constructed on landfill on the Hudson and on decking over the East River. Here, for the first time, is a proposal for opening up the former working waterfront to recreation. A new park would be placed along each river in the northern sections of the district, complementing Battery Park at the south end. In an effort to provide venues for a population of office workers and local residents to enjoy the beauty and respite of the waterfront, community plazas would be located at seven sites along the rivers. One of these sites would connect the World Trade Center, then in construction in an isolated location, directly to the Hudson River. A waterfront esplanade encircles the entire district.

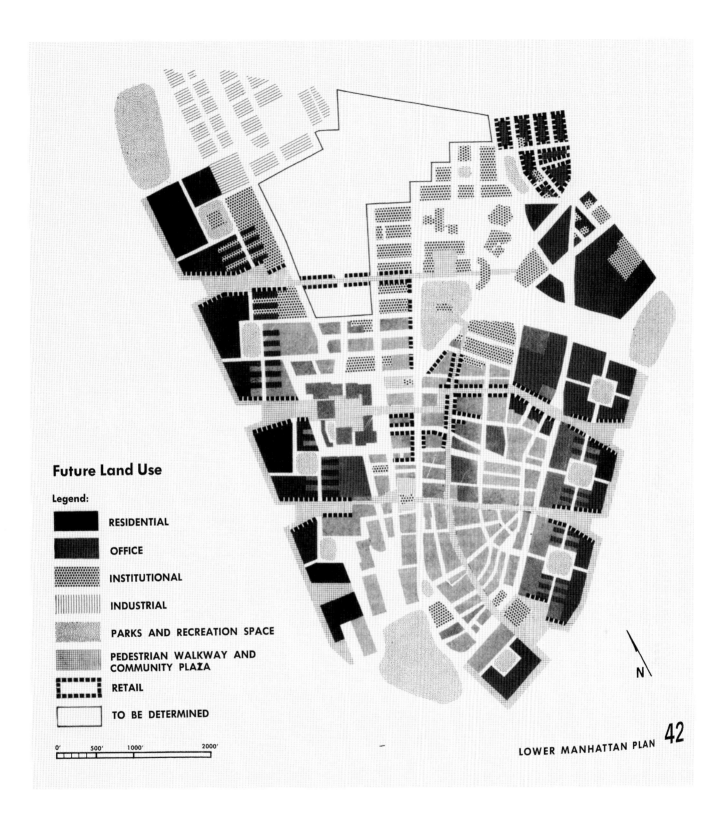

Future Land Use

Legend:

- RESIDENTIAL
- OFFICE
- INSTITUTIONAL
- INDUSTRIAL
- PARKS AND RECREATION SPACE
- PEDESTRIAN WALKWAY AND COMMUNITY PLAZA
- RETAIL
- TO BE DETERMINED

0' 500' 1000' 2000'

N

LOWER MANHATTAN PLAN 42

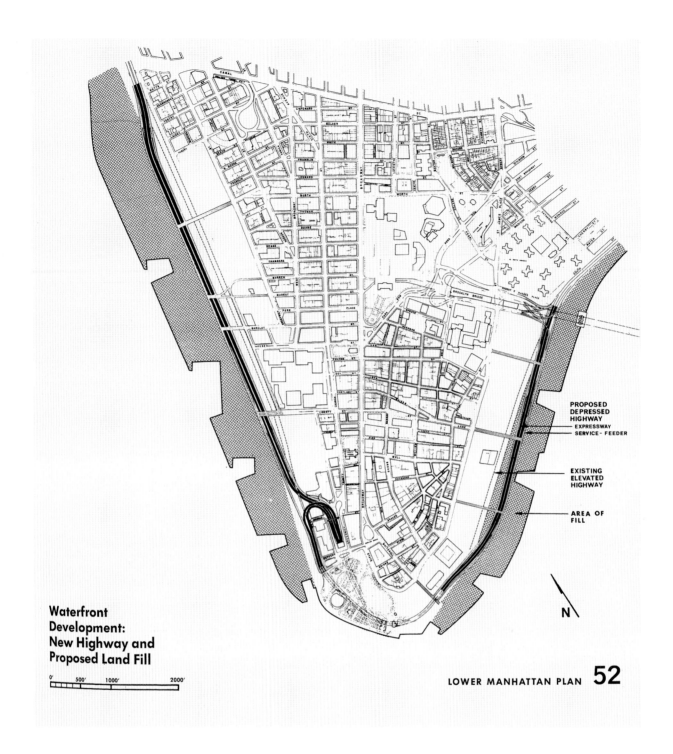

Waterfront
Development:
New Highway and
Proposed Land Fill

0'   500'   1000'   2000'

PROPOSED
DEPRESSED
HIGHWAY
EXPRESSWAY
SERVICE-FEEDER

EXISTING
ELEVATED
HIGHWAY

AREA OF
FILL

N

LOWER MANHATTAN PLAN **52**

**The Lower Manhattan Plan, map
indicating highway and land fill
proposals, 1966**

In addition to the obsolete and dilapidated piers, the elevated Miller Highway,
which ran above Twelfth Avenue parallel to the Hudson River, as well as the
East River highways, were crumbling.
They were also blocking access to the
riverfronts. The solution shown on this
plan—a depressed highway that would
run on landfill outside of the existing
East and Hudson River bulkheads—is the
first gleaning of what would eventually
become Westway.

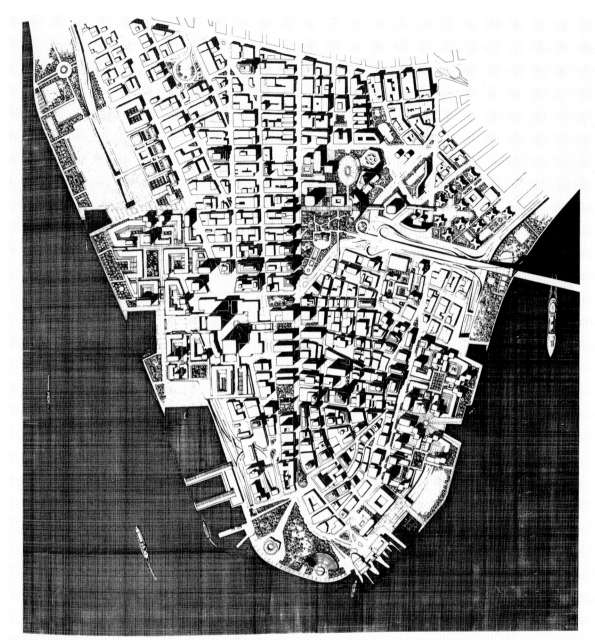

The Lower Manhattan Plan, map indicating development sites, 1966

With maritime commerce now largely moved to a containerport on vast flatlands in New Jersey and smaller, breakbulk facilities on piers in Brooklyn and Staten Island, the city had committed not to redevelop the Lower Manhattan Hudson River waterfront for shipping. But there is a holdout shown on one of the maps in the plan. Stage 1 Site Development shows two piers, a connected warehouse, and an open basin extending from Battery Park north to a block south of the World Trade Center.

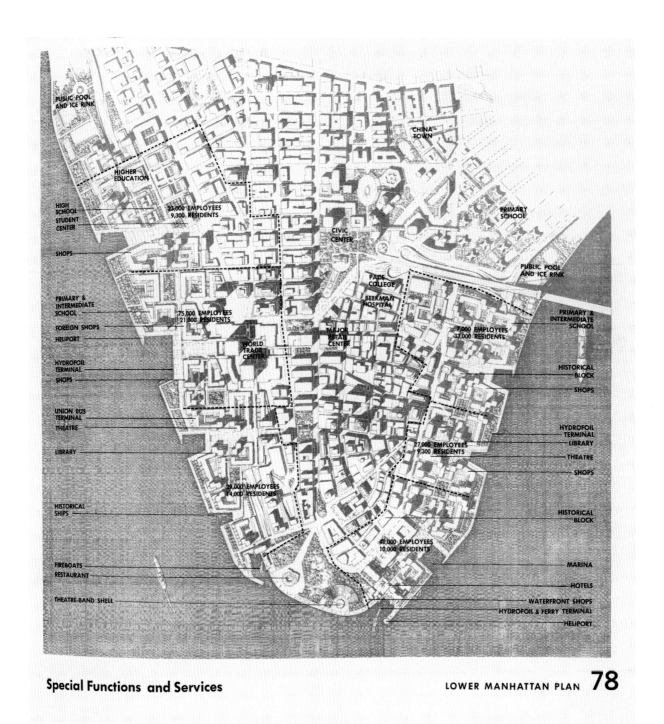

PUBLIC POOL
AND ICE RINK

HIGHER
EDUCATION

CHINA-
TOWN

HIGH
SCHOOL
STUDENT
CENTER

23,000 EMPLOYEES
9,300 RESIDENTS

PRIMARY
SCHOOL

CIVIC
CENTER

SHOPS

PRIMARY &
INTERMEDIATE
SCHOOL

PACE
COLLEGE

PUBLIC POOL
AND ICE RINK

75,000 EMPLOYEES
21,000 RESIDENTS

BEEKMAN
HOSPITAL

PRIMARY &
INTERMEDIATE
SCHOOL

FOREIGN SHOPS

HELIPORT

MAJOR
RETAIL
CENTER

7,000 EMPLOYEES
33,000 RESIDENTS

HYDROFOIL
TERMINAL

WORLD
TRADE
CENTER

HISTORICAL
BLOCK

SHOPS

SHOPS

UNION BUS
TERMINAL

HYDROFOIL
TERMINAL

THEATRE

27,000 EMPLOYEES
9,300 RESIDENTS

LIBRARY

LIBRARY

THEATRE

SHOPS

29,000 EMPLOYEES
14,000 RESIDENTS

HISTORICAL
SHIPS

HISTORICAL
BLOCK

48,000 EMPLOYEES
10,000 RESIDENTS

FIREBOATS

MARINA

RESTAURANT

HOTELS

THEATRE-BAND SHELL

WATERFRONT SHOPS

HYDROFOIL & FERRY TERMINAL

HELIPORT

Special Functions and Services

LOWER MANHATTAN PLAN 78

The Lower Manhattan Plan, map indicating special functions and services, 1966

The final Lower Manhattan Plan is shown in three-dimensional details. A mix of residential, commercial and recreational use is depicted on filled land from the Brooklyn Bridge, to the south, around the tip of Manhattan, and north to Canal Street. High- and low-rise residential and commercial structures on the upland alongside the landfill provide what the plan describes as "windows on the water" to varied landscapes bordered by an esplanade.

Lower Manhattan showing the World Trade Center, c. 1972

This image includes portions of what would become ninety acres of landfill on the west side of Lower Manhattan. This newly made land is located in one of the areas recommended for development in the 1966 plan. The material for what would become the last expansion of the city's waterfront was relatively cheap. The site provided a place to dispose of the debris excavated for the construction of the nearby World Trade Center and for the harbor dredging that was needed to accommodate deeper-draft ships. Though in a location preserved in the 1958 DLMA plan for steamship piers, this photograph shows work in progress for what would become Battery Park City, the commercial and walk-to-work residential community designed to allay the concerns of David Rockefeller and the DLMA since the 1950s. Perhaps in deference to their earlier plan, and certainly to city policy that a maritime economy be maintained, the piers to the north of the landfill still appear viable for shipping. An additional icon in this image is the elevated Miller Highway that prohibits access to the Hudson River from the nearly finished World Trade Center.

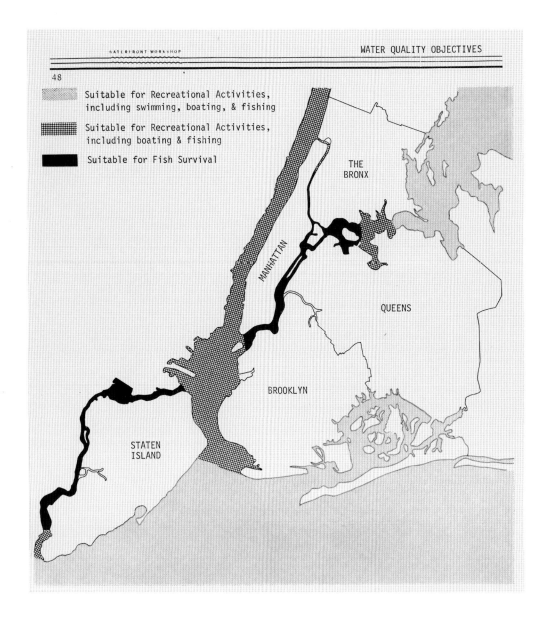

Suitable for Recreational Activities, including swimming, boating, & fishing

Suitable for Recreational Activities, including boating & fishing

Suitable for Fish Survival

THE BRONX

MANHATTAN

QUEENS

BROOKLYN

STATEN ISLAND

New York Department of City Planning, map indicating water quality objectives, 1974

By 1974 City Planning officials had concluded that the then 570 miles of New York City waterfront had potential but needed a plan. This document would be unlike the city's first waterfront plan published by the Dock Department in 1871. At that time, the Dock Department was responding to the "disgraceful" conditions of the wharves and piers that served over ten thousand vessels in foreign, coastal, and domestic trade. The emphasis was on the improvement of the commercial waterfront. No mention was made of housing, and only one spokesman at official hearings pressed for a largely recreational shoreline, with of course, occasional opportunities for shipping.

A century later, city planners had a different view. Prompted by blocks of empty West Side piers, state legislation that required public access through residential properties, and the 1972 Federal Water Pollution Control Act, which mandated "zero discharge into the waterways," recreation in and on the edge of the Hudson River was no longer merely a possibility but a reality. As is clear in the map from City Planning's 1974 Waterfront Workshop, within a decade New Yorkers would be able not only to promenade along the Battery Park City waterfront, but also to fish and paddle in kayaks in the Hudson. On the East Side, the future was in "floating parks on barges." The city budget in 1974 even contained $5.5 million for an experimental, four-acre park to float in the East River north of the Brooklyn Bridge. A floating pool was a possible adjunct.

Photographic montage showing park proposed as part of Westway, 1974

By the early 1970s, the elevated Miller Highway was in extreme disrepair and in danger of collapse. Here was opportunity both for new development and to improve the environment. A highway, funded mostly by the federal government, would extend under newly created land between the bulkhead and east of the pierhead line, from the Battery to 59th Street. Half of the 700 acres of new land was proposed for housing; just under a quarter would be park and esplanade extending north-ward from Battery Park City to Riverside Park. But "Westway," as it came to be known, came under attack by citizens, professionals, and public agency staff from the beginning. They questioned the availability of funds to complete the project, the placement and type of the various uses, and risks to air and water quality. Community Boards, local elected officials, and even Hugh Carey, who was running for New York State Governor, opposed the plan.

Proponents tried to sell Westway as best they could. Michael Lazar, the City Transportation Commissioner, and John Zuccotti, chair of the New York City Department of Planning, issued a report that contained a photograph showing what the park on top of the landfill could be. Instead of a drawing by landscape consultants, this image is a doctored photograph of the landfill that would become Battery Park City. Slightly to the north of the World Trade Center is a single prone reader. A huddle of football players, a food cart, and various athletes are standing or running about on a sandy surface. Trees and skyscrapers, includ-ing part of the World Trade Center, can be seen in the background.

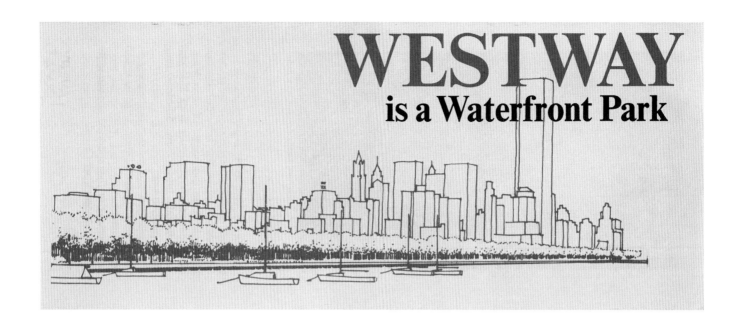

Cover of New York Chamber of Commerce and Industry, *Westway Is a Waterfront Park*, 1978

This image is included in a pamphlet published by the Westway Coalition, under the auspices of the New York Chamber of Commerce and Industry. The group's objective was to get residents on board and to capture a vocal constituency by selling Westway as a park. Similar to the doctored photograph in the City report, this sketch shows a thick line of trees in full leaf, backed by skyscrapers including the World Trade Center. To appeal to recreational sailors, boats are moored in the apparently calm waters of the Hudson. While the Westway Coalition tried to gather open-space supporters, the New York State Office of Parks and Historic Preservation (NYSOPHP) hired the Philadelphia architectural firm of Venturi, Rauch & Scott Brown to design the park.

New York Chamber of Commerce and Industry, Map indicating route of proposed Westway development on new land created along the Hudson River shoreline, 1978

United States Federal Highway Administration, Map of Selected Modified Outboard Alternative, known as Westway, 1977

A map of the Westway route on new land (right) is further indication of how desperate the group was to highlight the importance of the park. A thick overlay of green extends northward from Battery Park City. The highway exists under the green. There is no evidence of the residential, commercial, industrial, and other developments that were shown in the 1977 Final Environmental Impact Statement (far right).

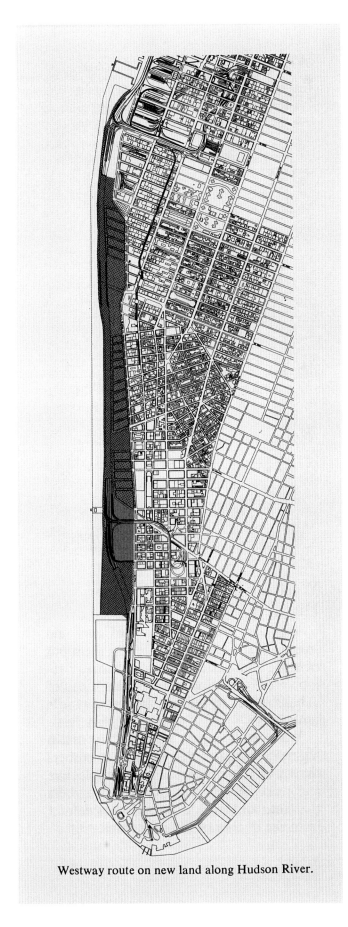

Westway route on new land along Hudson River.

Fred R. Conrad, "Amost Their Own Beach," *New York Times*, **May 16, 1977**

New York City residents Suellen Epstein and James Biederman packed up a copy of the Sunday *New York Times*, which they had bought at Morgan's Market at Hudson and Reade Street, and climbed through holes in a hurricane fence for their "day at the beach" on the Battery Park City landfill. They are sunbathing on a tract of bare, new land that was in the process of settling prior to construction of a 92-acre housing and commercial development. This photograph represents the reality of a hoped-for scene alluded to in a city planning document published a decade earlier. Here is a Lower Manhattan waterfront site serving the recreational needs of residents, framed by the magnificence of the Twin Towers of the World Trade Center, the Lower Manhattan skyline, and, on the far right, New York Harbor. Unseen, at the photographer's back is the Hudson River. The following summer the sunbathers would have shared part of the beach with a sculpture show by Creative Time, a not-for-profit organization that presents public art exhibitions. By 1980 shovels were in the ground, and the waterfront beach was no longer accessible.

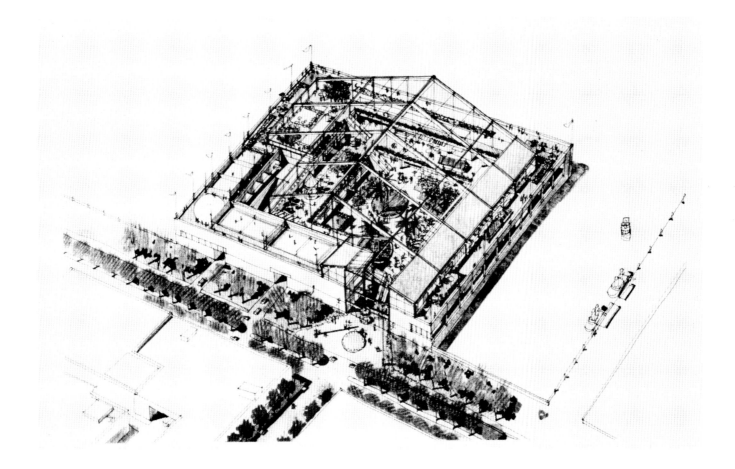

**Parks Council, Rendering of
proposed Pier 40, 1978**

The demise of Westway created new pressure to deal with a waterfront that no longer served shipping and was a blot on the new residential neighborhoods. Advocacy groups such as the Parks Council stepped in, echoing the sentiment seen in the early parks and playgrounds movement, including the Trinity Church Men's Committee study of Battery Park in 1914. In 1977 the Parks Council turned to the West Side waterfront, working to create a constituency to create and open a ribbon of green space along the length of the Hudson River from Battery Park City north. This image of Pier 40 is one of dozens in this booklet that show ideas for converting decrepit shipping piers into public open space. Here the Boston urban design consultant Stephen Carr envisioned a wide variety of recreational facilities, from a glass-enclosed botanical garden to rooftop tennis courts. Before long, Pier 40 and its newly constructed ballfields would become home to prime recreation space for schools and youth sport leagues and the ribbon of park running alongside it would become one of the city's most treasured waterfront amenities: Hudson River Park.

10

Remaking Times Square

1980–2000

*The irony is that Times Square represents in many ways the
epitome of free-market capitalism. But its transformation
is due more to government intervention than just about any
other development in the country.*

—Tim Tompkins, president of the Times Square Alliance, 2010[1]

In the wake of the controversial urban renewal efforts of the 1960s and the
withdrawal of direct federal funding in the 1970s, the reimagining of other
areas of New York was both more measured and more focused on creating
new commercial—rather than residential or cultural—spaces. The regeneration of Times Square and West 42nd Street between 1980 and 2000 set a
precedent for this type of development in many respects, most notably for
the way the city and state worked together with multiple developer partners. It also served as a template for the concept of public development
corporations playing a primary role as agents of physical transformation
and regeneration—a formula that would subsequently be used successfully
in mixed-use urban renewal projects across the city.

Times Square owes much of its storied history to a historical anomaly.
The bowtie configuration of roads created by the intersection of Broadway
and Seventh Avenue at 42nd Street, and indeed Broadway as a whole as it
winds north of Houston Street, was not part of the original Commissioners'
Plan. Once known as Longacre Square, the area became one of the most
vibrant destinations in Manhattan, a position that can be traced back to its

association with the entertainment industry in the late nineteenth and early twentieth centuries. Live theater in New York did not, however, start in Times Square. Originally centered around Union Square, a critical mass of live entertainment had moved to what was known as the Tenderloin District in the West 30s by the late nineteenth century. At the turn of the twentieth century, it was migrating further north on the West Side as garment manufacturing businesses expanded and put upward pressures on real estate prices in the Tenderloin. The opening of the IRT subway and the New York Times Building in 1904 and the construction of luxury hotels and ornate theaters during the same period cemented Times Square's reputation as a destination for New Yorkers and visitors alike.

Decline of Times Square

The area around Times Square and 42nd Street flourished as a mecca for live theater through the 1920s, but a combination of factors conspired to transform its offerings during the subsequent decades. The rise of the movies offered a cheaper alternative form of entertainment to live theater. The repeal of Prohibition in 1933 took its toll as well, leading to the emergence of watering holes featuring burlesque shows and honky-tonk music and theaters presenting old action movies. Showy billboard advertising emerged in the 1950s and 1960s as a way to make money on buildings that were unmarketable to commercial tenants.

By the early 1970s, Times Square, once the legendary "Crossroads of the World," had become lodged in the popular imagination as a forbidding, crime-ridden area. Though still containing the city's largest aggregation of legitimate theaters, the area was also home to drug dealers and prostitutes, as well as a large number of cinemas that presented pornographic movies. Times Square became a symbol of the decline in the city as a whole, beset with a financial crisis, rampant crime, and a broken transit system.

The subsequent effort to transform and clean up 42nd Street was born of the city's need to remain relevant economically, and specifically its determination

to halt the ongoing exodus of the middle class to surrounding suburbs. Programs to revitalize the area began in the late 1970s, on the heels of the financial crisis. The city set up an Office of Midtown Enforcement in 1976, following a United States Supreme Court decision ratifying the constitutionality of using zoning ordinances to restrict and criminalize the proliferation of "adult" movie theaters. Months before the ruling, the New York City Board of Estimate had passed the nation's first legislation prohibiting the establishment of "massage parlors."

While attempts to control the so-called sex industry were underway, so too were changes in the area's physical characteristics. In 1976 the original Times Tower, which had prompted the renaming of Longacre Square in 1904, was reimagined as a tourist-friendly facility. In 1979 the New York City Planning Commission embarked on a study focused on exploring responses to the increasing density and congestion defining the eastern side of Midtown, including the stimulation of growth in the less developed western portion of the district. Within two years, with the prospect of increased development in Times Square, plans to create a pedestrian mall in the area—dating back to the 1960s—resurfaced. Though the plan initially had the city's backing, local theater owners were opposed to it, and it was never realized.[2]

In 1980 the city proposed a new plan to be overseen by the New York State Urban Development Corporation through its Times Square Redevelopment Corporation subsidiary, an agency wielding both municipal and state authority. The plan was an ambitious one, stretching from Seventh to Eighth Avenues along the blocks bounded by 40th and 42nd Streets and involving 13 acres, 74 parcels, and more than 8 million square feet of development rights. It included a hotel, trade mart, considerable retail, a redevelopment of the Times Square subway station, and four massive office towers located at the intersections 42nd Street with Broadway and Seventh Avenue. With the city short of funds, the money to condemn and acquire the land, as well as to construct the towers and rebuild the existing subway station, was expected to come from the private sector, with repayment via tax abatements. A Request for Proposals soliciting developer partners was issued in 1981.

The successful bidders, George Klein and the Prudential Insurance Company, proposed a complex of office towers at Times Square planned and designed by Philip Johnson and John Burgee Architects. Perhaps drawing inspiration from the stylistically coordinated design of nearby Rockefeller Center, Johnson and Burgee's scheme, presented to the public at the end of 1983, called for four limestone-clad towers, ranging in height from twenty-nine to fifty-six stories and terminating in dramatic mansard roofs. But the project was plagued by widespread debate and opposition within the architectural and planning communities, by rival developers, and among the general public. The subject of dozens of lawsuits over the next five years, it was never built.[3]

Revival of 42nd Street

Despite a stalemate in the plan to activate the footprint of Times Square itself, several factors would together initiate a change in the wider area's fortunes. After years of political infighting, the construction of a hotel, first proposed by the architect-developer John Portman in 1972, finally got underway along Broadway at 45th Street. Challenged by architectural preservationists who had objected to the required demolition of three distinguished theaters that stood on the site, court rulings eventually allowed the theaters to be demolished and the Marriott Marquis hotel to be opened on the site in 1985.

The construction of the Marriott hotel was significant as a symbol of commercial confidence in the area, but it was important for other reasons as well. The architectural loss of the theaters on the site moved the city to establish the Theater Advisory Council, which in turn led the Landmarks Preservation Commission to designate more than two dozen theaters as landmarks by 1987. This had a strong impact on stabilizing the area, retaining positive aspects of its character and history, and ensuring that the area would retain a mixed-use dimension.

Other efforts to respond to development pressure in the area were underway during this time, including substantial zoning changes intended to support development and legitimate entertainment uses in the area. In the early 1980s, after comprehensive review, the city established a Special Midtown Zoning District in response to perceived real-estate market pressures. In 1987 the City Planning Commission, building upon the initial study and working with the Public Development Corporation, drafted guidelines for a special "theater sub-district" in the area. The zoning ordinances specified the number, size, type, and placement of new illuminated signs required in the core of the new district, ensuring animated facades into the foreseeable future.

Visions for a revitalized 42nd Street between Seventh and Eighth Avenues continued to be developed by architects, designers, and artists, largely overseen by the 42nd Street Development Corporation, a non-profit established in 1976 to steward the transformation of the corridor as a whole. In 1987, using funding from the earlier aborted deal, the 42nd Street Development Corporation engaged Robert A.M. Stern Architects and Hardy Holzman Pfeiffer Associates to reimagine a revived block incorporating restored theaters. Working with the Landmarks Preservation Commission, the corporation examined the historical value of the area's theaters, approximately fifty in all, and sought to protect many that had not been previously designated as individual landmarks.

The New Victory, built in 1900 by the theater impresario Oscar Hammerstein as the Republic, was the first of the landmarked theaters to be restored. As realized by Hardy Holzman Pfeifer, the theater reopened in 1995 as a children's theater, as if to signify clearly the dramatic changes occurring along 42nd Street. The firm completed the equally extensive renovation of the New Amsterdam Theater (1903) in 1997 for the Disney Corporation, which further signaled the area's acceptability for family entertainment and served as an essential component of the area's transformation.

By the early 1990s, the approach to achieving a reimagined Times Square had shifted significantly from the vision proposed by Mayor Ed Koch in 1980. Instead of an ambitious master plan, simpler design guidelines for the sites now in public control were issued. An RFP issued in 1994 did not require developers to front cash to acquire land as the previous one had; the state had already condemned most of what was required to transfer the requisite air rights to the corner sites. Nor were developers asked to fund the renovation of the Times Square subway station; instead the Metropolitan Transportation Authority (MTA), operator of the subway, undertook and paid for this work.

Ultimately, the four corner sites at the Times Square bowtie would be awarded to three different developers rather than to one, as had been anticipated.[4] With the construction of these four towers over the next decade, the Times Square area would be doubly transformed, returning to its former glory as a cacophonous celebration of illuminated signage and becoming a desirable location for corporate offices. By the mid-1990s, the area also began to attract significant investment by retailers, including numerous themed restaurants, a long-standing Times Square tradition dating back to Maxim's and "the lobster palaces" that catered to well-heeled theater-goers during the first decade of the twentieth century.

As if to further reclaim its historic past, beginning in the late 1980s, the area west of Times Square was rediscovered as a residential neighborhood, recalling its claim to being a fashionable residential neighborhood at the turn of the century. Forty-second Street between Ninth and Tenth Avenue had proven untenable as the site for high-end residential development as recently as 1977, when Manhattan Plaza, originally intended as an upmarket development, was reconfigured and opened as federally subsidized affordable housing for a mixed population comprising people working in the performing arts, neighborhood residents, and the elderly. By the late 1980s, the redevelopment of Times Square seemed a safer bet, and a decade later, a slew of residential towers, promoted for their proximity to Midtown office buildings, had been completed west of Times Square.

By the dawn of the twenty-first century, Times Square and 42nd Street, an area that had for many represented all that was wrong with the financially beleaguered city, was transformed. The changes had been catalyzed and sustained not only by shifting urban attitudes and real estate markets, but also to a great extent by government action, including the creation of the Special Midtown Zoning District and the subsequent passage of new signage-friendly zoning ordinances. The journey from squalor to success—as a thriving around-the-clock district for entertainment, business, and residential life, served up with a bit of the historic razzle-dazzle long associated with Times Square—was complete.

Billboards in Longacre Square, 1898

Before Times Square was Times Square, it was Longacre Square, a name taken from a commercial street in London. The moniker was a logical one, stemming from the land use common to the district in both cities. Horse dealerships, carriage factories, and stables were the main businesses during the area's initial transition from residential to commercial use. The commercial concentration itself hardly made for public value at the time; rather it was a history of amusement and the characters drawn to the area, even before theaters became its main attraction. It was associated with horseplay, on several levels, and given the early nickname "Thieves Lair." A change in character came with the illumination of the theaters in the late 1880s, followed shortly thereafter by outdoor lamps—note the street lamp at the extreme left—street signs, and lighted entrances to public places, and the decision in 1901 to build New York's first underground rapid transit system, the Interborough Rapid Transit Company (IRT).

**Times Square subway station
on opening day, 1904**

The opening of the Times Square subway station transformed the intersection of 42nd Street and Broadway into a major crossroads. Designated a crosstown thoroughfare when the city grid was laid out in 1811, it was not officially opened until 1837. In the half century from 1850 to 1900, the city's foremost east–west thoroughfare had moved northward three times, from 14th Street to 23rd Street, then to 34th Street, before settling at 42nd Street in 1915, largely because of the path of the new IRT subway that connected Times Square and Grand Central with points south and north. Superior transit also gave it a lock on the "Rialto," as the Theater District was called: entertainment districts require a centrality of location to best serve residents, suburbanites and visitors, and the Times Square subway station transported almost 5 million customers in 1905, its first full year of operation.

Times Square: The Center of New York, 1905

Times Square got its name upon the completion of the landmark New York Times Tower in 1905. Through a series of adroit actions, Adolph S. Ochs, owner and publisher of the *Times*, succeeded in forging a public identity between his newspaper and what he perceived could be the renown of an "internationally celebrated crossroad." First, he selected the area's most visible site, the small triangular piece of the block at the southern end of the Times Square "bowtie" created by the X-crossing of Broadway and Seventh Avenue. He then tore down the Pabst Hotel and built for his headquarters a 25-story building in Italian-Renaissance style faced in limestone, terra-cotta, and brick. The Times Tower was at the time the second tallest building in the city and, reportedly, visible from a distance of twelve miles. With the building's dedication timed to welcome in the New Year on December 31, 1904, the Times staged a carefully orchestrated gala attended by thousands of New Yorkers who watched a fireworks display launched from the still-unfinished tower. This was Ochs's third, but not final, signature move. In 1907, after safety concerns led to a city-wide ban on fireworks, the New Year's Eve event was refined with the addition of a giant, electrically lighted ball dropped from the 70-foot flag pole of the Times Tower, immediately marking the site as a stage for municipal celebrations. Over the years, increasing popularity and promotion turned the annual rite into a beloved national custom. The prestige of its tower married with the new subway line opened up tremendous real estate opportunities in the area. The vacant parcel evident in the forefront of this image would not be vacant for long.

Hammerstein's Victoria Theater, 1904

The enduring image of Times Square as "The Great White Way" locked into place during a relatively short period of time. Between 1899 and 1920, thirteen theaters were built on West 42nd Street, beginning with impresario Oscar Hammerstein I's theaters, the Victoria and the Republic, and including the most lavish of all, the legendary New Amsterdam, an elaborate Art Nouveau design constructed in 1903. Many more theaters were built on nearby streets, driven by fierce competition between the six-member Theatrical Syndicate, a trust owning numerous theaters, and independent producers, in particular the Shubert Brothers, who set out to challenge the Syndicate. Fashionable hotels such as the Astor, the Claridge, the Knickerbocker, and the Rossmore came soon after, as did elaborate roof gardens, racy cabarets, and fancy restaurants catering to upper-class patrons. Between 1893 and 1927, at least eighty-five theaters were constructed in an area from 38th to 63rd Streets between Sixth and Eighth Avenues before the Theater District consolidated around Times Square, which at its height—theatrical activity peaked during the 1927–28 season when 264 shows opened in the district—drew in sixty-eight theaters.

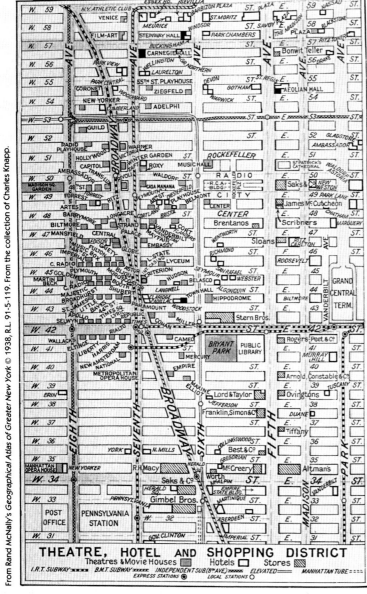

126

Map of the Theater District indicating theaters, hotels, and stores, 1938

During the first quarter of the twentieth century, the agglomeration of legitimate theaters and nightlife activity defined an entire district surrounding Times Square stretching north to 53rd Street from Broadway to Eighth Avenue. Commercial extravagance rather than aesthetic discipline set the prevailing tone for Times Square, and it was precisely this tone that gave the district its legendary distinctiveness, and, most importantly, national influence. Times Square became America's great central marketplace for commercial culture. As fashions in popular entertainment evolved over time, a succession of new businesses moved into Times Square: first film, then movies, vaudeville, cabaret, popular music—"Tin Pan Alley," as the industry was known—then radio. The scope and depth of the entertainment infrastructure centered in Times Square was vast, encompassing network radio producers and national print-news houses, dance studios, rehearsal halls, musical-instrument shops, costumers, theatrical agents, publicity brokers, and other ancillary show-business activities. The city's large and growing metropolitan market gave New York, and Times Square in particular, a commanding edge over other cities as the nation's entertainment center.

202:—42nd Street-Looking East from 6th Avenue, New York

**View east from Times Square
along 42nd Street, 1936**

Times Square's growth and prosperity as a national entertainment center were directly tied to the city's newly emergent Midtown business district, growing so rapidly that it would soon eclipse the city's historic business center in Lower Manhattan. Its development in the early part of the twentieth century took place at a time when, nationally, tourism was simultaneously expanding the market for entertainment and the drawing power of Times Square. For business-men and their entourages coming to New York, the buying trips, conventions, trade shows, or financial transactions provided the pretext for visiting, but they were not the sole reason for doing so. Rather, it was the combination of business contacts and personal pleasure that brought New York so many tourists. What tourists wanted was not always the uplifting art museums, historical monuments, and parks, but rather the satisfaction of good plays, enjoyable meals, rides about town, memorable views from observation decks, and live music and entertainment at nightclubs and roof gardens. All of that was avail-able in Times Square, and though the venues would change over the decades, few tourists would leave New York City without visiting it—the city's number one tourist destination.

Times Square parade commemorating the 300th anniversary of Broadway, 1926

As the central public place of New York City, Times Square has been a place of celebration, a place for parades, a place to announce big events to the world at large. In 1926 a parade through Times Square proudly marked the 300th anniversary of Broadway, the oldest north–south main thoroughfare in the city. Since parts of Broadway preceded the grid that the Commissioners' Plan of 1811 imposed on the island, it crosses midtown Manhattan diagonally, intersecting with both the east–west streets and north–south avenues. At Times Square, Broadway intersects with Seventh Avenue, and the crossing of streets creates a distinctive X-shaped open space, colloquially called a "square." The bowtie, five blocks running from West 43rd Street to West 47th Street, marks out two triangles: one, from the Times Tower at 43rd Street to 45th Street, and a second, from 45th to 47th Streets. Completing the bowtie at the northern end is Duffy Square, named for the bronze statue of Francis P. Duffy, a heroic World War I army chaplain of New York's "Fighting 69th" Infantry Regiment, who officiated at Holy Cross Church on the north side of 42nd Street just off Eighth Avenue. Duffy Square and the statue of Father Duffy were dedicated by Mayor Fiorello La Guardia on May 2, 1937. The statue of Duffy and the square itself were listed on the National Register of Historic Places in 2001.

hOTEL AſTOR *TIMEſ SQUARE* NEW YORK
At the Croſſroadſ of the world
F. A. muſchen heim

Astor Hotel, Times Square, c. 1940

The "bowtie" lays out a near-perfect visual landscape for commercial signage. The east–west width married with the north–south length of the X defines a visual framework for outdoor advertising display. Decade after decade, advertisers festooned the facades of buildings with promotional signs, their branded products marking eras of commercial cultural history. One of the earliest brands to bring its product to Times Square was Coca-Cola, in 1920; in 1923, neon lighting was added to bring a new dimension to the billboard. The neon sign, which measured 75 by 100 feet, flashed the message "Drink Coca-Cola, Delicious and Refreshing" to the public. It was the second-largest electric sign in the world at the time. Then in 1932, the Coca-Cola sign moved to the 47th street location evident in this postcard of Times Square at night. More prominent in this nighttime image is the Four Roses whiskey "spectacular." This branded advertisement, made up of 4,000 incandescent lights and thousands of feet of neon tubes, staged a display of two long-stemmed roses "growing" up the 100-foot sign frame above the Studebaker Building at 48th Street. Designed by the master maker of memorable signs, Douglas Leigh, the Four Roses spectacular debuted in 1938.

Times Square, early 1960s

In sharp contrast to the sleaze and socio-economic chaos of the times, this view of Times Square looks too clean and orderly. Figured in the center facing the Times Tower and looking southward is the statue of George M. Cohan, the multitalented American entertainer, playwright, composer, and lyricist who was known as the "man who owned Broadway" and the father of American musical comedy. His eight-foot bronze statue at 46th Street was dedicated in 1959. In the early 1960s, Times Square was entering a spiral of decay and decline. The grand picture palaces of Times Square were gone or disappearing, including the Roxy (1927, demolished in 1960) and the Paramount (1927, closed in 1964 and converted to office and retail use). The Hotel Astor (whose sign can be seen in the postcard above), the first important hotel in the square (1904), was closed and demolished in 1967. The Loew's State Theater (1921) (whose vertical neon sign can be seen on the left side of the postcard) hung on until 1987, when it was replaced with an office tower, now known as the Bertelsmann Building.

Times Square, early 1970s

Whatever else was happening (or not) in Times Square, the "bowtie" remained a commanding public space as well as a physical framework for giant signs. Just beneath the Castro Convertibles sign is the original "tkts" (pronounced phonetically as spelled-out "tee kay tee ess") discount-ticket booth operated by the Theater Development Fund. Inaugurated by Mayor John V. Lindsay in 1973, the pipe-and-canvas booth at West 47th Street was installed as a temporary structure. Working with a miniscule budget at a time when the city was experiencing great fiscal distress and was on the verge of bankruptcy, the architects Mayers & Schiff Associates cleverly developed a design plan based on renting, rather than buying, the pavilion's parts; ticket sales were conducted from a rented construction trailer. The "tkts" logo on a white canvas ribbon interwoven through the pipe armature around and on top of the construction trailer became an icon of the place, while the activity associated with the tkts discount-ticket booth helped keep Broadway ticket sales alive. The "temporary" structure lasted until 2008, when it was replaced with a new, decidedly upscale piece of functional public sculpture—a bright-red grand staircase rising sixteen feet to give visitors an equally grand view of public activity in Times Square—designed by Australian architects John Choi and Tai Rophia.

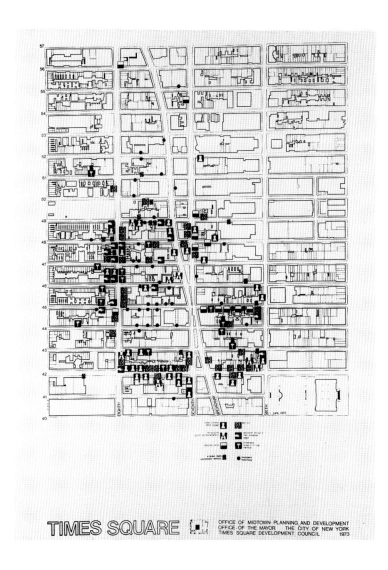

TIMES SQUARE

OFFICE OF MIDTOWN PLANNING AND DEVELOPMENT
OFFICE OF THE MAYOR   THE CITY OF NEW YORK
TIMES SQUARE DEVELOPMENT COUNCIL   1973

Midtown Vice Map, 1973

Vice Central was another name for Times Square. Massage parlors, spas, peep shows, live burlesque shows, adult book and video stores, theaters specializing in porn movies, and presumed prostitution, or "pross," hotels—it was all concentrated around Times Square, as shown in this 1973 map prepared by the Office of Midtown Planning and Development, which had been created by Mayor Lindsay to begin a cleanup of Times Square and vicinity. This world-known precinct of New York, the city's symbolic soul, was a civic embarrassment, and in moral terms, a cesspool of epic proportions in need of thorough sanitization. The perception of wide-spread decline and depravity was vast, yet not new. At the turn of the twentieth century, commercial sex seemed to define the Midtown area, and houses of prostitution were commonplace in Longacre Square. In 1901 "Soubrette Row," the moniker for the French-run bordellos of West 39th Street, had moved to West 43rd Street, an infamous block where almost every house was a brothel. Sex-related businesses were quite profitable, and in 1970, the pornography business in Midtown had just begun to locate its best customers—the vast population of office workers proximate to West 42nd Street, who on either side of the journey home were within striking distance of Times Square. The people count was huge, higher than that of Rockefeller Center: approximately 49,000 persons entered 42nd Street between Sixth Avenue and Eighth Avenue during the morning rush hours compared with about 12,000 at Rockefeller Center. By middle-class standards of behavior, the intensity of vice conditions, its associated crimes as well as loitering and street peddling on West 42nd Street provided a ready impetus for a cleanup. Plus, here was an immense desire on the part of city officials and cultural leaders to see the area brought back to its former greatness. By 1980 the city had taken charge and adopted a real estate strategy to clean up the infamous block—the "Deuce" in cultural argot; it joined forces with the state to redevelop West 42nd Street with "good" commercial uses to drive out the "bad."

42nd Street at Night, 1985

West 42nd Street was once a movie haven, a "Movie-Goers' Mecca." With ten of its fourteen movie theaters showing first-run releases of general and action-adventure movies at low prices several times a day, it was a unique movie entertainment center for the city, drawing audiences from all five boroughs. Movies appeared on West 42nd Street in the 1930s, replacing legitimate theater as the social and economic power of that "class entertainment" had begun to fade. Movies occupied an economic niche between audiences for whom theater was too expensive, vaudeville too crude, and nickelodeons too dark, dirty, and cheap. However, the theaters on West 42nd Street lacked the size and splendor of the many new movie places being built on or near Broadway, and carved out a niche featuring "grinders," reruns of older movies emphasizing action and violence that appealed to a male rather than a female audience. Throughout the 1970s and 1980s, mixed messages sallied forth from marquees advertising constantly changing fare: mainstream Hollywood— *Fifth of July, Gremlins, License to Kill, Of Human Bondage;* action fare and martial arts—*Buried Alive, Borderline, Kung Fu;* sexploitation—*Hot Saddle Tramp, Ginger's Wet Dreams, Scent of Sex, Ultimate Sensation.* These movie houses became symbolic of West 42nd Street's decay. Consequently, movie use was omitted from the initial redevelopment plan for the area and only later, gradually and in a limited way, sanctioned as a permitted use.

Lou Stoumen, *West 42nd Street as Male Turf*, 1981

The world of 42nd Street was a place definitively marked "male turf," a world of sex shops, action movies, and retail stores that catered to primarily male taste. The street's sexist and pornographic visual imagery provided a prime field site for the 1970s activist group Women Against Pornography, which offered twice-weekly bus tours of the street. The social behavior of the place so vividly portrayed in John Schlesinger's Academy-Award winning film *Midnight Cowboy* (1969), a then-shocking tale of the dark side of the street's squalid subculture, not only offended middle-class sensibilities, but also offered up a powerful and sad indictment of urban depravity.

In confronting the problems of Times Square, by 1980, city officials had come to the conclusion that they were dealing with an intractable situation where the prescriptive solution had to change public perception as well as reality. The danger and morally repulsive aspects had to disappear, and the place had to be transformed, made safe and attractive for the middle class as a center for office work as well as for entertainment.

The failure of earlier approaches— policing and law enforcement, pedestrian malls, streetscape improvements—created the context for the 180-degree shift in city policy: the decision to exercise its powers of eminent domain to sanitize the area through almost wholesale clearance. This was the first time New York City had used condemnation for a commercial project, and it did so after concluding that in this particular instance private development was not going to lead redevelopment on its own on West 42nd Street.

Irving Browning, *Times Square at Night*, 1923

The dramatic excitement and syncopated dazzle of Times Square has been expressed in the blaze of lights affixed to marquees, theater signs, billboard advertisements, and promotional displays. The magic and lushness of city lights, an ancient symbol of the contrast between city life and rural areas, seemed to know no bounds in Times Square. They were blazing, multicolored, animated, fantastic—always a spectacle. For good reason, the lights of Times Square bestowed upon it the enduring image as "The Great White Way."

Sky signs, as roof-top billboards were first called, were viewed as a terrible blight, visual pollution on the public environment by city elitists who advocated for legislation to ban them by controlling their height (willfully violated, unenforced by the city, overturned by state courts which declared signage to be an aesthetic concern), by getting them taxed (politically dead-ended), and by shaming advertisers, who proved to be virtually shameless.

In 1918 the New York City Zoning Commission finally ruled that billboards were a "nonconforming" use in residential districts. The self-interest of other groups, in particular the Fifth Avenue Association, which feared that electric signs would spill out of Times Square where they had been allowed under the city's new zoning ordinance of 1916, succeeded in 1922 in getting the city's Board of Aldermen to pass a law banning all "projecting and illuminating" signs on Fifth Avenue between Washington Square and 110th Street. Tight controls on signs everywhere around Times Square had the effect of intensifying the glitter and concentrating it in that one sanctioned area, where signage flourished. The effect solidified the image of Times Square as a place of popular culture, bright lights, and the messy vitality of commercial culture.

Camel cigarettes sign in Times Square, c. 1942

Spectacular billboards put up by national advertisers, like the Camel sign designed by Douglas Leigh, hold an enduring place in the glorious history of signage in Times Square. One of the most photographed and memorable images of Times Square, the Camel Man blew the illusion of a giant smoke ring every four seconds around the clock for decades from a billboard mounted on the Claridge Hotel on Broadway between 43rd and 44th Streets. During World War II, the image switched from soldiers to sailors to airmen, but the puffing never stopped until the hotel, which served as a location for the film *Midnight Cowboy* and as a background for Woody Allen's film *Radio Days*, was replaced by an office building and movie theater in 1972. As a barometer of commercial culture, however, signage in Times Square not so long ago sadly registered its urban malaise. Throughout most of the 1970s, the most memorable skyward visions of Times Square chronicled by the area's photographers singled out images of vacant spaces adjacent to demolished spectaculars, including the Camel sign, and "for rent" signs on what had been since the 1920s a jungle of billboards along Broadway. The national energy crisis of 1973 dampened the commercial logic of exuberant advertising spectaculars by making them appear wasteful, but even earlier the dazzle had disappeared as sex became the square's best-known industry. The city's mid-1970s fiscal crisis further exacerbated the downward trajectory. The lights went out as advertisers canceled their displays, leaving the billboards blank.

**Charles M. Weiss, *Times Square Relit
by Japanese firms*, 1985**

The deeply depressed urban condition that gripped Times Square in the 1970s was but a metaphor for a wider retreat from cities taking place across the nation. The myopia of the situation was peculiarly American. It had an analogue, however, in the domestic tunnel vision obscuring the latent power of Times Square as an advertising venue, despite the decay and decrepitude that prevailed during that time. Japanese consumer-product manufacturers knew the tourist appeal of the place; they understood better than any other group of brand merchandisers the transportability of the icon's branded location and they pioneered a re-lighting of the place. Sony came first, in 1965; in the 1970s, Canon, JVC, Midori, Panasonic, and Suntory broke the darkness of Times Square with large, bright neon super-signs full of animation. More came in the early 1980s, and most of the district's

signs advertised Japanese products. The proliferation of Japanese advertisers during this period involved more than just prescient advertising logic, however.

The Japanese corporate executives behind these decisions shared similar career paths and a nostalgic attachment to Manhattan from their experiences in the city during the 1950s, when they had whiled away many an evening in Times Square. To many of them, to be in Times Square represented success—a statement of having become a company that could have such a sign in "the center of the world." There was pride and prestige in just being able to be there. That the square was physically in decline did not seem to weaken the motive: the image of the place looked fine at night when the signs were lit, and, seen on television, the signs were way above the grit and decay on the streets below.

Prototypical block of Broadway between 46th and 47th Streets demonstrating municipal regulations intended to promote commercial signage, 2001

After much controversy over the initial plan for the redevelopment of Times Square at 42nd Street, the Department of City Planning was tasked with developing an urban design plan to maintain the visual character of Time Square in the bow-tie area as new development occurred. The staff needed to identify those elements that gave Times Square its special character and translate them into technical standards, and then draft regulations that once approved would become a part of the city's zoning law. This would be something of a balancing act since these regulations would have to resolve the conflict between the city's efforts to stimulate westward expansion of the high-rent corporate-style office buildings of Midtown yet protect the Times Square theater economy and legacy. They would need to ensure the district's identity as a flashy and flamboyant, electrically charged entertainment center. The act of legislating for chaotic, rambunctious diversity—gaudy bad taste to some— was counterintuitive, and certainly ironic, as an objective of city planning. And the truly vexing issue was how to mandate diversity by legislation in an environment that had evolved through the spontaneous actions of competitors trying to outshine one another. The planners identified "prototypical" blocks characteristic of Times Square and used them as a template for developing closely matching design controls that could function as as-of-right zoning regulations applicable to all future development. Packed into eight dense pages of zoning text, the special Times Square signage and urban design requirements were specific and inclusive. To clarify the requirements for illumination, staff had to invent a measurement system known as "Light Unit Times Square" (LUTS), though a more ironic name for the regulatory light measure might have been LUST. The inventions embedded in these regulations for signage were groundbreaking.

42nd Street Renewed, 2001

By 1997 West 42nd Street was morphing into a ribbon of popular entertainment venues capitalized by the biggest corporate names in business: Disney, Warner Brothers, Sony, AMC, Madame Tussaud's, SFX, Entertainment, MTC Networks, and ABC's "Good Morning America." Real estate values had skyrocketed. Economic pressures had ignited changes in land use on seedy Eighth Avenue, and in the aged Garment District. The street that *Rolling Stone* magazine in 1981 called the "sleaziest block in America" was now a family-entertainment venue, complete with a children's theater, The New Victory.

The transformation had even become a model for other cities. The entertainment focus of the new 42nd Street came only after a rescripting of the redevelopment plan for the street begun in mid-1991, in the depths of a real estate recession. By that time, the original plan for the redevelopment of the street could have been reasonably considered a "great planning disaster," and as planners cast about for a way to rescue the failing project, they resorted to its cultural origins. The original cleanup plan sought to make the street safe for corporate investment by eliminating the deviant subculture of Times Square. In the second plan, the public sector was promoting a new set of values representative of its antithesis in program and design. It was a radical shift in planning vision for a high-profile project. This second chance was a rare event—and a great success.

**The Disney Corporation's presence
on 42nd Street and Seventh Avenue,
1998**

The Walt Disney Company's decision in 1993 to come to 42nd Street and renovate the legendary New Amsterdam Theater created a strong momentum for the entertainment-focused plan for "The Deuce." Disney had been on a strategic quest in search of a Broadway platform for launching its new live-theatrical production worldwide, and there was no better place than Times Square. For eager public officials, the media giant's commitment to 42nd Street symbolized something beyond a marquee tenancy: it conferred middle-class respectability on the street and this triggered intense corporate interest from competing brand-oriented entertainment retailers seeking a similarly visible geographic identity for mass distribution. The pattern of what attracted business to West 42nd Street was not new, only the players. The undisciplined, messy, and chaotic urban environment stood in stark contrast to the type of controlled environment corporate executives were used to dealing with in selling the Disney brand; indeed, just across Eighth Avenue is the Port Authority Bus Terminal, a point of entry for some 180,000 daily commuters. In time, company executives came to realize that they could not control the guest experience; from Disney's perspective, it could only start inside the theater.

Times Square transformed, 2001

Inside the physical shell that marked the transformation of Times Square lay an economic transformation: a localized concentration of jobs in the creative fields of media and entertainment built upon the district's legacy to the nation of network radio broadcasting, Broadway theater production, Hollywood-movie distribution, and the image-brokering business of public relations. That is what contributed to the new crackling energy of Times Square.

The almost combustible social and economic diversity of the place, so different from other city districts where greater visual order and economic or residential homogeneity prevail, is what ultimately would mark the true iconic legacy and unchanged reality of Times Square. Times Square in the twenty-first century remains an irregularity, no doubt part of its appeal to the many who come to New York and must experience the place. It is still a public place, a very public place—a place where demonstrations take place, where hundreds of thousands come to celebrate New Year's Eve, where congestion signals success. It is the quintessential urban place, not really predicable, however cleaned up it looks, however benign its latest activities.

Laying the Groundwork

1. Frances Milton Trollope, *Domestic Manners of the Americans* (London: Whittaker, Treacher & Co., 1832), 227.

2. Henry Hudson's first mate, as quoted in Russell Shorto, "The Accidental Legacy of Henry Hudson" in Geert Mak and Russell Shorto, *1609: The Forgotten History of Hudson, Amsterdam and New York* (New York: Henry Hudson Foundation, 2009), 45.

3. Three years later, the city's first brickyard opened, leading to Stuyvesant's legacy as the man who "found New York City a wood town and left it a brick one."

4. Edwin G. Burrows and Mike Wallace, *Gotham: A History of New York City to 1898* (New York: Oxford University Press, 1999), 188.

5. Michel Guillaume de Crèvecocur, Lettres d'un Cultivateur, Américain, écrites à W.S., écuyer depuis l'Année 1770, jusqu'à 1781 (2 vols., 1784), as published in *Magazine of American History*, 2 (1878), 749; as quoted in Bayrd Still, *Mirror for Gotham: New York as Seen by Contemporaries from Dutch Days to the Present* (New York: New York University Press, 1956), 16.

6. [Anon.], "Journal of an Irishman at the Close of the American Revolution," as quoted in Still, *Mirror for Gotham*, 43.

The Formative Years

1. Ed Glaeser, "Reflection" in Hilary Ballon, ed., *The Greatest Grid: The Master Plan of Manhattan 1811–2011* (New York: Museum of the City of New York and Columbia University Press, 2011), 209.

2. Joseph François Mangin to Common Council, December 17, 1798, manuscript letter, New York City Municipal Archives, as quoted in Gerard Koeppel, *City on a Grid: How New York Became New York* (Boston: Da Capo, 2015), 373.

3. It is far from clear how innovative the grid plan actually was, with some historians arguing that it was more a resuscitation of an earlier plan by Cassimir T. H. Goerck than an original idea. For further discussion, see Koeppel, *City on a Grid*.

4. Gouverneur Morris, Simeon DeWitt, and John Rutherford, "Remarks of Commissioners for Laying Out Streets and Roads in the City of New York, under the Act of April 3, 1807," as quoted in Marguerite Holloway, *The Measure of Manhattan: The Tumultuous Career and Surprising Legacy of John Randell, Jr., Cartographer, Surveyor, Inventor* (New York: W. W. Norton, 2013), 151.

5. Ballon, *The Greatest Grid*, 87.

6. The fire dealt a fierce blow to the burgeoning insurance industry in New York, which had grown rapidly on the back of expanding maritime trade volumes in the decades after the Revolutionary War.

Twenty-three of the twenty-six insurance companies in New York went bankrupt as a result of the losses incurred in the 1835 fire, setting the stage for the growth of the insurance industry 120 miles to the northeast in Hartford, Connecticut.

7. The Manhattan Water Company was also permitted to use excess funds for banking, a business that would prove far more lucrative and lead to the growth of the Bank of Manhattan, which would later merge with the Chase National Bank to become the Chase Manhattan Bank.

8. *Frank Leslie's Illustrated Newspaper* (August 16, 1873): 363, as quoted in Tyler Anbinder, *Five Points: The Nineteenth-Century New York City Neighborhood that Invented Tap Dance, Stole Elections, and Became the World's Most Notorious Slum* (New York: Free Press, 2001), 1.

9. Burrows and Wallace, *Gotham*, 794.

10. Frederick Law Olmsted as quoted in Burrows and Wallace, *Gotham*, 794.

The Rise of the Apartment

1. Moses King, *King's Handbook of New York City: An Outline History and Description of the American Metropolis* (Boston, Mass.: Moses King, 1892), 242–43.

2. For extensive discussions of a broad spectrum of housing types from the 1860s through the 1890s, with particular attention to the apartment building type, see Robert A.M. Stern, Thomas Mellins, and David Fishman, *New York 1880: Architecture and Urbanism in the Gilded Age* (New York: Monacelli Press, 1999), 494–568.

3. Jacob A. Riis, *How the Other Half Lives: Studies among the Tenements of New York* (New York: Charles Scribner's Sons, 1890).

Moving the People

1. E. B. White, "Here is New York," *Holiday* 5 (April 1949): 36.

2. John H. White Jr., *Horse Cars, Cable Cars and Omnibuses* (New York: Dover, 1974), vi.

3. *New York Herald* (October 2, 1864), as quoted in Clifton Hood, *722 Miles: The Building of the Subways and How They Transformed New York* (New York: Simon & Schuster, 1993), 42.

4. In 1883, as a member of the New York State Assembly, Theodore Roosevelt introduced a bill to cap elevated railway fares at five cents.

5. King, *King's Handbook of New York City*, 138.

6. "Gould Is Grabbing Again," *New York Times* (October 27, 1892): 9.

7. Benson Bobrick, *Labyrinths of Iron: Subways in History, Myth, Art, Technology, and War* (New York: Quill, 1986), 210.

8. Kyle Kirschling, *An Economic Analysis of Rapid Transit in New York: 187--2010*, https://clio.columbia.edu.catalog/20811368, acquired May 22, 2014.

The Evolution of the Skyscraper

1. Cass Gilbert, "The Financial Importance of Rapid Building," *Engineering Record* 41 (June 30, 1900): 624.

2. Montgomery Schuyler, "The Field of Art: The Skyscraper Problem," *Scribner's Magazine* 34 (July 1, 1903): 253.

3. Ada Louise Huxtable, *The Tall Building Artistically Reconsidered: The Search for a Skyscraper Style* (New York: Pantheon, 1982), 23.

4. George Warrington Steevens as quoted in Schuyler, "The Skyscraper Problem": 255.

5. The Woolworth Company retained an office in the Woolworth Building until selling the structure in 1998.

6. Cass Gilbert as quoted in "The Woolworth Building, Most Modern Example of the Fireproof Skyscraper . . . How It Was Built," in *The Real Estate Magazine* 2 (July 1912): 56.

7. Paul Goldberger, *The Skyscraper* (New York: Knopf, 1982), 44.

8. See Carol Willis, *Form Follows Finance: Skyscrapers and Skylines in New York and Chicago* (New York: Princeton Architectural Press, 1995), 9.

9. Willis, *Form Follows Finance*, 68.

10. Edward M. Bassett, *Zoning: The Laws, Administration, and Court Decisions during the First Twenty Years* (New York: Russell Sage Foundation, 1940), 24–25.

Housing the People

1. Fiorello LaGuardia, radio broadcast, WNYC, October 1938.

2. Constitution of the State of New York Article XVIII, Social Welfare, adopted by the Constitutional Convention of 1938 and approved by a vote of the people, November 8, 1938; see https://www.dos.ny.gov/constitution.htm.

3. Fiorello LaGuardia, as quoted in "Housing," *Survey* 72 (June 1936): 25.

The Making of Midtown

1. Sheldon Cheney, *The New World Architecture* (London: Longmans, Green, 1930), 120

2. Goldberger, *The Skyscraper,* 98–99.

3. In 1920, during a severe post–World War I housing shortage, New York State enacted Emergency Rent Laws, granting state courts power to review the "reasonableness" of rent increases. The laws expired in 1929. In 1943, during World War II, with housing once again in short supply, the state reinstituted rent regulation.

Urban Renewal

1. Robert Moses, public statement, 1974, as quoted by Paul Goldberger, "Robert Moses, Master Builder, Is Dead at 92," *New York Times* (July 30, 1981): 1, B18–19.

2. Jane Jacobs, interview by Eve Auchincloss and Nancy Lynch, *Mademoiselle* (October 1962), as quoted in Jane Jacobs, *The Last Interview and Other Conversations* (Brooklyn: Melville House, 2016).

3. Jane Jacobs, *The Death and Life of Great American Cities* (New York: Random House, 1961).

4. Philharmonic Hall was reamed Avery Fisher Hall in 1973, which was in turn renamed David Geffen Hall in 2015.

5. Sociologist Marshall Berman placed Robert Moses's highway projects within a broad social and political context. For his assessment of the defeat of the Lower Manhattan Expressway and the subsequent development of SoHo, see Marshall Berman, *All That Is Solid Melts into Air* (New York: Simon and Schuster, 1982), 337–38.

Plunz Portfolio

AUTHOR'S NOTE: Some aspects of this essay were first explored in 1994 with Columbia Urban Design Student Mica Thanner (MSAUD '94). Mica was a joint degree candidate with Urban Planning, and I served as advisor for his dissertation on *Lincoln Square: The Dramatic Transformation of a Neighborhood*. I much admired Mica's passion and diligence as we worked closely in defining much of what now, after a long hiatus, whose efforts have been essential to its completion.

1. From Bob Dylan lyrics written for "Committee to Stop the Lower Manhattan Expressway." Resistance to the project and Bob Dylan's role is described in Anthony Flint, *Wrestling with Moses: How Jane Jacobs Took on New York's Master Builder and Transformed the American City* (New York: Random House), 2009. See also Ben Yakas, "Did Bob Dylan Write A Protest Song About Robert Moses?" *The Gothamist*, published June 26, 2015, accessed December 7, 2015, available at: http://gothamist.com/2015/06/26/bob_dylan_robert_moses.php. Original is in "Joint Committee to Stop Lower Manhattan Expressway," 1964–1965; Greenwich House Records; TAM 139; Box 106; Folder 5; Tamiment Library/Robert F. Wagner Labor Archives, Elmer Holmes Bobst Library, New York University Libraries.

2. "66% in City Area Moved in 1950's," *New York Times,* July 28, 1962, 21, accessed December 4, 2015.

3. Robert A. Caro, *The Power Broker: Robert Moses and the Fall of New York* (New York: Alfred A. Knopf, 1974), 849.

4. An estimate given in Michael Powell, "A Tale of Two Cities," *New York Times,* May 6, 2007. Of late, historical revisionism has revisited the Moses legacy, and especially the monumental and critical Moses biography. What remains least explored are the long-term effects of cultural displacement.

5. Berman, *All That Is Solid Melts into Air: The Experience of Modernity,"* 290–312.

6. William Shakespeare, Romeo and Juliet : West Side Story / Book by Arthur Laurents; Music by Leonard Bernstein ; Lyrics by Stephen Sondheim ; Introduction by Norris Houghton; Notes by John Bettenbender (New York: Dell, 1965).

7. City of New York, Committee on Slum Clearance, *Preliminary Report Lincoln Square Project* (New York, July 20, 1956), 13.

8. Samuel Zipp, *Manhattan Projects: The Rise and Fall of Urban Renewal in New York* (New York: Oxford University Press, 2010), chapter 4.

9. Dan Sullivan, "Theatre: Jets vs. Sharks," *New York Times*, 1968, web. Also see Zipp, *Manhattan Projects*, 247–49.

10. Julie Bloom, "Rekindling Robbins, a Step at a Time," *New York Times*, March 4, 2009, web.

11. Marcy Sacks, *Before Harlem: The Black Experience in New York City before World War I* (Philadelphia: University of Pennsylvania, 2006), 76.

12. Sacks, 81–83.

13. Community Council of Greater New York Research Bureau, *Population of Puerto Rican Birth or Parentage, New York City, 1950; Data for Boroughs, Health Areas, and Census Tracts* (New York, 1952), table 3-C.

14. Michael Thanner. *Lincoln Square. The Dramatic Transformation of a Neighborhood.* Columbia University, 1994. Print. M.S. Thesis. Avery Classics. 16–17.

15. Richard Plunz, Michael Sheridan, and Alexander Garvin, "Deadlock Plus 50: On Public Housing in New York," *Urban Planning Today: A Harvard Design Magazine Reader,* vol. 3 (Minneapolis: University of Minnesota Press, 2006), chapter 2.

16. Richard Plunz, *A History of Housing in New York City. Dwelling Type and Social Change in the American Metropolis.* (New York: Columbia University Press, 1990), 291–92.

17. William Zeckendorf with Edward McCreary, *The Autobiography of William Zeckendorf* (New York: Holt, Rinehart and Winston, 1970), 238.

18. Edgar B, Young, *Lincoln Center, the Building of an Institution* (New York: New York University Press, 1980), 45.

19. Victoria Newhouse, *Wallace K. Harrison, Architect* (New York: Rizzoli, 1989), 251.

20. *The Neighborhood That Disappeared*, directed by Mary Paley and John Romeo (Albany, NY: Omikronicles, 2014), DVD; *Echoes From The Neighborhood That Disappeared*, directed by Mary Paley and John Russell Cring (Albany, NY: Omnikronicles, 2015), DVD.

21. Louis Wirth, "Urbanism as a Way of Life," *American Journal of Sociology*, 44, no. 1 (1938): 1–24, http://www.jstor.org/stable/2768119.

22. Charles Grutzner, "Stevens Expands Lincoln Sq. Plans," *New York Times*, October 27, 1956, 15, web, accessed December 11, 2015.

23. New York Department of City Planning, *Transcript of Public Hearing before the City Planning Commission, September 11, 1957, in the Matter of the Lincoln Square Urban Renewal Plan and Project* (New York, 1957), 102.

24. Robert Moses, *Public Works: A Dangerous Trade* (New York: McGraw-Hill, 1970), 529.

25. David Gottehrer, ed., *New York City in Crisis [a Study in Depth of Urban Sickness] Prepared by the New York Herald Tribune Staff under the Direction of Barry Gottehrer* (New York: D. McKay, 1965) 108–9.

26. Newhouse, *Wallace K. Harrison*, 36–38, 105–106, 200, 204.

27. Andrew Cusack, "Boullée's Opera," January 9, 2008, accessed January 13, 2016, http://www.andrewcusack.com/2008/etienne-louis-boullee-opera.

28. "Symbol of U.S. Culture—An Estimate of Stimulus of the Arts That Is Inherent in Lincoln Center," *New York Times*, July 23 1956; Joel Schwartz, *The New York Approach: Robert Moses, Urban Liberals, and Redevelopment of the Inner City* (Columbus: Ohio State University Press, 1993).

29. Howard Taubman, "New Cultural Vista for the City," *New York Times*, April 22, 1956, vi:76.

30. Martin Duberman, *The Worlds of Lincoln Kirstein* (New York: Alfred A. Knopf, 2007), 521.

31. Caro, *The Power Broker*, 1014.

32. Zeckendorf, *The Autobiography of William Zeckendorf*, 238.

33. Linda Ocasio, *Welcome to Amsterdam Houses* (Teaneck, NJ: The Author, 2007).

34. David W. Dunlap, "1959–75 | The Rise and Fall of the West (Side)," *New York Times*, August 27, 2015, accessed January 14, 2016, http://www.nytimes.com/2015/08/28/insider/1959-75-the-rise-and-fall-of-the-west-side.html.

35. The politics surrounding the destruction of the Met have been variously described. See Gregory Gilmartin, *Shaping the City: New York and the Municipal Art Society* (New York: Clarkson Potter, 1995), 377–78.

36. Michael Whitney Straight, *Nancy Hanks: An Intimate Portrait: The Creation of a National Commitment to the Arts* (Durham, NC: Duke University Press, 1988), 77.

37. Theodore Strongin, "Wreckers Begin Demolishing Met," *New York Times*, January 18, 1967.

38. Nathan Silver, *Lost New York* (New York: Weathervane Books, 1967), 226–27.

39. The evolution of the plaza design is summarized in Robert A. M. Stern, Thomas Mellins, and David Fishman, *New York 1960: Architecture and Urbanism between the Second World War and the Bicentennial* (New York: Monacelli Press, 1995), 710–13.

40. Brendan Gill, "The Skyline," *New Yorker*, August 19, 1991, accessed November 25, 2015, http://archives.newyorker.com/?i=1991-08-19#folio=054.

41. Plunz, *A History of Housing in New York City*, 41, 103, 106, 118.

42. The struggle with acoustics and renaming was well-documented by Gill, "The Skyline," August 19, 1991.

43. Edgar B. Young, *Lincoln Center, the Building of an Institution* (New York: New York University Press, 1980), 46; 48.

44. Robert Curvin and Bruce Porter, *Blackout Looting. New York City, July 13, 1977* (New York City: Gardner, 1979). Also see Pete Hammill, "Cursing the Darkness in the Blackout of 1977," *New York Daily News*, originally published in print July 15, 1977, published on web July 12, 2015, accessed October 20, 2015, http://www.nydailynews.com/opinion/pete-hamill-cursing-darkness-blackout-1977-article-1.2284199

45. Caro, *The Power Broker*, 1024.

46. New York Committee on Slum Clearance, *Riverside-Amsterdam, Manhattan; Slum Clearance Plan under Title I of the Housing Act of 1949 as Amended. [Report to Mayor Wagner and the Board of Estimate]* (New York, 1958).

47. Jen Rubin, "Weekend History: How One Store Fought to Survive the Blackout and Looting of '77," *West Side Rag*, April 14, 2014, accessed October 29, 2015, http://www.westsiderag.com/2014/04/05/uws-history-how-one-store-fought-to-survive-the-blackout-and-looting-of-77.

48. All three struggles are well described in Flint, *Wrestling with Moses*, 2009.

49. In 1965, toward the end of this odyssey, Moses produced a chronology of the many attempts to realize his project. See *Lower Manhattan Elevated Expressway* (New York: Triborough Bridge and Tunnel Authority, 1965).

50. New York City Department of City Planning, *SoHo/NoHo Occupancy Survey (1983)* (New York City: Department of City Planning, May 1985), 31, 35.

51. A gallery plan is published in Kaisa Broner's *New York Face à Son Patrimoine: Préservation Du Patrimoine Architectural Urbain à New York, Analyse de la Méthodologie, Étude de cas sur le Secteur Historique De SoHo* (Brussels: Pierre Mardaga, 1986), 212. For Soho development also see: James R. Hudson, *The Unanticipated City: Loft Conversions in Lower Manhattan* (Amherst: U of Massachusetts, 1987). Also see: Sharon Zukin, *Loft Living: Culture and Capital in Urban Change* (Baltimore. Johns Hopkins University Press, 1982).

Remaking Lower Manhattan

1. New York City Council, Legislative Panel on Waterfront Development, *The Future of New York City's Waterfront* (New York, 1989), 3.

2. Angus Gillespie, *Twin Towers: The Life of New York City's World Trade Center* (New Brunswick, N.J.: Rutgers University Press, 1999), 33.

3. Austin J. Tobin, "The World Trade Center: Symbol of Future Leadership," *Westsider* 29 (1964): 86.

4. "The opposition to the World Trade Center . . . stems from all the major builders of New York City," noted Robert Kopple, executive director of the opposition group known as the Committee for a Reasonable World Trade Center in the the spring of 1964. See Clayton Knowles, "All Major Builders Are Said to Oppose World Trade Center," *New York Times* (March 9, 1964): 31.

5. Ada Louise Huxtable, "Who's Afraid of the Big, Bad Buildings?" *New York Times* (May 29, 1966): 14.

6. Paul Goldberger, "Battery Park City Is a Triumph of Urban Design, *New York Times* (August 31, 1986), II: 23.

Remaking Times Square

1. Tim Tompkins as quoted by Charles V. Bagli, "After Thirty Years, Times Square Rebirth Is Complete," *New York Times* (December 3, 2010): A17.

2. The plan, initiated by Fred Pappert, was known as the City@42nd Street. Mayor Koch was quick to condemn the plan, which he likened to Disneyland.

3. In 1989 Philip Johnson and John Burgee Architects issued a revised design calling for a group of buildings, each distinctly different from each other, with some incorporating large swathes of colorful illuminated signage. This iteration, also widely criticized in both the architectural and general press, languished as well.

4. One site was developed by Rudin Management, one by the Durst Organization, and two by Boston Properties.

Abbreviations

SBDOYL — Seymour B. Durst Old York Library Collection, Avery Architectural & Fine Arts Library, Columbia University

SBDOYL, CPC — Seymour B. Durst Old York Library collection of postcards, Avery Architectural & Fine Arts Library, Columbia University

SBDOYL, PLC — The Seymour B. Durst Old York Library Photograph and Lithograph Collection, ca. 1850s–1980s. Avery Architectural & Fine Arts Library, Columbia University

Laying the Groundwork

22. *Book of New York* (New York: Priv. print. for American Bankers Association, 1922), cover. The Seymour B. Durst Old York Library Collection, Avery Architectural & Fine Arts Library, Columbia University F128.3 B86

23. *Book of New York*. The "Hartgers View" of New York (above); New York, 1922 (below). SBDOYL F128.3 B86

24. New York in the Beginning. The Southern Point. The Seymour B. Durst Old York Library Photograph and Lithograph Collection, c. 1850s–1980s. Avery Architectural & Fine Arts Library, Columbia University. Lithographs-Valentine's Views, Box 37, Album 1

25 top. View of the "Graft," or Canal, in Broad Street, and the Fish Bridge, 1659. Julia B. Colton, *Annals of Old Manhattan, 1609–1694* (New York: Brentano's, 1901), illustration facing page 142. SBDOYL F128.4 C72

25 bottom. Governor Stuyvesant's house, erected 1658, afterwards called "The Whitehall." Colton, *Annals of Old Manhattan, 1609–1694*), illustration facing page 211. SBDOYL F128.4 C72

26 top. The West India Company's House, Haarlemmer Straat, Amsterdam, 1623–1647. Thomas A. Janvier, *The Dutch Founding of New York* (New York: Harper & Brothers, 1903), illustration facing p. 30. SBDOYL F122.1 J34

26 bottom. The Town House (Stadt Huys), New York, 1670. Colton, *Annals of Old Manhattan, 1609–1694* illustration facing page 96. SBDOYL F122.1 J34

27. The Jansson-Visscher Map, with a view of New Amsterdam drawn before the year 1653. SBDOYL F122.1 J34

28. The Duke's Plan, 1664. Janvier, *The Dutch Founding of New York*, illustration facing p. 188. SBDOYL F122.1 J34

29. Attributed to Carel Allard (c. 1648–1709) *Totius Neobelgii Nova et*

Accuratissima Tabula Restituto view, c. 1700). Museum of the City of New York 29.100.2199

30. The Blockhouse and City Gate (Foot of the present Wall Street). Colton, *Annals of Old Manhattan, 1609–1694*, illustration facing page 220. SBDOYL F128.4 C72

31. No.1 Residence of Jacob Leisler on the Strand (now Whitehall Street, N.Y.). The First Brick Dwelling Erected in the City. SBDOYL, PLC. Lithographs-Valentine's Views Box 37, Album 1,

32. George Hayward, *The Ferry House*, 1746. SBDOYL, PLC Lithographs-Valentine's Views Box 36, Folder 9

33. George Hayward, *View of Harlaem from Morisania in the Province of New York*, September 1765. Lithographs-Valentine's Views Box 36.1, folder 4. SBDOYL, PLC. Lithographs-Valentine's Views Box 37, Album 1.

34. Plan of the City of New York, 1767. Henry Collins Brown, *Fifth Avenue Old and New* (New York: Fifth Avenue Association, 1924), 16. SBDOYL AA735 N4 B81

35. The Ratzer Map of New York City, 1767 (New York?: Longmans, Green, 18--?). SBDOYL AA735 N4 R195

36. Burns's Coffee-House in 1765. SBDOYL, PLC. Lithographs-Valentine's Views; Box 36.1, Folder 6

37. *Représentation du Feu Terrible à Nouvelle Yorck*. Engraving (hand-colored) by André Basset [1776?] Courtesy of the Library of Congress. Prints and Photographs Division

38. View of the Inauguration of Washington as seen from Broad Street. SBDOYL,PLC. Lithographs-Valentine's Views Box 37, Album 1

39. "It was a warm bright summer morning that these two that these two political chieftans stood before each other prepared for mortal combat." [Duel of Aaron Burr and Alexander Hamilton, July 11, 1804, in Hoboken, N.J.] Martha J. Lamb, *History of the City of New York, Its Origin, Rise and Progress* (New York: A.S. Barnes, 1877–96), 492. SBDOYL F128.47 H31 1896

40–41. Charles Balthazar Julien Févret de Saint-Mémin, *A View of the City of New-York from Brooklyn Heights, foot of Pierrepont St. in 1798* (New York, 1861?). SBDOYL F128.37 S25 1861g FFF

The Formative Years

50–51. This map of the city of New York and island of Manhattan, as laid out by the commissioners appointed by the legislature, April 3d, 1807 is respectfully dedicated to the mayor, aldermen and commonalty thereof by their most obedient servant Wm. Bridges, city surveyor; engraved by P. Maverick (New York, 1811). SBDOYL AA735 N4Q3 B76 FFF

52–53. Samuel Marks, A new map of the City of New York: comprising all the late improvements, compiled and corrected from authentic documents, designed to accompany the Description of New York (New York: S. Marks, 1827). SBDOYL AA735 N4 M3196 F

54–55. Charles Magnus, New-York city & county map: with vicinity entire, Brooklyn, Williamsburgh, Jersey City & c. in the 79th year of the independence of the United States. (New York: Charles Magnus, 1855?). SBDOYL AA735 N4 M265 F

57. David H. Burr, Map of the country twenty-five miles round the city of New-York. (New York: David H. Burr, 1831) SBDOYL AA735 N4 B945 F

58. Fulton Street [Collect Pond to Fulton Street] Page from J. Clarence Davies scrapbook/Museum of the City of New York. X2012.61.15.48

59. W. H. Bartlett, The Park and City Hall, New York [New York, 184_?]. SBDOYL AA735 N4 B275

60. Northwest corner of Fulton Street and Broadway, 1829 [New York, 18__?]. SBDOYL AA735 N4 N815 S

61. City Hotel, Trinity & Grace Churches, Broadway. Archibald L. Dick, City Hotel, Trinity & Grace Churches, Broadway: Broadway; drawn & engraved on steel by A. Dick; printed by J. & G. Neal (New York: Peabody & C., 1831). SBDOYL AA735 N4 D55 S

62–63. Hydrographic map of the counties of New-York, Westchester and Putnam: and also showing the line of the Croton Aqueduct. T. Schramke, Description of the New-York Croton Aqueduct (New York and Berlin: Mundt, 1846) SBDOYL TD225.N5 S3 1946g

64–65. Egbert L. Viele, Map of the lands included in the Central Park (New York, 1856). SBDOYL AA9065 N4 V651 FFF

65. M. (Matthew) Dripps, Plan of Central Park [New York, 186_?]. SBDOYL AA9065 N4 D83 S

66. South gate house, new reservoir, during construction. Viewed in the direction of the east water entrance. D.T. Valentine's Manual, 1862 (after page 188). SBDOYL, PLC. Lithographs-Valentine's Views, Box 36.1, Folder 8.

67. George Hayward, View in Central Park. Southward from the Arsenal 5th Ave & 64th St. June, 1858. for D. T. Valentine's Manual, 1859. SBDOYL,PLC. Lithographs-Valentine's Views, Box 36.1, Folder 1

68–69. Asa Coolidge Warren, [Scene on the Lake in Central Park] [graphic] (New York: D. Appleton & Co., 1869). SBDOYL AA735 N4 W25 FFF

The Rise of the Apartment

75 left. A whole block of dumb-bell tenement houses built under the laws in force in 1900 [model]. Robert W. De Forest, The Tenement

House Problem (New York: MacMillan, 1903), illustration facing p. 10. SBDOYL HD7304.N5 D3

75 right. Typical dumb-bell tenement, built under the laws in force in 1900. De Forest, The Tenement House Problem, 8. SBDOYL HD7304 N5 D3

76. Orchard Street, c. 1900. Postcard. Courtesy of Andrew Dolkart

77 top. Mr. White's Model Tenements--Brooklyn, 1879. Interior Court or Park. De Forest, The Tenement House Problem, illustration facing p. 97. SBDOYL HD7304.N5 D3

77 bottom left. City Suburban Homes 78th Street and Avenue A. SBDOYL, CPC. Box no. 29, Item no. 214

77 bottom right. Kitchen. Model Tenements, New York. The City and Suburban Co., De Forest, The Tenement House Problem, illustration facing p. 108. SBDOYL HD7304.N5 D3

78. 100 Central Park with Majestic Hotel & Dakota Ap. N.Y. City. SBDOYL, CPC. Box no. 22, Item no. 88

79 left. Kendall Court. Apartment Houses of the Metropolis (New York: G.C. Hesselgren, 1908), 170. SBDOYL AA7860 Ap12 F

79 right. Kendall Court, plan of upper floors. Apartment Houses of the Metropolis, 171. SBDOYL AA7860 Ap12 F

80. The Langham. Apartment Houses of the Metropolis, 18. SBDOYL AA7860 Ap12 F

81 top. The Langham. One-half plan of 2nd, 4th, 6th, 8th, 10th floors. Other half similar. Apartment Houses of the Metropolis, 18. SBDOYL AA7860 Ap12 F

81 middle left. Langham. Driveway. Apartment Houses of the Metropolis, 18. SBDOYL AA7860 Ap12 F

81 middle right. The Langham. A drawing room. Style, "Adam." Apartment Houses of the Metropolis, 18. SBDOYL AA7860 Ap12 F

81 bottom left. The Langham. A dining room. Style, "Colonial." Apartment Houses of the Metropolis, 18. SBDOYL AA7860 Ap12 F

81 bottom right. The Langham. A dining room. Style, "Elizabethan." Apartment Houses of the Metropolis, 18. SBDOYL AA7860 Ap12 F

82. Three-family Tenements. New York Tenement House Department, Fifth Report of the Tenement House Department of the City of New York (New York: Martin B. Brown, 1909), 35. SBDOYL AA7880 N48

83 left. Typical floor plan of a two-family dwelling. New York Tenement House Department, Fifth Report of the Tenement House Department of the City of New York, 53. SBDOYL AA7880 N48

83 right. Typical floor plan of three-story, three-family tenement. New York Tenement House Department, Fifth Report of the Tenement House Department of the City of New York, 53. SBDOYL AA7880 N48

84 left. Irving Underhill, 998 Fifth Avenue. Museum of the City of New York x 2010.28.265

84 right. 998 Fifth Avenue, typical floorplan. Pease & Elliman, *Catalog of East Side New York Apartment Plans* (New York: Pease & Elliman, 1925?), 50. SBDOYL AA7860 P32

85 left. 898 Park Avenue. R.W. Sexton, *American Apartment Houses of Today* (New York: Architectural Book Publishing, 1926), 77. SBDOYL AA7860 Se9 F

85 right. Upper and lower floors of typical duplex apartment. Apartment house at 898 Park Avenue. Sexton, *American Apartment Houses of Today*, 78. SBDOYL AA7860 Se9 F

86 left. Gainsborough Studios. *Apartment Houses of the Metropolis*, 218. SBDOYL AA7860 Ap12 F

86 right. Gainsborough Studios. Typical floor plan. *Apartment Houses of the Metropolis*), 218. SBDOYL AA7860 Ap12 F

87 top. 77 Park Avenue. Sexton, *American Apartment Houses of Today*, 45. SBDOYL AA7860 Se9 F

87 bottom. Typical floor plan, 77 Park Avenue. The apartments are featured by exceptionally large rooms. The living rooms averaging 15 x 25 feet. *American Apartment Houses of Today*, 45. SBDOYL AA7860 Se9 F

88. The Oliver Cromwell Apartment Hotel. SBDOYL, CPC. Box 21, Item 219.

89 left. The Sherry-Netherland, Fifth Avenue, at 59th Street, as seen from Central Park. SBDOYL, CPC. Box 15, Item 220

89 right. The Panhellenic, New York City, showing new apartments under construction. SBDOYL, CPC. Box 57, Item 228

90 left. The Cloister and the Manor in Tudor City. SBDOYL, CPC. Box 29, Item 250

90 right. Prospect Tower in Tudor City. SBDOYL, CPC. Box 29, Item 249

91. A Glimpse of the Private Parks in Tudor City. SBDOYL, CPC. Box no. 29, Item no. 252

Moving the People

99. Irving Underhill, Manhattan Bridge under construction, March 23, 1909. Library of Congress, 90710122

100. East Side of Greenwich Street, corner of Morris Street, December, 1867. William Fullerton, *The First Elevated Railroads in Manhattan and the Bronx of the City of New York; The Story of Their Development and Progress* (New York: New-York Historical Society, 1936), 64. SBDOYL TF840 R4

101 top. A stone viaduct elevated railroad. Proposed in 1833 as a solution of New York's rapid transit problem. Fullerton, *The First Elevated Railroads in Manhattan and the Bronx of the City of New York*, 55. SBDOYL TF840 R4

101 bottom. First Elevated Railroad on Greenwich Street South of Morris Street. Fullerton, *The First Elevated Railroads in Manhattan and the Bronx of the City of New York*, 65. SBDOYL TF840 R4

102 top. A Proposed Elevated Railroad for Broadway Patented by Richard P. Morgan, 1869. Fullerton, *The First Elevated Railroads in Manhattan and the Bronx of the City of New York*, 59. SBDOYL TF840 R4

102 bottom. Dr. Rufus H. Gilbert's Patented Plan for a Proposed Elevated Structure on Sixth Avenue, trains to be operated by atmospheric pressure in steel enclosures, 1874–75. Fullerton, *The First Elevated Railroads in Manhattan and the Bronx of the City of New York*, 56. SBDOYL TF840 R4

103 top. *Illustrated Description of the Broadway Pneumatic Underground Railway, with a Full Description of the Atmospheric Machinery, and the Great Tunneling Machine* (New York: S.W. Green, printer, 1870), 4. SBDOYL TF238 N53129 1890g

103 bottom. *Illustrated Description of the Broadway Pneumatic Underground Railway, with a Full Description of the Atmospheric Machinery, and the Great Tunneling Machine* (New York: S.W. Green, printer, 1870), 9. SBDOYL TF238 N53129 1890g

104. Plan for Building Arcade without Interruption to Travel. New York Parcel Dispatch Company, Voice of the Press on the New York Arcade Railway, 115 Broadway: 1886 (New York, 1886), frontispiece. SBDOYL HE4491.N2 N49 1886g

105. Arcade Railway cross-section. New York Parcel Dispatch Company, *Voice of the Press on the New York Arcade Railway, 115 Broadway*: 1886 (New York, 1886), 42. SBDOYL HE4491.N2 N49 1886g

106. Fifth Avenue looking north from 42nd Street, New York. SBDOYL, CPC

107. Darracq taxis, New York. National Motor Museum/Getty Images

108. Demolition of 42nd Street el spur. SBDOYL, PLC. Box 21, Folder 6

108–9. Last Elevated Train. SBDOYL, PLC. Box 21, Folder 6A

110. Riverside Park proposed cross-section, looking north. Photograph of drawing by Sielke. SBDOYL, PLC. Box 17, Folder 3A

111. View of south portal of First Avenue tunnel looking over the southeast corner of the U.N. site towards the new widened bridge at 42nd Street. SBDOYL, PLC. Box 12, Folder 3B

The Evolution of the Skyscraper

119. Bird's-eye View of the Southern End of New York and Brooklyn, Showing the Projected Suspension–bridge over the East River from the Western Terminus in Printing-House Square, drawn by Theodore Russell Davis (New York, 1870). SBDOYL AA735 N4 D29 FF

120. City Hall and Newspaper Row. SBDOYL, CPC. Box 56, Item 325

121. Nos. 40–51 Broadway. *Both Sides of Broadway from Bowling Green to Central Park, New York City,* Rudolph M. De Leeuw, compiler (New York: De Leeuw Riehl, 1910), 49. SBDOYL AA735 N4 D39

122. Broad Street and Curb Brokers, New York. SBDOYL, CPC. Box 19, Item 15

123. Map showing Value per Square Foot in Dollars of New York Real Estate. Richard M. Hurd, *Principles of City Land Values* (New York: Record and Guide, 1911), 158. SBDOYL AA9058 H93

124. Looking into Madison Square, New York [showing Metropolitan Tower at left] SBDOYL, CPC. Box 16, Item 171

125. Cover, *New York Times* supplement, January 1, 1905. Courtesy of Mark Tomasko

126. Batiment Singer [Singer Building], 149 Broadway, New York. SBDOYL, CPC. Box 6, Item 303

127. Equitable Building and Singer Tower. SBDOYL, CPC. Box 53, Item 43

128. New York Skyline, Showing Skyline of Manhattan from Jersey City. SBDOYL, CPC Box 54, Item 39

129. Entire Manhattan Island from an altitude of 16,000 feet, Fairchild Aerial Survey, Inc. SBDOYL, CPC. Box 54, Item 1

130. Setback principles typical examples. New York Commission on Building Districts and Restrictions, Final Report, June 2, 1916 (New York: City of New York Board of Estimate and Apportionment, Committee on the City Plan, 1916), 62. Avery Architectural & Fine Arts Library AA9054 N422

131. Study for maximum mass permitted by the 1916 New York City Building Zoning Resolution. Renderings by Hugh Ferriss based on diagrams by Harvey Wiley Corbett. Courtesy of Skyscraper Museum

133. Chrysler Building, New York. SBDOYL, CPC Box 8, Item 43

135. Aerial view of the Empire State Building. © Fotoseal SBDOYL, CPC. Box 7, Item 481

136. Berenice Abbott, *Seventh Avenue Looking North from 35th Street.* Berenice Abbott for Federal Art Project / Museum of the City of New York. 43.131.1.67

137. View from Central Park showing Hotel Pierre, Sherry-Netherland Hotel, and Savoy-Plaza Hotel. Skyscraper Museum

Housing the People

145. Yard of a tenement. SBDOYL Box 24, Item 334

146. Survey of housing built by private developers, institutions, labor unions and cooperatives, 1930–34. Werner Hegeman, *City Planning: Housing* (New York: Architectural Book Publishing, 1938), 140. Avery Architectural & Fine Arts Library, Columbia University. AA9090 H362

147. History in capsule form: 4 housing stages in 4 blocks. Federal Emergency Administration of Public Works, United States Housing Authority, *Harlem River Houses* (Washington: U.S. Govt. Print. Off., 1937), unpaginated. SBDOYL AA7545 Un3733

148. View of gardens in Paul Laurence Dunbar Apartments, New York City, looking toward Seventh Avenue entrance. SBDOYL, CPC, Box no. 29, Item no. 225

149. Paul Dunbar Garden Apartments. Site plan. *Architectural Record* 63 (March 1928), 272. Avery Architectural & Fine Arts Library, Columbia University. AB Ar44

150. Henry Wright, Analysis of Sunnyside Gardens and Paul Dunbar Apartments, 1929 *Architectural Record* 65 (March 1929): 213.

151. Cover, Federal Emergency Administration of Public Works, *Harlem River Houses.* SBDOYL AA7545 Un3733

152. Harlem River Houses site plan. *Harlem River Houses.* SBDOYL AA7545 Un3733

153. What you will find. *Harlem River Houses*, 10. SBDOYL AA7545 Un3733

154. Manhattanville residents earn diverse incomes. Elizabeth R. Hepner, *Morningside-Manhattanvill Rebuilds—A Chronological Account of Redevelopment in the Morningside-Manhattanville area, with Special Reference to the Development of Morningside Gardens* (New York: Morningside Heights, Inc., 1955), 9. SBDOYL AA9127 N4Ur1 H41

155. Hepner, *Morningside-Manhattanville Rebuilds*, 10. SBDOYL AA9127 N4Ur1 H41

156. Residential floor space. Harrison, Ballard & Allen, *Plan for the Rezoning of New York City; A Report Submitted to the City Planning Commission* (New York, 1950), 27. SBDOYL AA9054 H24

157. How many families? Harrison, Ballard & Allen, *Plan for the Rezoning of New York City*, 17. SBDOYL AA9054 H24

158. Cover, Hepner, *Morningside-Manhattanville Rebuilds.* SBDOYL AA9127 N4Ur1 H41

159. Reference map, Hepner, *Morningside-Manhattanville Rebuilds*, opposite page 1. SBDOYL AA9127 N4Ur1 H41

160. Typical floor plan. Morningside Gardens, Hepner, *Morningside-Manhattanville Rebuilds*, 28. SBDOYL AA9127 N4Ur1 H41

161. Proposed Activities Diagram. Architects' Renewal Committee in Harlem, *East Harlem Triangle Plan* (New York: Architects' Renewal Committee, 1968), 51. SBDOYL AA9127 N4 Ar253 F

The Making of Midtown

167. The Prometheus Fountain, Rockefeller Center. SBDOYL, CPC Box 53, Item 475

168 left. RCA Building Rockefeller Center at night. SBDOYL, CPC. Box 50, 258

168 right. *Atlas* sculpture by Lee Lawrie in Rockefeller Center. SBDOYL, CPC. Box 55, Item 184

169 top. Looking South from Observation Roof of RCA Building; photograph by Ratcliffe. SBDOYL, CPC. Box 55, Item 157

169 bottom. Looking North from Observation Roof of RCA Building. SBDOYL, CPC Box 55, Item 164

170. Entrance to Lincoln Tunnel; photograph by Keystone. SBDOYL, CPC Box 35, Item 458

171. East Side Airlines Terminal. SBDOYL, CPC Box 35, Item 537

172. East 34th Street and the Empire State Building. SBDOYL, CPC Box 35, Item 332

173. Bird's eye view east from Times Square; Thomas Airviews, 1974. SBDOYl, PLC. Box 1, Folder 3A.

174. 44 W 44th St. The Royalton Hotel. SBDOYL, PCP Box no. 14, Item no. 238

175 top. A View of the United Nations Headquarters from Across the East River. SBDOYL, CPC. Box 49, Item 441

175 bottom. A View of the General Assembly Hall in the United Nations Permanent Headquarters. SBDOYL, CPC. Box 49, Item 442

176. Proposal for Grand Central, Fellheimer & Wagner, Architects, September, 1954. SBDOYL, PLC. Box 20, Folder 4

177. Grand Central Terminal. SBDOYL, PLC. Box 20, Folder 5

178 left. Helmsley-Spear, Inc., Midtown Office Building Map (New York: Helmsley-Spear, Inc., 1970?). SBDOYL AA735 N4 H36

178 right. Landauer Midtown Manhattan Map. New York: Stanton & Hawthorne, 1979. SBDOYL AA735 N4 L15

179. Map of Midtown Manhattan in Detailed Axonometric Projection. New York: Anderson Isometric Maps, 1980. SBDOYL AA735 N4 An223

180. World Trade Center SBDOYL, CPC Box 53, Item 264

181 left. Map of Midtown Manhattan in Detailed Axonometric Projection (New York: Anderson Isometric Maps, 1980). SBDOYL AA735 N4 An223

181 right. Map of Midtown Manhattan in Detailed Axonometric Projection (New York: Manhattan Map Co., 1985). SBDOYL AA735 N4 An2231

Urban Renewal

187. Frederick Kelly, *Musicians in Washington Square*, 1962. Frederick Kelly/Museum of the City of New York. 2001. 59. 21

188. Jerome Robbins directing scene for the motion picture *West Side Story*, 1961. Billy Rose Theatre Division, The New York Public Library for the Performing Arts, Astor, Lenox and Tilden Foundations

189 left. Map of San Juan Hill area, 1934. G.W. Bromley & Co., Manhattan Land Book (New York: G.W. Bromley & Co., 1934), plate 86. SBDOYL AA9127 N4 B782 1934 F

189 right. Map of San Juan Hill area, 1970. G.W. Bromley & Co., Manhattan Land Book of the City of New York (New York: G.W. Bromley, 1970), plate 86. SBDOYL AA735 N4 B782 1970 F

190. Slum Clearance Progress: Title I, NYC (New York, N.Y.: Committee on Slum Clearance, 1956), 11. SBDOYL HT177.N5 S58 1957g

191. Block lot and house number map. New York Committee on Slum Clearance, Lincoln Square: Slum Clearance Plan under Title 1 of the Housing Act of 1949 as Amended (New York, 1956), 63. SBDOYL AA9127 N4 N4943

192. Scheme for Metropolitan Opera House at Lincoln Center, fall 1955. Rendering by Hugh Ferriss. negative in Wallace K Harrison architectural drawings and papers, 1913–1986. Avery Drawings & Archives. Avery Architectural & Fine Arts Library, Columbia University

193. Webb & Knapp, *Lincoln Square Progress: Lincoln Square Cornerstone Ceremony, June 27, 1961* [New York: Webb & Knapp, 1961?], cover. SBDOYL AA9127 N4 W38

194. Interior of Metropolitan Opera House. SBDOYL, COC Box 34, Item 203

195. Lincoln Center for the Performing Arts, New York State Theater. SBDOYL, CPC. Box 34, Item 138

196. Lincoln Center for the Performing Arts, Philharmonic Hall. SBDOYL, CPC. Box 34, Item 139

197. Lincoln Plaza Towers promotional brochure (New York: J.J. Sopher & Co., Inc., 1979?). Illustration of lobby. SBDOYL NA7862.N5 L46 1973g F

198. Alan Rubin, *Looting on Upper West Side during Blackout*, 1977. Courtesy of Alan Rubin

199. *Lower Manhattan Elevated Expressway* (New York: Triborough Bridge and Tunnel Authority, 1965), 1. SBDOYL AA9052 T7344

Remaking Lower Manhattan

206. The Aquarium, with public baths at sea wall. SBDOYL, CPC Box 1, Item 53

207. Battery Park—The Natural Playground of the Lower West Side. *A Social Survey of the Washington Street District of New York City*, Instituted and Conducted by Trinity Church Men's Committee October, 1914 (New York, 1914?). SBDOYL HN80.N5 N5

208. The docks along West Street. SBDOYL, CPC, Box 2, Item 51

209 left. Existing Waterfront Use. Downtown-Lower Manhattan Association, *Lower Manhattan: Recommended Land Use, Redevelopment Areas, Traffic Improvements* (New York, 1958), 32. SBDOYL AA9127 N4 D753

209 right. Recommended development areas. Downtown-Lower Manhattan Association, *Lower Manhattan: Recommended Land Use, Redevelopment Areas, Traffic Improvements*, 41. SBDOYL AA9127 N4 D753

210. Growth of Manhattan Island, 1650–1980. *The Lower Manhattan Plan: Summary of Report/Wallace McHarg, Roberts, and Todd; Whittlesey, Conklin and Rossant; Alan M. Voorhees & Associates, Inc.*; prepared for the New York City Planning Commission (New York: The Commission, 1966), unpaginated. Avery Architectural & Fine Arts Library, Columbia University. AA9127 N4 N48254

211. Cross-Island Sections: Looking North at Wall Street 1950–1980. *The Lower Manhattan Plan: The 1966 Vision for Downtown New York.* Essays by Ann Buttenwieser, Paul Wilen, and James Rossant; Carol Willis, editor (New York: Princeton Architectural Press: Skyscraper Museum, 2002). Avery Architectural & Fine Arts Library, Columbia University. AA9127 N4 B98

212. Land Use: Basic Concepts. *The Lower Manhattan Plan: Summary of Report/Wallace McHarg, Roberts, and Todd; Whittlesey, Conklin and Rossant; Alan M. Voorhees & Associates, Inc.* Avery Architectural & Fine Arts Library, Columbia University. AA9127 N4 N48254

213. Future Land Use. *The Lower Manhattan Plan: The 1966 Vision for Downtown New York*. Avery Architectural & Fine Arts Library, Columbia University. AA9127 N4 B98

214. Waterfront Development: New Highway and Proposed Land Fill, *The Lower Manhattan Plan: The 1966 Vision for Downtown New York.* Avery Architectural & Fine Arts Library, Columbia University. AA9127 N4 B98

215. Site Development: Stage I, *The Lower Manhattan Plan: The 1966 Vision for Downtown New York*. Avery Architectural & Fine Arts Library, Columbia University. AA9127 N4 B98

216. Special Functions and Services, *The Lower Manhattan Plan: The 1966 Vision for Downtown New York*. Avery Architectural & Fine Arts Library, Columbia University. AA9127 N4 B98

217. Skyview Survey, Lower Manhattan, East View south of Brooklyn Bridge, showing World Trade Center under construction with Battery Park landfill. SBDOYL, PLC

218. Water quality objectives, New York Department of City Planning, *The New York City Waterfront: Comprehensive Planning Workshop* (New York: New York City Planning Commission, 1974), 48. SBDOYL AA9127 N4W2 N484

219. This montage shows how the large park proposed as part of Westway alignment would appear against the Tribeca skyline. Michael J. Lazar, *Land Use: Recommendations: A Report to the Working Committee of the West Side Highway Project* (New York?,1974), 17. Avery Architectural & Fine Arts Library, Columbia University. AA9127 N4T6 L45

220. *Westway Is a Waterfront Park* (New York: New York Chamber of Commerce and Industry, 1978), cover. SBDOYL HE336.E94 W47 1978g

221 left. *Westway Is a Waterfront Park*, unpaginated. SBDOYL HE336. E94 W47 1978g

221 right. Selected Modified Outboard alternative known as Westway. United Sites Federal Highway Administration, *West Side Highway Project: Final Environmental Impact Statement* (Albany, N.Y., 1977?). SBDOYL AA9127 N4T6 Un33

222. "Almost Their Own Beach," *New York Times*; May 16, 1977; photograph by Fred R. Conrad. Redux

223. Pier 40. *Hudson River Park Esplanade Park: A Design Concept for the West Side Waterfront* (New York: The Parks Council, 1987). SBDOYL AA9127 N4W2 H86

Remaking Times Square

229. Longacre Square's billboards, 1898. Brown Brothers

230. The Times Building entrance to the Times Square subway station, c. 1904. Robert L. Bracklow Photograph Collection. 66000-456. New-York Historical Society. Lynne B. Sagalyn, *Times Square Roulette: Remaking the City Icon* (Cambridge, Mass.: MIT Press, 2001). SBDOYL AA9127 N4 Sa 18

231. Times Square: The Center of New York. SBDOYL, CPC Box 21, Item 6

232. Hammerstein's Victoria Theater at the northwest corner of 42nd Street and Seventh Avenue, 1904. Byron Company (New York, N.Y.)/ The Museum of the City of New York. 93.1.1. 20361 Sagalyn, *Times Square Roulette: Remaking the City Icon* (Cambridge, Mass.: MIT Press, 2001). SBDOYL AA9127 N4 Sa 18

233. The Theater District, 1938, dense with theaters, hotels, and stores. Rand McNally's Geographical Atlas of Greater New York, 1938. From the collection of Charles Knapp. William R. Taylor, ed., *Inventing Times Square* (Russell Sage Foundation, New York, N.Y., 1991). Avery Architectural & Fine Arts Library, Columbia University. AA735 N4 T23

234. Looking East from Times Square at 42nd Street, 1936. Postcard. Courtesy of Lynne B. Sagalyn

235. Celebrating Broadway's 300th birthday with parade through Times Square 1926. Redux New York Sagalyn, *Times Square Roulette: Remaking the City Icon*, 27. SBDOYL AA9127 N4 Sa 18

236. Hotel Astor, Times Square, New York, at the Crossroads of the World. SBDOYL, CPC Box 50, Item 249

237. "Crossroads of the World," early 1960s. Postcard. Courtesy of Lynne B. Sagalyn

238. Times Square. New York City. "Crossroads of the World." SBDOYL, CPC Box 50, Item 451

239. Midtown Vice Map, 1973. Cartographer: Office of Midtown Planning and Development. Office of Midtown Planning and Development, Office of the Mayor, 1973.

240. Glittering West 42nd Street at Night. SBDOYL, CPC Box 53, Item 459

241. Lou Stoumen, *West 42nd Street as Male Turf*, c. 1980. Lou Stoumen Trust. Sagalyn, *Times Square Roulette* SBDOYL AA9127 N4 Sa 18

242. Irving Browning, *Broadway on a Rainy Night. Times Square.* Undated. Browning Photograph Collection 71397. New-York Historical Society. Sagalyn, *Times Square Roulette*. SBDOYL AA9127 N4 Sa 18

243. Camel cigarettes sign in Times Square. Private Collection. Darcy Tell, *Times Square Spectacular: Lighting Up Broadway* (New York: Smithsonian, 2007). Avery Architectural & Fine Arts Library AA735 N4 T23

244. Charles M. Weiss, *Times Square Relit by Japanese Firms*, 1985. Courtesy of Charles M. Weiss. Sagalyn, *Times Square Roulette*. SBDOYL AA9127 N4 Sa 18

245. Gary Hack, Prototypical block of Broadway between 46th and 47th streets demonstrating municipal regulations intended to promote commercial signage, 2001. Courtesy of Gary Hack. Sagalyn, *Times Square Roulette*. SBDOYL AA9127 N4 Sa 18

246. Gary Hack, 42nd Street renewed, c. 2001. Courtesy of Gary Hack. Sagalyn, *Times Square Roulette*. SBDOYL AA9127 N4 Sa 18

247. Gary Hack, The Disney Corporation's presence on 42nd Street, c. 2001. Courtesy of Gary Hack. Sagalyn, *Times Square Roulette*. SBDOYL AA9127 N4 Sa 18

248–9. Gary Hack, Times Square transformed, 2001. Courtesy of Gary Hack. Sagalyn, *Times Square Roulette*. SBDOYL AA9127 N4 Sa 18

ACKNOWLEDGMENTS

Any project with as many constituent parts as *New York Rising* requires the participation of many people. From the outset, Christine Sala, Architecture Librarian at Columbia University's Avery Architecture & Fine Arts Library, mined her seemingly inexhaustible knowledge of, and enthusiasm for, the Durst Collection to make an invaluable contribution to this book. Without her knowledge and imagination, this book would not have been possible. Margaret Smithglass, Avery's Registrar and Digital Content Librarian was similarly indispensable in her expert stewardship of the image production process. We are also deeply appreciative for the unflagging support and guidance of Carole Ann Fabian, Avery Librarian, who played a critical role in launching this project, and we thank as well her entire staff, including Katherine Chibnick, Paula Gabbard, Teresa Harris, and Lena Newman.

We give our heartfelt thanks to all of the scholars whose contributions form the intellectual foundation of this book; we are grateful that they took time to immerse themselves in the Durst Collection and used their expertise to illuminate this rich material for other scholars, students, and the general public alike.

In particular, we want to note the contribution of the late Hilary Ballon, whose scholarship throughout her life set a widely admired standard; her portfolio in this book may indeed be the last of her many published works. *New York Rising* would not have come to fruition without the help of Mark Wigley and Amale Andros, former and current Deans of the Columbia University Graduate School of Architecture, Planning and Preservation, as well as Leah Cohen, James Graham, and Esther Turay. GSAPP alumni Andy Golubitsky, Shivam Jumani, Julia Lewis, and Sandra Mercado contributed mightily to our research efforts. We thank Dwight Primiano for photographing the Durst Collection material so flawlessly. We also thank all those who assisted in the book's production, including Yve Ludwig, who produced a clear and elegant design, and Michael Vagnetti, production director at The Monacelli Press. Finally, this project would not have come to completion without Gianfranco Monacelli's support as well as that of the Durst family. We hope this book will serve as a tribute to their multi-generational commitment to preserving and celebrating New York's historical legacy.